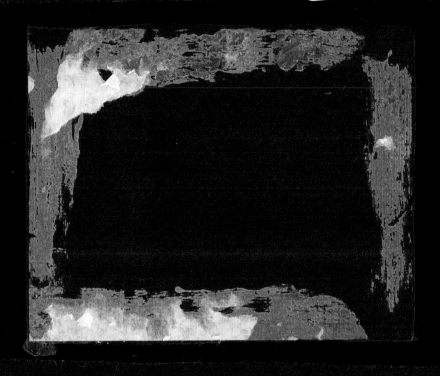

**Such
Men
as
Billy
the
Kid**

Such Men as Billy the Kid

Joel Jacobsen

The Lincoln County War Reconsidered

University of Nebraska Press
Lincoln and London

© 1994 by the
University of
Nebraska Press.
All rights reserved
Manufactured in
the United States
of America. The
paper in this book
meets the minimum
requirements of
American National
Standard for
Information Sciences –
Permanence of
Paper for Printed
Library Materials,
ANSI Z39.48–1984.
Library of Congress
Cataloging-in-
Publication Data
Jacobsen, Joel, 1959 –
Such men as Billy
the Kid : the Lincoln
County war recon-
sidered / by Joel
Jacobsen. p. cm.
Includes biblio-
graphical references
(p.) and index.
ISBN 0-8032-2576-8
(cl : alk. paper)
1. Lincoln County
(N.M.) – History.
2. Billy, the Kid.
3. Frontier and
pioneer life – New
Mexico – Lincoln
County.   I. Title.
F802.L7J33   1994
978.9'64 – DC20
93-42105 CIP

To Carla

Contents

Author's Note

In quotations from original sources, punctuation and spelling have been conformed to modern usage. A few trivial grammatical errors have been corrected. In addition, some of the testimony gathered by Special Agent Frank Angel is in the clumsy third-person affidavit form, in which the first sentence announces that "so-and-so says" and each succeeding sentence begins with "that." I have changed such testimony to normal English, deleting the "thats" and switching the third-person singular to the first person. Finally, I have ruthlessly suppressed that annoying lawyer's tic, the use of "said" to specify a person whose identity is not in doubt ("said Billy the Kid"). These changes do not alter the meaning of any passage.

I cannot begin to express the depth of my gratitude to my late father, Lynn C. Jacobsen, for his support, guidance, and love during my nine years of work on this project. I owe irredeemable debts of gratitude to my mother, Eloise Tittle Jacobsen; to my brother, Mark Jacobsen, for much valuable advice and a professional historian's critique of the manuscript; to Steven Voien and Lydia Bird, for many years of friendship and in particular for their invaluable comments on early drafts; to Robyn Bell and the late Marvin Mudrick, my teachers; to Alexander and Scott Jacobsen, who lived their first years with a father whose workday stretched unreasonably into the night; and especially to Carla Beauchamp, who was there from the beginning.

Preface

When I was eleven or twelve years old, my parents stopped the station wagon at a roadside museum in Fort Sumner, a dusty crossroads town in eastern New Mexico. The museum's prize exhibit was a dilapidated wooden door spotted with traces of a color that might have been dried blood or might just as easily have been brown paint. The holes in the door could have been bullet holes. Billy the Kid was supposed to have been shot against that door.

Studying the door, ignoring my big brother's wise-guy skepticism, I realized for the first time that Billy the Kid wasn't a tall-tale fantasy like Pecos Bill or Paul Bunyan, as I had hazily supposed. He was a real person, who bled real blood (or perhaps brown paint); he was even a New Mexican, like me. I began trying to find out about him, and became familiar with the phrase "Lincoln County War" without having any clear idea what it signified.

Years later I made a concerted effort to finally get the story straight. I searched libraries and bookstores for a history that would give me the facts and also tell the story in a lively narrative. I discovered no such book existed.

There was no shortage of books on the Lincoln County War. With the notable exceptions of works by Maurice Fulton and William Keleher, however, most of them were fiction, whether they admitted it or not. Worse, they conventionalized the story by importing stereotypes from movie westerns, giving us the usual late-show crowd of one-note characters. Trying to jazz up the story, these hordes of writers invariably only succeeded in making it hackneyed.

Robert Utley and Frederick Nolan have done much to improve the situation in the last few years. But their more academic approach, which deliberately downplays the drama, has its own drawbacks. In *High Noon in Lincoln: Violence on the Western Frontier* (Albuquerque: University of New Mexico Press, 1987), Utley asserts that the Lincoln County War was a "war without heroes," a phrase echoed in the preface to Nolan's dauntingly complete *The Lincoln County War: A Documentary History* (Norman: University of Oklahoma Press, 1992). But judging the actions of real people against the standard of heroism – the standard established by Gary Cooper in the real *High Noon* – is also distorting. The lurid colors of the fictionalizers are bleached out, but what remains is sometimes colorless.

The subtitle of Utley's book, which promises to extract broad generalizations from the conflict, illustrates a second shortcoming of the conventional scholarly approach: a tendency to downplay the uniqueness of events by insisting on their broader significance.

I believe the story of Lincoln County's troubles is far more interesting than it is historically significant, and it's interesting because it wasn't typical of anything at all. It represents a unique confluence of enduring American themes, such as violence and vigilantism, and more subtle variations on them, such as the establishment of legal and social norms in the newly settled wilderness. Gilded Age capitalism and political corruption were the motors behind elaborate legal (or at least legalistic) machinations. Litigiousness spread like smallpox, as everybody sued or brought charges against everybody else. The press piled on enthusiastically, fanning the flames and creating America's most enduring (so far) instant celebrity, Billy the Kid, whose fifteen minutes of fame have stretched into their second century.

The inescapable American theme of race is present everywhere: Anglos and Hispanics formed alliances based on mutual antipathies but still referred to themselves as Americans and Mexicans, members of different nations; the black troopers of the segregated cavalry were led by white officers; the Mescalero Apaches were robbed by the Interior Department agent given paternalistic charge of their well-being. There's even a strange echo of Ulster in the way Irish Catholic immigrants banded together against an Englishman allied with Celtic-surnamed Presbyterians. The legends of the cowboy, of the cavalry to the rescue, and even (in a cameo appearance) of the Texas Rangers all get a workout, incidentally discrediting the West-as-myth. Even Henry James's theme of the relationship between the old world and the new appears in the controversies kicked up by the Londoner John Tunstall.

Other "wars" of the western frontier were, by comparison, mere feuds, and so attempts to draw parallels inevitably diminish the uniqueness of what happened in Lincoln County. And while there may have been no heroes fit to be played by John Wayne (especially not John Chisum, who *was* played by John Wayne), people in New Mexico in the 1870s were recognizably human, full of moral complexities, wishing to do the right thing but capable of rationalizing almost anything.

As I try to make clear in the narrative that follows, I believe the citizens of Lincoln County perceived a moral dimension to their troubles. It wasn't good versus evil; it wasn't even a two-sided struggle, but rather a whole series of struggles, each posing a new set of hard and sometimes dangerous choices between better and worse.

I hope I have written the book I wanted to read all those years ago.

Part One

THE FALL OF
THE HOUSE

*Mr. John H. Tunstall
came to this county,
opened a store and
by his straightfor-
ward course made
friends with the people
who preferred to
trade with him rather
than with Murphy,
Dolan & Riley. This
caused the enmity of
them against Tunstall.*

Juan B. Patrón, June 6, 1878

In This Corner

1

The United States Army invaded Mexico in 1846. The northernmost Mexican state proved farcically unable to defend itself after its governor (correctly assessing the odds) fled south, and so New Mexico Territory was formed. The blessings of annexation were not universally appreciated: the territory's first American governor was killed in an unsuccessful revolt.

But in practical terms the conquest made little difference to most New Mexicans. What had once been a forgotten dry extremity of the Spanish Empire, and later Mexico's northern frontier, became the American frontier, but things continued much as they had during the previous two somnolent centuries.

A thin ribbon of Pueblo Indian and Spanish settlements traced the course of the Rio Grande from Taos in the north to El Paso to the south. East of the Rio Grande and flowing south in rough parallel was the Pecos River. The Pecos watered pasturage so lush that Coronado's expeditionary force rode in grass up to its stirrups, yet neither the Pueblo Indians nor the Spanish had ever settled its lower reaches.

One reason for the lack of settlement was the Mescalero Apaches, who resented intrusions. Another reason, at least as important, was geographical isolation: it took four days for a person on horseback to ride from the Rio Grande to the southern Pecos valley.[1] Nature had constructed an ingenious double barricade between the rivers. The harsh desert known as the Journada del Muerte, or dead man's journey, is succeeded by a gigantic extinct volcano, the Sierra Blanca, soaring twelve thousand feet and snowcapped much of the year.

Consequently, at the time of the American annexation, the lower Pecos remained largely devoid of permanent settlement.[2] The 1870 census, however, found 1,803 settlers. The intervening event that made settlement possible was the Civil War. In 1861 a Texas Confederate army invaded New Mexico, routing the hastily formed New Mexico Volunteers and capturing the Rio Grande settlements. In California, an energetic soldier named James Carleton raised a Union army that heroically quick marched across the Mojave Desert and the wilds of Arizona, racing to New Mexico's rescue.[3]

But it takes time to raise an army, train it, and then walk with it from California to Santa Fe. In the meantime, Colonel John Slough led a Union army from Colorado that routed the rebels at the Battle of Glorieta. Carleton arrived in New Mexico with his genius for organization and his desert-hardened army to discover that the Civil War in New Mexico was already over.

But he was too resourceful a leader to squander his opportunity for military glory. He cast his eye about for alternative battlefields, and soon the Mescalero Apaches were confined to a reservation on the flanks of the Sierra Blanca. To keep an eye on the Apaches, troops were stationed at nearby Fort Stanton. And the government began searching for farmers and stock raisers who could provide the necessary foodstuffs for the reservation and the fort.

Suddenly, the lower Pecos was inhabitable. The Apache threat was nearly eliminated and a local economy sprang up, full grown, to feed the inmates and guards of Sierra Blanca's open-air prison. Part of the military reservation was "thrown open" to settlement, in the words of the statute. A new county was formed, one that eventually encompassed all of southeastern New Mexico, an impossible thirty thousand square miles – the size of Connecticut, Massachusetts, New Hampshire, and Vermont combined.[4]

The California Column provided settlers for Lincoln County, since Carleton's soldiers were mustered out in New Mexico with no transportation home. The marooned vets formed the core of Lincoln County's pioneers. Consequently, a surprisingly high percentage of the fighters in the Lincoln County War had combat experience. Life in Lincoln County, with its overwhelmingly male society and sudden violence was, in fact, much like life in an army camp, but without the discipline.

In the view of his many enemies, Alexander McSween was the cause of the Lincoln County War. He and his wife Sue arrived in Lincoln in March

1875. Sue was thirty and her husband was probably a year or two older; they had been married for a year and a half. Sue was born in Pennsylvania but raised in Kansas. A photograph has come down to us depicting her in early middle age and showing a face of greater sturdiness than beauty. But sturdiness was what counted in New Mexico Territory. Sue was involved only peripherally in the early skirmishes of the Lincoln County War, but when the showdown came, she waded resolutely into battle and kept up the fight long after most of the men had, in one way or another, retired from the field.

Her husband was a lawyer who had studied at Washington University and practiced in Kansas. His stationery boasted: "For punctuality and responsibility I refer to any business man in this city."[5] They made a prominent enough match that their wedding was noted with sophomoric ribbing in *The Atcheson Champion*: "Roll up your sleeves, Mac, and pitch into business now; no more excuses old boy."[6] Other than that, virtually nothing is known of Alexander McSween's life prior to his arrival in Lincoln. The historian William Keleher discovered that an Alec McSween was adopted by a Scottish settler on Prince Edward Island at about the right time, but nothing except the coincidence of names suggests Canadian Alec grew into Lincoln's Alexander. A photograph shows a young man with a sweeping handlebar mustache, fair hair, smooth skin, and eyes that seem to slant upwards, as if pulled taut by that tight skin. There is little in that face of the calm sturdiness of his wife.

McSween was devout: he held church services in his living room (attended by Billy the Kid) and didn't drink in a county that swam in whiskey. Even after the killings began, he bragged in a newspaper article that he owned no firearm except a shotgun for hunting. But McSween was also exceptionally ambitious. He developed a successful practice, with clients all over the territory, and eventually brought in his brother-in-law as partner to help him with the caseload. He also promoted various business ventures, which were less successful.

Sometimes the competing impulses of righteousness and relentless striving worked in tandem: McSween was instrumental in bringing a Presbyterian missionary to Lincoln and purchased land on which he planned to erect the sprawling county's first Protestant church and a school. But sometimes ambition got the upper hand. McSween could be combative, even grasping. Although he must have seemed a terrible hypocrite to his enemies, the secret of his personality was his absolute sincerity both as a Christian and as a young man on the make.

The two factions of the Lincoln County War were known to contemporaries as McSween men and Murphy men. But when he first hung out his shingle in Lincoln, McSween was Murphy's lawyer.

Lawrence Murphy, the managing partner of Lincoln County's largest store, was a tall, thin Irishman with a red beard neatly trimmed into a goatee and a prominent forehead unencumbered by hair. A candidate for melanoma in the desert sun, with a pasty complexion that refused to tan, he was described by a contemporary as a "city man," fastidious about his looks and the black suits that set him apart from the cowboys and soldiers who formed his clientele.[7]

Murphy grew up in County Wexford, where the Atlantic Ocean meets the Irish Sea. He was fourteen when the potato crop failed in 1845. The population of Ireland nearly halved during the cataclysm of famine, with the demographic reduction divided fairly evenly between "death" and "emigration." Murphy emigrated, joined the United States Army, and served in the new territories of the West. When civil war broke out, he enlisted in the New Mexico Volunteers and served as Kit Carson's quartermaster. After the war, he became post trader to Fort Stanton. His mercantile career had begun.

Fort Stanton — not a stockade, but a collection of frame buildings built around a central parade ground, with no thought given to defense — was built where the Rio Bonito valley widens into a windswept bowl. Murphy and his partner, Emil Fritz, profited handsomely from the soldiers' boredom and isolation until the day in late summer 1873 when one of their employees, James J. Dolan, tried to shoot an officer.

Murphy, Fritz, and Dolan were expelled from the fort. In September they opened a new store in Lincoln town, named L. G. Murphy & Co.

Their timing could not have been worse. The postwar boom that swept Ulysses S. Grant to his second presidential term ended with sickening abruptness. A string of bank failures culminated in the September 18 collapse of Jay Cooke & Co., which ushered in the Panic of 1873.

The panic and the long depression it heralded are lost to popular memory today only because they are overshadowed by the more recent but distinctly similar 1929 crash. The stock market was mobbed by investors frantic to dump their holdings at any price. A long list of financial firms failed in the first thirty-six hours, and banks suffered ruinous runs.[8]

As the economy crashed on Wall Street, L. G. Murphy & Co. pressed ahead with the construction of its new building, the most imposing structure in the entire county (it later became the county courthouse). Called "the big store" or, most often, "the House," the building was a two-story adobe with a pitched roof and a long balcony. Shaded by the balcony was a broad front porch, an ideal spot for loungers to monitor traffic up and down Lincoln's single street. The second floor provided living quarters for Murphy, Dolan, and other House men.

Then as now, Lincoln was approached from the east on a road that climbs steadily up the flanks of the Sierra Blanca, weaving in precise imitation of the meanderings of the Rio Bonito. Hills rise on both sides, creating a long, sloping valley. The valley narrows to a bottleneck and then, around a bend, opens up again on Lincoln, a series of adobes along the southern bank. Across the river, steep piñon-covered hills rise precipitously to a narrow ridge.

Lincoln, at 5,750 feet, is a mountain town. Even in the height of summer the meager atmosphere lacks the capacity to retain solar heat, so blistering days are relieved by cool evenings. Tall deciduous trees, nourished by the Bonito, shade the street. It is a pleasant spot, but no more than a hamlet. The imposing House rises from the foothills with an air of slightly loony grandeur. How could tiny Lincoln support such a grand store?

It couldn't, and Murphy never intended that it should. Referring to the House as a "store" is almost misleading. Its most important function was as a commodity brokerage house. The federal government let out contracts for beef and grain to supply the fort and reservation. There were no competing suppliers for many commodities within two hundred miles: the contractors were forced to buy from the House, and local farmers and stock raisers had little choice where to sell. It was a nice little monopoly.[9]

Murphy was a banker, too, setting up farmers on credit and outfitting them with everything from seeds to threshers in exchange for the promised delivery of x pounds of grain or beef in the fall. If a farmer fulfilled his obligations, Murphy made a tidy profit. If he failed, Murphy repossessed the equipment and foreclosed on the farm. He had a monopoly in the loan business, too.

The House also sold everything anyone in Lincoln needed, from bridles to soap balls, canned fruit to shirt collars, axle grease to shawl pins.[10] It also housed a saloon, whose biggest customer was Murphy himself.

The picture emerges of a courtly man, with a high-domed white forehead and small squinting eyes, in starched collar and thin black cravat, slightly unsure on his feet, the proprietor of a wonderful little money-making machine high up in the piney foothills of the Sierra Blanca. Just the thing, one might think, to weather the panic. But within five years of its founding in Lincoln town, the House went bankrupt.

The story of the House's collapse is the story of the Lincoln County War. Juan Patrón, a Notre Dame graduate who became chairman of the Lincoln County Commission and then speaker of the territorial House of Representatives while still in his twenties, set the scene:

> I know a great many circumstances which lead me to believe that the cause of the present troubles is the result of oppression of the people for quite a number of years. . . . The farmers have been complaining greatly as to the one-sided settlements had with the firm of Murphy & Co. They had been induced to buy merchandise of them under an agreement that they should be paid a fixed price for their produce, but when a settlement was had the goods were charged at exorbitant prices and the produce turned in at prices to suit them (M & Co.).[11]

George Van Sickle was one of the complaining farmers. He told a federal investigator in 1878:

> I am well acquainted with L. G. Murphy, J. J. Dolan and J. A. Riley and have been so since they commenced business in [Lincoln] County. Their reputation for honesty and fair dealing has been uniformly low. As a matter of business they done as they pleased. They intimidated, oppressed and crushed people who were obliged to deal with them. They were a gigantic monopoly. If they done wrong, there appeared there was no redress, as they were reported to control the Courts. . . . The people generally complain of their surrounding themselves with murderers, thieves and desperadoes to carry out their ends; complain that they have ruined farmers by exacting and collecting unjust amounts [and] by obliging them to part with their produce to pay such debts at prices to suit them; complain that they have taken contracts for corn at rates at which the required supplies cannot be raised; complain that they have swindled those who dealt with them. "The House," as they are called here, never suffered competition if they could help it.[12]

Godfrey Gauss, a German immigrant who made his living as a ranch house cook, had his story, too:

I know L. G. Murphy; he has treated me very badly. I hired his brewery for a year. I wrote him that I wanted it in writing, [but] he wrote me that as long as I held to my bargain he would to his. I thereon commenced the business of brewing and had been there about two months, and at that time I had 400 gallons of beer ready, when Murphy sent Dolan & Mathews with arms and told me that I must leave, claiming that he had sold the brewery.

I was forced to leave and sell him my beer at forty cents a gallon. It was worth then seventy-five cents per gallon. I could not take the beer away because I had nothing to put it in, and he well knew that I could not take it away. [He] told me to come down & settle. My account was made out & then they owed me $160 and they not having the money the next day thereafter they made me another statement in which they owed me only about $28. I do not think that they had sold the brewery and I believe that it still belongs to them.

This is only a sample of the way they did business throughout the county – and they would fix up their accounts to suit themselves.[13]

Of course, it is to be expected that a monopolist will exploit his monopoly. But "exploit" is exactly what the House failed to do to Gauss – it stole the golden eggs, then killed the goose that laid them. A ruthlessness that had little to do with the profit motive was at work. As Alexander McSween testified, "L. G. Murphy & Co. were absolute monarchs of Lincoln County and ruled their subjects (the farmers & others) with an oppressive iron heel."[14]

The Fritz Insurance Policy

2

McSween had plenty of opportunity to observe the House's predations, but he was an unlikely candidate to become a hostile witness. The House was his most important client. McSween performed the disagreeable business of suing debtors and then seizing the pound of flesh. He kept 10 percent of the money he collected.[1] This meant that McSween, who didn't even own a pistol, was the House's enforcer.

An important aspect of the House's control over county affairs was Lawrence Murphy's position as probate judge. Probate judges were the highest elected judges in the territory; the three district judges, who doubled as Supreme Court justices, were appointed by the president. The biggest battles involving probate courts weren't between the bickering bereaved, but between territorial and federal politicians scrapping for turf. Territorial legislators wanted control over their territory's court system, and the way to acquire control was to expand the probate court's jurisdiction at the expense of the federal appointees.[2]

For this reason, Probate Judge Murphy had considerably more power than his title suggests. Some of his powers were curiosities: he could punish runaway children by putting them to work on road gangs. He was responsible for whipping "vagrants and those who have no visible means of support" into shape. He oversaw trade with the Mescaleros, which meant he was the local official in charge of making sure his firm lived up to its obligations. The probate judge also controlled the county treasury, with everything that implied.[3]

Most important, though, Murphy was a one-man court of appeals. Most decisions of Lincoln County's five justices of the peace were appealed to probate court, and no further appeal was allowed. If Murphy didn't like a J. P.'s ruling in a particular case, he fixed the matter.[4]

The judge's business partner was Major (Brevet Colonel) Emil Fritz. Fritz, a German, was a good businessman and a moderating influence on Murphy. The House prospered while he was around and failed after his death.

Photographs of Emil Fritz show a dour-faced, bony man with a thick black beard and sunken eyes. The dour expression in part reflected the tedium of the photographic process, but it was also an effect of tuberculosis. Lincoln County's high altitude and dry climate kept Fritz's illness at bay. Nevertheless, he was dying. In the fall of 1873, he returned to Stuttgart and died in his wet, cold, and low-lying hometown a few months later.

After Fritz's death the House became strictly an Irish affair. Jimmy Dolan bought into the business; later on, so did John Riley, who was born on an island in Dingle Bay and fled during the famine.

For a year or more, Fritz's partner, the probate judge, took no steps to administer his estate.[5] The reason for the delay is exactly what one would suspect: Murphy owed Fritz money. For years Fritz, a bachelor, had plowed his profits back into the business. Upon his death, his heirs were entitled to liquidate his share of partnership and recover the reinvested profits – which, according to one calculation, added up to the astronomical sum of $70,000.[6] Murphy chose not to open probate, and for many months the debt, which was recorded only on the House's own books, remained undiscovered and unpaid.

Juan Patrón observed Murphy's political machinations up close. He told a federal investigator:

> L. G. Murphy controlled everything that there was any money in – and dictated who should run for office and who should not – at one time going into a convention of the people who were to select persons who were to run for offices which the people had to give, knowing that the convention was opposed to him, overthrew the table, destroyed the stationery and told them you might as well try to stop the waves of the ocean with a fork as try and oppose me.[7]

In 1875, the fork stopped the waves. A Lincoln County grand jury investigation revealed that $20,000 in tax collections had disappeared. Judge Murphy escaped being indicted, but he was forced to resign.[8] Florencio Gonzáles, a former territorial legislator, was elected to take Murphy's place as probate judge at a special election.

Only Murphy knew the full implications of Gonzáles's election: probate of the Fritz estate could no longer be avoided. But everyone could see the House's grip on the county was loosening. As far as Juan Patrón was concerned, the political divisions in the county could be easily accounted for: "the people were divided into two parties, the Mexican element standing by me, and the American, the soldiers, & Murphy against me."[9] Murphy's replacement by Gonzáles meant the balance of power was shifting.

All of the land conquered by the United States in the Mexican War suffered the same ethnic division. The Americans were invaders in 1846, colonizers thirty years later. The offhand use of "Mexican" to describe families that had lived in this American territory for generations illustrated a central paradox of life on the southwestern frontier: the natives were foreigners.

There was a small silver lining to Murphy's downfall. His cautious, conservative partner had insured his own life, and the $10,000 death benefit was due and payable. Fritz's choice of an underwriter, however, was unfortunate – insured and insurer died at about the same time. By the time Gonzáles took office, the affairs of the Merchants Life Insurance Company of New York were being wound up, and the receiver refused to pay the $10,000.

Someone would have to go to New York to straighten things out. The travel would be expensive, but the amount of money involved justified the cost. In the Lincoln County of the 1870s, cowboys received two dollars per day and a cow cost fifteen dollars; $10,000 went a long way.[10] Moreover, the long-term economic trend, brought about by the postwar return to "hard money," was persistent deflation, making the $10,000 more valuable with each passing day. So the administrator of the Fritz estate, William Brady (yet another famine refugee from Ireland), hired McSween, the House's enforcer, to squeeze money out of the receiver.

McSween ran into problems as soon as he hit New York City. Spiegelberg Bros., a family-run firm that made a fortune outfitting traders along the Santa Fe Trail, claimed that Lawrence Murphy had assigned them the proceeds from the insurance policy in partial payment of the House's debts. This was probably true, but beside the point; Murphy had no authority to assign it. Nonetheless, the Spiegelberg claim gave the receiver of the insolvent insurance company an excuse not to act. How could he know which claimant was entitled to the money?

A lawsuit would have been costly and time-consuming. So McSween, armed with his authority to compromise the policy, sat down to talk. The Spiegelbergs agreed to accept $700 cash to surrender their claim, possibly their estimation of its worth. But McSween didn't have $700 cash, and it was increasingly evident that squeezing money out of the receiver would take time. McSween killed both birds with a single stone by making a deal with the bankers Donnell, Lawson & Co.: the bank would advance the $700 and pressure the receiver; in return, it would accept a contingency fee. If it failed to collect the money, it didn't get paid.[11]

It was an elegant solution, but McSween returned to Lincoln without a penny of insurance money. Even worse, he had signed away thousands of dollars to Spiegelberg Bros. and the bank. Once McSween's own fee and expenses were figured in, Murphy's hypothetical gain was reduced to $6,000 or even less.

The House fired its lawyer. A year later the killings began.

Shortly before McSween left for New York, William Brady was elected sheriff of Lincoln County. He resigned as administrator of the Fritz estate and was replaced by Emil Fritz's brother and sister, Charles Fritz and Emilie Fritz Scholand. Mrs. Scholand spoke little English, and her brother was a drunk. Moreover, they disliked each other. In December 1876, shortly after he was fired by Murphy, McSween wrote to Charles Fritz:

> Whoever tells you I am trying to get that money for Mrs. Scholand states something of which he knows nothing – something manu-factured by himself. . . . I regret that you should mistrust me when I was working for you in good faith, spending even my own funds in further cause of the interests you represent. . . . I excuse you on ac-count of the pressure that may have been brought to bear upon you.[12]

The identity of the unnamed "whoever" bringing pressure to bear was revealed a year and a half later, when McSween testified: "On my return to Lincoln [from New York] I found J. H. Riley was exceedingly angry and was trying to cause trouble."[13] Riley succeeded.

The Kid's Youth

3

Billy the Kid was born in 1859, his mother was Catherine McCarty, and his given name was Henry. Armed with these three facts, generations of history buffs have descended on the birth records of New York, Indiana, Ohio, Illinois, and County Limerick, and in each place have found solid indications that a Henry McCarty or McCarthy was born there in 1859 or thereabouts. But since Henry was one of the nineteenth century's favorite names, persevering researchers could undoubtedly locate the birth of a Henry McCarty or McCarthy in 1859 in almost any corner of the world with a substantial Irish population.[1]

The trail warms up at the close of the Civil War, by which time Catherine McCarty, a widow with two sons, had found her way to Indianapolis. From this date on, sightings of the family, like sightings of a fugitive as the cops close in, become more frequent and more reliable.

By 1870 Mrs. McCarty was a landowner in Wichita – the family was already well along on its westward migration. She lived with an ex-soldier named William Henry Harrison Antrim. She took in laundry while Antrim tried his hand at farming. Evidently neither business flourished: in less than three years the ménage headed westward again. On March 1, 1873, Antrim married Catherine in the beautifully austere adobe First Presbyterian Church in Santa Fe. Her two sons are listed in the church registry as witnesses. The family set up house in Silver City, a mining camp high in the mountainous southwest corner of the territory, where Antrim hunted for the advertised silver.

Antrim is a county in the far northeastern corner of Ireland. But as a surname, Antrim is unheard of in Ireland, as outlandish as Massachusetts, suggesting some confusion between the surname and place of origin lines on an immigration application.

Antrim's first three names have a more obvious origin: he was born in 1842, one year after the untimely end of the Harrison administration. The fact that Antrim was named for a Scotch-Irish president confirms his ethnicity. Billy the Kid's stepfather was an Orangeman, which explains why a woman with a good Irish Catholic name like McCarty remarried in a Presbyterian church.

Many of young Henry's Silver City schoolmates, and even his old schoolteacher, stepped forward briefly into the limelight of his spectacular career to tell curious historians about the outlaw's youth. All of it, without exception, was to the effect that Henry was a normal boy, a good boy, an unexceptional boy.[2] The only peculiarity is endearingly wholesome: Henry, who liked to sing, used to perform in amateur theatricals. A woman who knew him later in life said he sang the hymns in a pleasing tenor while attending Presbyterian services at McSween's house. The story might even be true.

Catherine McCarty Antrim died of tuberculosis in September 1874, when Henry was fifteen. He continued in school for one more year, working for room and board in a hotel whose landlord later said he was the only employee who never stole anything.

The following September, however, Henry found himself in jail. The local newspaper, *The Grant County Herald,* told the tale:

Henry McCarty, who was arrested on Thursday and committed to jail to await the action of the grand jury, upon the charge of stealing clothes from Charley Soo and Sam Chung, celestials sans cue, sans Joss sticks, escaped from prison yesterday through the chimney. It is believed that Henry was simply the tool of "Sombrero Jack," who done the stealing whilst Henry done the hiding. Jack has skinned out.[3]

The peculiar flippancy of the reporting reveals how lightly Silver City's grown-ups took the incident. But Henry, who didn't stop to read his reviews, took the matter very seriously indeed. The "celestials" in question were Chinese; the clothes were laundry. The crime was petty, and it is usually assumed the Grant County sheriff wanted to give the boy a good scare. By the second night, young Henry was good and scared: according to legend, he shimmied up the chimney and lit out for Arizona Territory.

He found work as a ranch hand, working on an itinerant basis, moving from ranch to ranch according to the cycle of bovine life. This was the usual life for cowboys, accepting work where it could be found. Not too surprisingly, the slender teenager became known as Kid, or sometimes Kid Antrim. Since he was known in Silver City as McCarty (that's what the newspaper called him) Antrim was an alias.

After two years in Arizona, the Kid got into a fight with a blacksmith named Frank Cahill. As the newspapers reported, "Bad names were applied each to the other."[4] A blacksmith working all day on forge and bellows would tend to be well muscled, while all accounts agree that the Kid looked even younger than his age. The results were predictable. Picking himself off the floor, the Kid got even. Cahill died from the bullet wound. The Kid, now eighteen years old, was arrested and imprisoned at Camp Grant, the nearby army post.

With the expansive interpretation given to the concept of self-defense on the frontier, the odds of acquittal were good. That, however, was a wager Henry preferred not to make; he escaped from the Camp Grant guardhouse. The sentry fired two or three shots at his receding figure, to no effect. Normally two or three shots might sound the alarm in a military post, but the Kid had timed his escape well: he slipped away in the heat and commotion of a soldiers' holiday – the sort of social function where two or three shots was the expected sound of boys at play – and headed east into New Mexico.

A persistent legend, with just enough basis in fact to prevent extirpation, has the Kid teaming up Jesse Evans and the Boys, a gang of open and notorious, catch-me-if-you-can thieves and killers who terrorized southern New Mexico during a three-year reign in the late 1870s. If the legend were true, it would tell us a great deal about Henry. Jesse Evans and the Boys wouldn't allow an amateur to join their ranks.[5]

The closer the legend is examined, however, the less likely it appears to be true. First of all, no one ever actually identified the Kid as Evans's associate. That conclusion can be reached only by piecing together scraps of information from the local newspaper. The October 6, 1877, issue of *The Mesilla Valley Independent* contains an editorial polemic against Evans and his gang that accuses them of a multitude of sins, including the theft of a horse belonging to a Colonel Ledbetter. The editorial doesn't pretend to be a news report: it states that, in the course of their predations, the outlaws "found a copy of the *Independent,* and with the open-hearted liberality so characteristic of his class, Captain Evans did us the honor to announce that he intended to present us with a 'free pass to h–ll.'" A week later, the *Independent* reported that Colonel Ledbetter had unsuccessfully tracked the (unnamed) horse thieves, and that the following day "the party of thieves, among whom was Henry Antrim, were met in Cook's cañon by Mr. Carpenter." That's the sum total of the evidence linking the Kid to the Boys.

We're not told how Mr. Carpenter knew that the party he met was the party of thieves (did he recognize the horse?). We can't even be sure he knew Henry Antrim to recognize *him*. And the crusading *Independent* would have named the celebrity "captain" had he been present.

Once he reached Lincoln County, the Kid (now calling himself William Henry Bonney) found honest work as a cowboy – not the behavior of a professional criminal. Moreover, he and the Boys repeatedly tried to kill each other during the Lincoln County War, which hardly suggests a confederate bond.

But the most damning evidence against the report is its plausibility: joining an outlaw gang at age eighteen is exactly what we expect of Billy the Kid. It is nearly impossible to blot out our anachronistic awareness of his legend and focus instead on the skinny nobody he was then. Why would grown men like Jesse Evans and the Boys want to make him a partner in their business?

By late summer 1877, the newly renamed William Henry Bonney was in Seven Rivers. In her memoir, *My Girlhood among Outlaws*, Lily Klasner remembered Bonney this way:

> The Kid was as active and graceful as a cat. At Seven Rivers he practiced continually with pistol or rifle, often riding at a run and dodging behind the side of his mount to fire, as the Apaches did. He was very proud of his ability to pick up a handkerchief or other object from the ground while riding at a run.[6]

There is much to doubt in Klasner's book, many stories that bear the obvious distortions of repeated tellings. But there is little doubt Bonney practiced his riding and shooting. He was soon celebrated for his frightening facility: just nine months later an army colonel would harshly criticize Sue McSween for allowing "such men as Billy Kid" in her house.[7]

John Tunstall

4

On one of McSween's journeys to Santa Fe, he met a tall, sandy-haired Englishman with a young man's unconvincing beard. Just twenty-four years old, John Henry Tunstall was touring the West looking for investment opportunities. The only son of a well-to-do London businessman, he was ready to pump his father's money into any project that offered the prospect of multiplying it.[1]

To McSween, Tunstall's arrival must have seemed like an act of divine providence. Just as he lost one rich client, the House, he gained a new prospect. The timing was perfect in other ways, too. McSween had more on his mind than statute books. It was not the beauty of the mountain valleys and the softness of the summer evenings that kept him in Lincoln. He had big plans: he was going to build a church and a school, and he was going into business for himself. Only Murphy, Riley, and Dolan knew the inner workings of the House better than the House's former lawyer, and no one knew better that the House was almost insolvent. Who would supply the government contracts after the House was gone? All McSween lacked was capital.

The match of the frontier lawyer and the London merchant's son was less incongruous then than it might seem now, for the post-Civil War era saw enormous European investment in America. The official American policy of subsidizing expansion with grants of land and the unofficial Gilded Age policy of "anything goes" combined to make imperial sugarplums dance in the dreams of European capitalists.[2]

Moreover, the English were used to sending both their children and their capital overseas in the 1870s. The sun never set in those days, and John Tunstall's western swing began in Victoria, British Columbia, where his father's mercantile business maintained its most distant store.[3]

Outposts of empire were the usual stations for sons of the middle class, such as Tunstall, or younger sons of posher types. There were fortunes in Africa, Canada, India, and Asia simply waiting to be made. The colonial experience was also a training ground, and undoubtedly it was expected that Tunstall's experience in the Victoria store would prepare him for running the show back home.

This is standard stuff – and it fails utterly to explain why Tunstall abandoned his clerk's position in Victoria, traveling first to San Francisco and then to Santa Fe. His travels were a search for investment opportunities, but that, too, fails to explain his restless persistence. California was hardly used up in the 1870s, and it had the same pleasant climate then as now, without the overcrowding. But Tunstall turned his back on California and chose an amputated appendage of Latin America misruled by corrupt American politicians, eventually settling in the most remote and unpopulated corner of this most remote and backward territory.

At the back of beyond, Tunstall assured his family, "I shall be far happier than cuffed in white linen & coated in broadcloth, pedalling trifles to women with slim purses & slimmer education & refinement."[4] Such rugged snobbishness reveals the most important respect in which Tunstall differed from his new neighbors. He was English; he had money, education, and business experience. But the crucial difference was that he had no reason to be there. He was not driven by economic necessity, as were so many settlers during the lingering depression of the 1870s. He moved to Lincoln because he wanted to, not because there was nowhere else to go. He was drawn by a love of adventure, and he expected to be happy.

Tunstall knew life in Lincoln would be hard and perhaps dangerous. That was the point. He prided himself on his toughness. But he experienced Lincoln County as an outsider, as someone who threw himself into the game knowing he could withdraw at any time.

Tunstall was encouraged to travel to Lincoln County by Alexander McSween, whom he met in Santa Fe, and he rode into town with Juan Patrón, so there never was much doubt where he would stand in the gathering feud. In a letter home, Tunstall wrote that he liked Patrón but couldn't stand to watch him flog his horses.

Patrón had his reasons for pushing the horses. Tunstall may not have understood what a night in the mountains near Lincoln entailed, but Patrón wished to avoid the scene Tunstall described when the pair finally stopped for the night at the camp of some strangers: no dinner, inadequate blankets, bitter cold, and a five-day-old bun for breakfast.[5]

To top things off, their horses had wandered during the night, and Tunstall wound up walking seven miles looking for them. The strangers with whom they had shared the campsite were kind enough to hitch up the now-horseless buggy to the back of their wagon and tow it into town.

After describing the discomforts of the journey, Tunstall solemnly assured his parents, back home in Belsize Terrace, that Lincoln "is in miner's parlance about the 'toughest' little spot in America, which means the most lawless; a man can commit murder here with impunity."

Tunstall recounted a conversation with a man who told him that Ham Mills had recently killed someone for calling him a gringo. When Tunstall mildly suggested Mills "is rather bad medicine, I guess," the other replied, "Who? Ham Mills? . . . No! not a bit of it! you never saw a better fellow than Ham anywhere; he gets mad quick & shoots quick, but he's a good shot & never cripples; none of his men have ever known what hurt them & I really think he is sorry for it afterwards when he cools off."

Mills was, in fact, the former sheriff of Lincoln County. While he had indeed been convicted of manslaughter (and had been pardoned by the governor), the depiction of him as a wanton but accurate killer is an example of the leg-pulling, tall-tale humor of the frontier epitomized by Mark Twain's *Roughing It*. That Tunstall accepted the embellished story at face value, repeating it to his parents to impress upon them the character of the place, shows how impressed he was with the discomfort and dangerousness of his new life at the end of the earth.

Attempting to get a fix on Tunstall's personality by a close reading of his letters is tricky. His letters home were discursive, loving, excited, and cheerful appeals for money. He spent much of his time in New Mexico thinking up ways to make piles of money, and, it sometimes seems, spent the balance of his time trying to talk his father into advancing him the capital to finance his dreams of empire.

In March 1877, days after his twenty-fourth birthday, Tunstall wrote to his father about his "*latest* scheme for making money."[6] He explained that in Lincoln County, the army and Interior Department were cash customers for corn, hay, flour, and beef, and that freight costs from the settlements on the Rio Grande amounted to 1½ cents per pound – the equivalent of a protective tariff.

The way to make tons of money from the situation was obvious: corner the market in produce raised within the district, so that "Uncle Sam is compelled to patronise you & pour his almighty dollars into your lap." The way to do that was to open a store that would loan money to the local farmers and ranchers, or sell groceries to them on credit, in exchange for a promise to deliver x pounds of grain, hay, flour, or beef in the fall. "By this means," Tunstall told his parents, "T. can acquire a *controlling* interest in both these articles. The question then arises, is T. sure to get the [government] contracts? perhaps he may not, but whoever *does, must* come to T. to buy, or get 'bust.'"[7]

It was persuasive stuff. At least, it persuaded Tunstall senior to open his checkbook and advance the necessary cash. The store eventually opened, exactly along the lines outlined. And even today, anyone reading Tunstall's analysis for the first time is bound to be impressed by his reading of the situation. Tunstall's biographer Frederick Nolan comments, "The young adventurer's grasp of the economic situation in Lincoln County was incisive and correct."[8]

It was, but that shouldn't disguise the fact that he was describing the House. Every step in Tunstall's master plan had been taken, years before, by Lawrence Murphy. Whether Tunstall ever talked with Murphy and Dolan is unknown, but he did talk with McSween. Tunstall was clever and a good businessman. It doesn't detract from those qualities that, rather than concocting a master plan on his own, he agreed with McSween that the House was vulnerable to competition. The fact that Tunstall passed off the scheme as his own in his letter home was no more than good salesmanship. After all, why should Tunstall senior invest in Alexander McSween's plans?

Tunstall never mentioned Murphy, Dolan, or the House in any of his letters home. But the reference was clear when he told his parents, "I propose to confine my operations to Lincoln County, but I intend to handle it in such a way as to get the half of every dollar that is made in the county *by anyone*."[9]

Tunstall benefited greatly from the murder of a man named Bob Casey, one of Lincoln County's original Anglo settlers. Arriving just months after the close of the Civil War, Casey, a Confederate veteran from Texas, established a grist mill in the Rio Hondo valley, downstream from Lincoln. He also acquired some cattle and ran a modest operation on the Rio Felix, the tributary of the Pecos that gouged a valley parallel with the Bonito. But Casey never filed claim to his land; his ranch remained public domain.

In 1875 Casey was murdered by a man named William Wilson, who became not only the first but also the second person to be hanged in newly constituted Lincoln County. Wilson's inexperienced executioners may have suffered from stage fright when they made their debut. They let Wilson hang for nine and a half minutes, which sounds long enough, but wasn't. As Alexander McSween informed a correspondent, "Wilson was *well* hung – pronounced dead – showed signs of life in the coffin – was hung up the second time *con mucho gusto* until *really* dead."[10]

A year or two later the House obtained a judgment against the Casey estate, which in practical effect meant against his widow, who continued to run the grist mill. The judgment was for debt – the House sharks were closing in – and Sheriff William Brady, executing on the judgment, seized the entire Casey herd of over two hundred head of cattle. The herd was put up for auction.

At this point John Tunstall arrived in town looking for good land on which to run cattle, and his advisor Alexander McSween pointed him to the rich bottomland pastures of the Rio Felix. The water supply along the river was excellent. Best of all, the land was already improved, since the Casey family had been using it for a decade. Tunstall promptly filed on the land under the Desert Lands Act.

The Desert Lands Act allowed settlers to claim up to one square mile of designated tracts of public land for a down payment of just twenty-five cents an acre. You could acquire possession of a whole section of land for less than the cost of a mail coach ticket from St. Joseph to San Francisco.[11] A bargain. Or, as Mrs. Casey would have put it, a steal. Tunstall eventually acquired several thousand acres of prime grazing land – all of it land on which Bob Casey had once run his cattle.

Tunstall needed stock to run on his new ranch, and the Casey cattle auction was coming up fast. Tunstall dispatched McSween to attend the auction for him, and McSween put in a bid on Tunstall's behalf – at a fraction of the market price but more hard cash than the widow Casey was prepared to pay. Tunstall had his herd.[12]

The way Tunstall acquired his land and his cattle points up a couple of crucial facts about him. He was a shrewd businessman. He picked up a ranch and an entire herd for a song. But he was oblivious to the way others perceived him. Again and again we run across instances in which

Tunstall seemed not to understand quite how fully he had incurred the wrath of others. He was surprised, for example, when the Caseys took their revenge months later. Tunstall had a sort of emotional blind spot, based paradoxically on his honesty and forthrightness: he played the game fair and square, and he expected everyone else to be a good loser.

Almost immediately after succeeding to the Casey ranch and cattle, Tunstall began constructing his new store in Lincoln town. It was a traditional adobe structure, with solid walls several feet thick; today it houses the Lincoln post office. The building, located a short walk from McSween's home, was also intended to house McSween's law practice. In addition, Tunstall maintained an apartment in back. His ranch, on the Rio Felix, was many hours away over the steeply wooded ridge separating the parallel river valleys.

The sole outlet for Tunstall's dreamy, sentimental side in this spring and early summer of busy activity (other than his long letters home) was his love of horses. He was nuts about horses, purchased more whenever he could, described with delight their differing personalities and fretted about their ailments in his letters home, bestowed names on them, and chose his favorites. He prided himself on being a fine judge of horseflesh, but he also lavished affection on a U.S. Army reject he named Colonel. Colonel, a powerful chestnut, was rejected by the army for blindness. But it took more than loss of sight to discourage a horse lover of Tunstall's avidity. He told his parents:

> I have taught him to pick up his feet when I tell him we are coming to a bad place in the road, so that he does not strike it, & I can make him understand whether it is an up or down grade we are coming to. . . . He will come when I call him, & follow me around just as if he could see.[13]

Dolan and Chisum

5

In the spring of 1877, a few months after McSween's return from New York, Lawrence Murphy — his drinking out of control, already suffering from the cancer that would kill him eighteen months later — sold his interest in the House to his two partners, Jimmy Dolan and John Riley. Yet another Irishman, Jacob Mathews, also bought into the new enterprise, renamed J. J. Dolan & Co.

Jimmy Dolan grew up in the Irish slums of New York. In 1863, those slums exploded in the deadly draft riots. That same year, fifteen-year-old Jimmy Dolan joined the Union army, perhaps as a political statement, but more likely as an escape. After the war, in the regular army, he served time in several western outposts of greater or lesser desolation before hooking up with Murphy at Fort Stanton. He was wiry, dark-haired, with a snub nose and small, pinched features: a Yankee slum boy.

Murphy retired to his ranch near Carrizozo, northwest of Lincoln, where he ran cattle on no less than twenty square miles of unfenced range. According to a reporter for *The American Field,* "The house is furnished throughout with a luxuriousness and elegance of style which is utterly astonishing to one accustomed to the scant comforts of the ordinary ranch."[1] This tells us what happened to the $50,000 Emil Fritz reinvested in the House: Murphy took it. He spent his dead partner's share on his own ranch.

Selling the House when he did was the dying Murphy's crowning fraud. That the victims were his partners made his predatory circuit through Lincoln County complete.

That summer, Charles Fritz and Emilie Scholand petitioned Probate Judge Florencio Gonzáles for an order that the Fritz life insurance proceeds be paid to them. McSween suspected that Fritz wanted the money to pay off his own substantial debts to the House (leaving his surety, McSween, on the hook). He argued that the administrators shouldn't be allowed to get their hands on the money they were supposed to administer. Judge Gonzáles wasn't buying. On August 1, 1877, he requested Donnell, Lawson & Co., the New York City bankers, to deposit the insurance proceeds in the First National Bank of Santa Fe to the order of Charles Fritz.[2]

But the judge's letter was sent too late: Donnell, Lawson had already transferred the insurance proceeds, $7,148.49 – after deduction of its fees and the $700 advance – to McSween's St. Louis bank account.[3]

McSween filed a petition asking the judge to give him directions for distributing the money and also asking to be released from his bond. McSween's dilemma was twofold: his obligation as bondsman conflicted with his duty as attorney; his duty to prevent the looting of the estate conflicted with his duty to obey the administrators' directives. A much more basic conflict was also raised, of course: McSween could use the money.[4] For all of these reasons, he refused to do anything at all until ordered by the court. But the next term of probate court did not begin until January, five months away.[5]

By the time the insurance money came through, McSween was in business more or less in direct competition with the House. He was vice-president of the Lincoln County Bank. John Tunstall was the new bank's treasurer. John Chisum was president.

The mere mention of Chisum's name can conjure up romantic images of the Wild West, although he was born in Tennessee. His family moved to Texas just one year after the Battle of San Jacinto. Chisum was then twelve years old. He was thirty-five when the Civil War broke out. Already one of north Texas's most successful ranchers, he added to his fortune by inaugurating a series of long drives across Texas to the Red River ports that served the Confederacy. After the Union took control of the Mississippi, there were those envious souls who contended Chisum continued driving his cattle across Texas, all the way to New Orleans, where he accepted Union greenbacks for his stock.[6]

Chisum was a tall, lanky man with a high forehead, a prominent but dignified nose, and a mustache whose ends he sometimes waxed. His face was lined from long days in the southwestern sun, with fine crow's-feet gathering at the corners of his eyes.

In 1866, Charlie Goodnight and Oliver Loving created the Good-night-Loving Trail by wandering west and then north with a gigantic herd of longhorns, searching like characters in an existential drama sponsored by *The Wall Street Journal* for a market where they could re-alize a decent profit. The trail led from defeated and depressed Texas up the Pecos River through the territory of New Mexico and into the Rocky Mountains, where the federal government maintained its string of army forts and Indian reservations and paid top dollar for beef.

Goodnight and Loving were the first Texan cowmen to grasp the sig-nificance of the government contracts to let in the far West, but Chisum understood their potential. In 1867 he drove his herd into the Pecos River valley to stay, eventually building his home at South Spring River Ranch, where the Rio Hondo flows into the Pecos, some sixty miles downriver from Lincoln. The Bonito, Peñasco, and Felix flow more tamely now than when Chisum arrived in New Mexico, a consequence of flood control schemes and irrigation – and the overgrazing Chisum initiated. But in 1867, Chisum drove his herd of trail-thinned longhorns onto a pasture that had never been cropped by domestic animals.

Chisum later said he owned his ranch "by right of discovery,"[7] a re-mark that suggests something of his finely ironic humor, for he didn't own the land at all. It was government land, public domain, not yet opened for settlement (which meant the government paid top dollar to buy cattle fattened rent free on government land). Chisum's herd, esti-mated at fifty to ninety thousand head at its peak, simply took over the entire Pecos River valley from South Spring River Ranch to Fort Sum-ner, a distance of seventy miles.[8] A strip of land covering that entire dis-tance, and as wide across as a cow can wander from water in a day, con-stituted Chisum's ranch. And it all came free.

Chisum sold his cattle along the Goodnight-Loving Trail to the army posts of the Rocky Mountains, to the government posts in northern New Mexico and Arizona, and to the Santa Fe Trail civilian trade. Al-most the only available contracts he didn't have were those supplied by the House.

Fifty miles down the Pecos from Chisum's house was a town called Seven Rivers. Originally part of Doña Ana County, the Seven Rivers re-gion was joined to Lincoln County in early 1878. The townsite for Seven

Rivers was chosen spontaneously, so to speak – it was built in a field of persistent artesian wells. The town floated on an underground aquifer. The town doesn't exist today, since all the water long since spurted away, and the old townsite now basks on a dry lakebed. But in the 1870s, it was a tough little disorganized town, a center for the various small cattle operations of the southern Pecos valley.

In Lincoln town the small ranchers of Seven Rivers were called "Texans," regardless of their actual place of origin. The Texans were cowmen who had drifted westward looking for land and had found little squares of it south of Chisum's gigantic spread. They typically ran a few hundred to a thousand cattle; compared to Chisum, they were small fry. It was sometimes said that while Chisum's operation was the biggest industry in Lincoln County, rustling from Chisum was the second biggest. For the less honest of the Seven Rivers ranchers, blending "strays" into the herd was a cost-efficient way to raise cattle. The savings were passed on to J. J. Dolan & Co., which purchased cattle as an agent for government contractors – using Chisum's animals to underbid Chisum.

Chisum had given up on conventional brands, which could be easily disguised with the simple addition of a line here or dot there, developing instead the "long rail" brand, a single straight line seared along the animal's side from shoulder to hip. And when the long rail alone proved only partially effective, Chisum developed his most famous insignia, the jingle-bob earmark.

"Jingle-bob earmark" is a cheerful-sounding description of a barbaric practice: the animal's ear was split down the middle, two-thirds of the way to the head. The larger piece, supported by cartilage, would stand up and the smaller strip would flap loosely beside the animal's head.[9] The jingle-bob earmark was a hard mark to disguise.

When even the jingle-bob earmark failed to put an end to persistent rustling, Chisum organized the grandiloquently and somewhat ironically named "War on the Pecos." He gathered together thirty or so of his cowboys, armed them, and sent them south from South Spring River Ranch to the ranch of the Beckwith family, the most successful of the Seven Rivers ranchers.

On an earlier sweep through Seven Rivers, what might be termed a reconnaissance, John Chisum's brother Pitzer noticed a patch of newly turned earth near the Beckwith corrals. A shovel was procured, the earth was turned – and Pitzer dug up hundreds of split ears. The Seven Rivers men had hit upon the only way to disguise the jingle-bob earmark.[10] When the Beckwiths subsequently sold several hundred head of cattle in El Paso, Chisum decided it was time to act.

His "War on the Pecos" proceeded with comic-opera high seriousness. As the Chisum army approached, the Beckwith clan fortified itself inside the ranch house, and from an impossible distance of eight hundred yards or so the two sides took potshots at each other. Couriers were sent back and forth with dire threats and offers of safe conduct for the garrisoned women and children (who indignantly refused the offer). Chisum's men rounded up cattle grazing on the Beckwiths' land and herded northward what they ever afterward contended were Chisum cattle; that is, replacements for the one-eared cattle that had been sold down in El Paso. And the Beckwiths, not surprisingly, ever afterward accused Chisum of theft.

Andy Boyle, a Seven Rivers deputy sheriff (and the only law on the Pecos, since the sheriff lived 120 miles away in Mesilla), busied himself obtaining a warrant for Chisum's arrest, but nothing came of that either, and the faintly ludicrous "War on the Pecos" died down into a very serious blood feud.

In 1875 Chisum sold his entire herd to a St. Louis meatpacking firm, Hunter & Evans, for several hundred thousand dollars – the equivalent of several million today. Yet he stayed put, tending to his cattle. From his point of view, he received a fortune in cash and then continued living as he always had. From Hunter & Evans's point of view, who else would they hire to run their new ranch? No one knew the range, and the business, better than John Chisum.

The sale left Chisum flush with cash, searching for investments. Along came McSween with the idea for a bank. In the summer of 1877, the stationery was printed up, and the Lincoln County Bank was born.

Among its first customers was Jimmy Dolan, who needed a thousand dollars in a hurry.[11] It must have been humiliating for Dolan to borrow from his rival, and $1,000 wasn't nearly enough. The House, deeply in debt to the First National Bank of Santa Fe, was borrowing money to pay off debts: it had entered the shell-game stage of business failure.

Brewer to the Rescue

6

In the summer of 1877, about the time Henry McCarty returned to New Mexico from Arizona and changed his name to Bill Bonney, John Tunstall journeyed east to purchase supplies for his new store. On his way home some weeks later, Tunstall stopped overnight in Las Vegas, where his skin erupted with smallpox.[1] Thousands of miles from home, with no one to take care of him, he lay ill for an entire month, unable to resume his journey back to Lincoln. It is difficult to imagine a lonelier, more depressing experience. Tunstall, characteristically, never complained in his long letters home.

As Tunstall lay in a stranger's bed, trying not to die, the first in a succession of disasters struck his ranch down on the Rio Felix. Alexander McSween described it in a letter to *The Mesilla Valley Independent:*

September 18, 1877

This forenoon my horses and those of Mr. Tunstall were stolen from a ranche on the Rio Ruidoso. I valued my horses at seven hundred dollars; Tunstall's cost over one thousand dollars. Two of mine were fine black American horses; among Tunstall's were one of the handsomest mules in this section of country. Good citizens are in pursuit of the thieves and I hope they will overtake them and plunder.

For the recovery of these animals we will pay a liberal reward. The thieves were seen driving off the animals. "The boys" are known.

Yours, A. A. McSween[2]

Jesse Evans, the captain of the Boys, was short but solidly built, standing just over 5′5″ and weighing 150 pounds. His features were catalogued when he checked into a Texas penitentiary in 1880, serving time for the murder of a Texas Ranger: light hair, fair complexion, gray eyes.[3]

In 1877, Jesse was still just twenty-four years old, but he had built a formidable reputation. In June he had been acquitted of the murder of Quirino Fletcher in Las Cruces. Fletcher's body lay in the street over-night, suggesting he did not leave behind many mourners and giving a clue as to how Evans succeeded in proving he killed in self-defense. Just weeks after the verdict, Jesse was arrested again, this time in Paseo del Norte, Mexico (modern-day Juarez) for filibustering. Evans and the Boys (they gave their names as Johnson, Williams, Williams, and Jones) spent some time in a Mexican jail but were released when no one partic-ular charge could be pinned to them.[4]

Two years earlier, Evans participated in the dancehall murders of sev-eral soldiers in Mesilla, accomplished by firing through the windows. That particular slaughter was done in the company of John Kinney, Me-silla's most sophisticated criminal. Kinney began his flamboyant career as a butcher, literally. He vertically integrated his meatpacking opera-tion by employing criminals to steal the beef, a highly successful cost-cutting practice. He employed other criminals to protect his rustlers, and pretty soon he had a gang of professional outlaws on his payroll. Kinney was a frontier capo, the head of a family, running legitimate and illegitimate businesses side by side.[5] The district attorney, William Rynerson, wrote a letter to the governor complaining that the sheriff was too frightened to arrest Kinney. "The people are powerless. Ter-rorized."[6]

Kinney was Jesse Evans's teacher. After two years of study with the master, Jesse was ready to strike out on his own, moving to Lincoln County where he and the Boys found a ready market for their services. Jimmy Dolan had just opened a "cow camp" in Seven Rivers and needed a steady supply of low-price cattle. Evans and the Boys were effi-cient and businesslike in their rustling and could also provide a little muscle, when Dolan found it necessary. Their theft of Tunstall's and McSween's horses was a message.

As McSween reported in his letter to the editor of the *Independent*, "good citizens" were in pursuit of the horse thieves. The best of them was Tunstall's foreman Dick Brewer. Brewer was Jesse Evans's bête noire. Physically, they contrasted: Evans was short and blond while

Brewer was a large man (Tunstall described shaking his "big paw")[7] with dark curly hair and the sort of open handsomeness cameras love. Evans once told Brewer he saved his bullets specially for him, but Brewer triumphed in each of their encounters – a tribute not only to his courage and resourcefulness but also to his good sense not to press the issue on unpropitious occasions.

Brewer was a young man, still in his twenties, an immigrant from Wisconsin. Unlike many men who drifted west, he remained close to his family; his parents once visited him in Lincoln County. He purchased a farm on credit from the House upon his arrival, but the House played its usual trick of crediting his harvest against his debt at unreasonably low rates. One day Alexander McSween revealed that the House had never owned the farm in the first place. The House had simply taken over the land after the previous occupants left for Texas. Since the House never owned the farm, Brewer had been going ever deeper into debt for nothing.[8]

This revelation created some hard feelings on Brewer's part. He stopped making mortgage payments, which in turn caused some hard feelings on Jimmy Dolan's part. Rob Widenmann, a late arrival in Lincoln County, described what happened next:

I went to Brewer's ranch & while there J. J. Dolan accompanied by Wm Morton (the latter having the reputation of a desperate character in that county) came there and demanded that Brewer either leave the ranch or buy it of them, although it was known that Dolan had no title to it. Brewer replied that they had no title to the ranch, that he was living on it & had his crop in, but that if they would pay him for his improvements he would be willing to turn the ranch over to them rather than have trouble with them. Dolan declined the proposition & told Brewer that if the ranch was not turned over he would make it a personal matter with him, laying stress on the words "*personal matter with him*." Brewer said that he knew his rights and if necessary knew how to defend them. That he was not hunting any fuss, but that he did not run away from it. Dolan replied that if the ranch was not turned over Brewer would damned soon find what the fuss would be. At this time both Dolan and Morton were armed to the teeth.[9]

But Brewer didn't back down.

When the Boys stole Tunstall's horses, Brewer was working as Tunstall's foreman. He immediately started after the thieves, accompanied by two fellow farmers from the Rio Ruidoso, Charles Bowdre and Doc Scurlock – the beginning of a long association.[10] The three farmers tracked the stolen horses and mules over the flank of the volcano and across the desert all the way to Shedd's Ranch, high in the Organ Mountains near Mesilla. There they found the missing animals, including several that belonged to Brewer himself. They also found the Boys.

Tunstall told his parents what happened next. At the end of a long discussion, Evans said, in the reasonable tone of a businessman prepared to compromise, that he had no quarrel with Brewer, and if Brewer cared to, he was free to cut his own animals from the small herd and drive them back home. Brewer, with a loyalty that must have astonished Evans, said, "If you can't give me my horses without the Englishman's you can keep them all and go to hell."[11]

End of parley, beginning of feud. Brewer and Evans squared off almost as surrogates, each representing his own principal as well as himself. The collapse of their negotiations marks the true beginning of the Lincoln County War.

Brewer, Scurlock, and Bowdre left Shedd's Ranch and rode to Mesilla to obtain warrants for the arrest of the Boys. Apparently they expected to be able to encourage the Doña Ana County sheriff to raise a posse and recover the stolen animals. After all, the three men had tracked the animals and spoken with their thieves, who acknowledged the theft. The sheriff could hardly ask for more probable cause than that. But just because Brewer and his friends had the nerve to beard the lion in his den didn't mean the sheriff did. He did nothing.

Refusing to be frustrated, Brewer changed tactics. He rode back to Lincoln and had himself commissioned deputy constable by Lincoln's justice of the peace, John B. Wilson, becoming an auxiliary policeman with full power to raise his own posse.[12]

Three weeks later, on October 12, 1877, Brewer received word that the Boys could be found at the Seven Rivers ranch of Chisum's old nemeses, the Beckwiths. He dusted off the warrants and raised a posse of fifteen men, including Scurlock and Bowdre, and only then asked Sheriff Brady to join them. Turf was as important to law enforcement agencies then as it is today: a sheriff couldn't let himself be usurped by a deputy constable. So Brady saddled up and rode along, uncomfortably rehearsing in his mind all the sensible reservations that had previously occurred to his colleague in neighboring Doña Ana County.

At the confluence of the Peñasco and Pecos Rivers, Brady's nerve broke, and he announced his intention of returning to Lincoln. Brewer said he was going ahead even if he had to go alone. One by one, the fifteen men chose between Dick Brewer and their sheriff, and all fifteen chose to remain with Brewer. Shamed, Brady stuck with the group.

Brewer's posse found the Boys waiting for them in a lonely spot on the sunbaked rolling grasslands of the Beckwith ranch. The Boys were holed up in a *chozo,* a half-dugout built into the earth with solid adobe walls a foot or more thick — an ideal bunker, nearly impregnable, bristling with weaponry.

Laid up with smallpox in Las Vegas, Tunstall missed McSween's letter in the newspaper. Not until October 9, 1877, when he spoke with a traveler from Lincoln, did Tunstall learn of the Boys' depredations. He wrote his parents some weeks later that his horses and mules were stolen by "some desperadoes" at the head of a gang of one hundred men. "They had, it appears, threatened to kill McSween & Brewer & 'That Englishman' on sight, they were incited to make these threats by some people we know very well, against whom McS is bringing a lawsuit, with whom Brewer has a difficulty about a ranch, & whose business I have very nearly taken away."[13]

There is some exaggeration here, calculated to impress the folks back home with the Wild West's woolliness: Evans's band hardly numbered one hundred desperadoes (four was more like it), and if Evans had sworn to kill Brewer on sight, he missed a golden opportunity at Shedd's Ranch.[14] Nevertheless, the letter reveals Tunstall's understanding that the theft of his horses showed Jimmy Dolan's hand.

After four weeks in bed, listening to the church bells toll for victims of the epidemic, Tunstall was in no condition to travel. But he immediately ordered that his horse be fed, his buggy be greased, and his mess box be filled; the following morning he was on the road heading south. His horse, whom he had named Long Tom, had been boarded during his owner's illness. Before that had been boarded at the railhead in Trinidad while Tunstall journeyed back east. Horse and rider crowned their weeks of inactivity with forty miles the first day, forty the next, and forty the next, until they reached Lincoln on October 16, just three days after the departure of Brewer's posse.

Long Tom was put out to pasture to recuperate, but there was no rest for Tunstall. The goods and supplies he had ordered for his store arrived the same day he did, and he wound up sleeping among them "as a watchdog." It rained the next day and night, and his roof leaked, so he was up all night trying to fit his many crates and boxes into the few dry spots.

The following day, John Chisum gave the store its first business, sending in an order for various goods. Since the Boys had stolen his best animals, Tunstall had no choice but to press "a little rat of a white pony into service that Dick had thought was not even fit for service under the saddle," and which Jesse Evans apparently had not found worth the theft.[15] Tunstall hitched the runt to his loaded wagon and set out.

The White Mouse, as Tunstall derisively called the pony, was not strong enough for the task put to it. As night fell Tunstall was only part way to Chisum's ranch, somewhere in the long sloping funnel of the Hondo River valley. The persistent drizzle turned into driving sleet, and Tunstall's hands became too stiff with cold to hold the reins: he sat on the reins and pulled them with his fists. The White Mouse finally gave out altogether ten miles from any shelter, standing abjectly in the middle of the road, and no amount of whipping or coaxing could persuade it to continue. It had chosen to spend the night in a spot without water and without wood with which to make a fire. Tunstall spent that night walking in circles to keep warm. At dawn, he rehitched the pony and set out again for the Pecos. Just a few hours down the road he spied a group of horsemen heading his way. Minutes later he was shaking Dick Brewer's "great paw." He recorded the ensuing conversation for his parents' benefit: "But I thought you boys went out to round up some wild stock," he said, and Brewer laughed. Twenty or so riders were milling about on the road, and Tunstall, who had never seen any of the outlaws before, failed to recognize them.

"By God, Dick doesn't know if he's got us or we got him!" Jesse Evans said.

Tom Hill, one of the Boys, asked, "Well, have you got any whiskey, Englishman?"

"Merely a dram," Tunstall said. "If you knew me you would know I don't need any to keep my blood warm." Then he added a curious invitation: "But if you met me in Lincoln I would soak you if you wished."

"Well, we'll be in the jug then," Hill answered. "You can soak us there if you like."

To which Tunstall replied, "All right."

Sheriff Brady led the prisoners back to Lincoln. Brewer stayed behind and breakfasted with Tunstall, bringing him up to date on everything that had happened. The posse had found the Boys holed up in the *chozo* and pockmarked it with harmless gunfire. After everyone had wasted a fair amount of ammunition to no effect, it became clear that while the posse would find it difficult to overrun the *chozo,* the Boys would find it impossible to escape. There was no point in anyone getting himself killed needlessly, so the Boys surrendered.

Brewer said to Tunstall over breakfast, "They'll get out of jail sure as fate. They have more friends than enemies in this county. Brady will let them out for sure."

The posse disbanded, and Tunstall continued alone to Chisum's South Spring River Ranch. But no sooner were the four Boys locked inside Lincoln's new underground jail – a pit in the ground beneath a locked shed – than Brewer discovered the crowning disaster: Tunstall's entire herd, over two hundred head of cattle, had been stolen.

Of course, "stolen" is not the word Bob Casey's widow would have used. She thought of it as settling accounts with John Tunstall for appropriating the family ranch and herd. With Tunstall sick and his foreman occupied, Mrs. Casey had seized the opportunity, hiring cowboys to drive the herd back to her family's country in Texas.

Brewer immediately organized a second posse, enlisting six veterans of the previous campaign, and hit the road again. The posse pressed into service all of Tunstall's available horses, including poor Long Tom, and covered no less than fifty miles the first day. Luckily, Tunstall had ordered a case of carbines for his store, and the posse members helped themselves. The technology of weaponry was developing so quickly in the late nineteenth century that a late-model rifle was a different class of weapon than a rifle sold just a few years earlier. And, as Tunstall bragged to his parents, "You bet there was no discount on the way those boys could handle them."

As the small posse neared the Texas line, it became imperative to acquire fresh horses, so Dick Brewer and a second man stopped to haggle with a man who had some to sell. The locals said the posse might as well give up, since the herd was being driven by twenty-six Texans and seven tired men on jaded horses were no match. Tunstall wrote – and we can hear the pride with which he wrote it – that Brewer responded, "I don't care if there are 126, I mean to get back that herd."

Brewer must have felt a certain personal responsibility for the herd – that was a foreman's job. But the existence of a good motive doesn't explain the courage that allowed him to pursue rustlers with such epigrammatic élan. He always knew what to do and what to say while doing it.

It was essential that the herd be turned before reaching the Texas border, since the legal obstacles to extradition would have made it cheaper to buy a new herd in New Mexico. Moreover, while McSween had persuaded Lincoln's justice of the peace to issue a writ of replevin authorizing Brewer's counterstrike, the writ had no force outside the territory. So when Brewer and another man stopped to buy horses, the remaining five members of the posse pressed on, led by John Middleton. Tunstall described Middleton as "about the most desperate looking man I ever set eyes on (& that is not saying a *little*)," but he added that Middleton was "mild and composed."

Middleton and his four remaining companions caught up with the herd just ten miles from the border (or so they said – they wouldn't have admitted it if they thought they had crossed the line). The twenty-six Texan drovers of rumor turned out to be just seven men, but they still outnumbered the five posse members. With the border so close there was no time for delay. Middleton and his men galloped without warning toward the lead cattle, cutting them off and bringing the herd to a halt.

The seven drovers rode for a nearby low hill, dismounted, and unsheathed their rifles, threatening battle. Middleton spread his men across the hillside so as to avoid presenting a concentrated target. With their brand-new carbines at the ready, the posse advanced uphill. The drovers, who were hired men with no personal stake in the matter, surrendered the herd.

Once again, Tunstall learned of the excitement well after the fact. He completed his delivery to Chisum's ranch and bought a new horse from one of the Mormon settlers Chisum had encouraged to come live along the Pecos. Riding the Mormon Pussy (as he called his new horse), leading the White Mouse, Tunstall arrived back in Lincoln. There he was met by the local justice of the peace, J. B. Wilson, an old Mexican War veteran who had lived most of his adult life in the country.

"Well, Englishman, they seem bound to drive you out of the country," said the Justice of the Peace (an old fool who is about as much use as a fifth wheel would be on a coach). "How is that?" I said. "Well, all your cattle are driven off & I guess in Texas before now." "Good night," said I & drove on to see McSween to hear about it.

Tunstall's contempt for Wilson was misplaced. In the coming months, Justice Wilson would prove to be one of his most valuable allies. Indeed, Wilson had signed the papers Brewer carried with him as authority for driving the herd back to Tunstall's ranch along the Rio Felix.

Sheriff Brady and the Boys

7

That autumn, Dick Brewer hired a new cowboy for Tunstall's Rio Felix ranch. The new hand called himself Bill Bonney and was still just a teenager.

True to his word, Tunstall visited the imprisoned Boys. He told his parents that he chatted with them. "I got them pretty mad over a few things I told them that were too true to be palatable, but I never was notorious for 'rubbing the right way.'"[1]

The Boys kidded (or maybe it wasn't kidding) that Tunstall's mules were sold to a priest down in Old Mexico, that is, were beyond recall. Tunstall was not discouraged: "They found that I could joke as well as they could & we laughed a good deal. Some time after that I sent them a bottle of whiskey. I went to see them in gaol after that & joked them a good deal."

Evans was not impressed. He told Tunstall he was amused by the visits, since "what you want to know is where your mules are, & you don't get to find out."

Tunstall responded, according to his letter, that he never went begging for a woman and he certainly wouldn't go begging for some mules. He told Evans, "you should go to Hell & the mules too before I would ask you for them!" To which Evans replied, "Bully for you" (or words to that effect, which Tunstall spared his mother).

This exchange took place in the yard outside the jail. Tunstall wrote that when the Boys were ordered below to the cell, Evans invited him down for a visit. But Tunstall couldn't go without permission from the sheriff and Brady refused to give it. Tunstall commented, "He is an Irishman, a slave of whiskey & a man I think very little of, he is a tool."

Brady, we can be sure, thought equally little of moneyed Englishmen who used "Irishman" as an insult. He had immigrated from County Wexford and made a career in the army, eventually fetching up on the southwestern frontier, exactly as Murphy did. He departed from the pattern when he married an Hispanic woman and fathered no fewer than eight children, giving him a family life more stable, or at least more extensive, than anyone else involved in the Lincoln County War.[2]

Brady had a heavy oval face with drooping mustaches and a body like a sack of potatoes. He was elected the first sheriff of brand-new Lincoln County in 1869. Two years later he moved on to the territorial legislature, easily defeating incumbent representative Florencio Gonzáles. In 1876, with the scope of his political ambition receding, he returned to the post of sheriff.

A strange encounter took place in Tunstall's store a few days before Jesse Evans and the Boys escaped from jail. Alexander McSween described the scene in later testimony:

> Sheriff Brady came into Tunstall's store in a half intoxicated condition and indirectly accused Mr. Tunstall of giving the credit of the arrest of said outlaws to R. M. Brewer . . . and had considerable talk with Mr. Tunstall and among other things accused Mr. Tunstall of having tried to aid Baker, Evans, Hill and Davis to escape.[3]

The charge that Tunstall was trying to help the Boys escape is sensational enough that it is easy to overlook Brady's first point. It seems that Tunstall was telling everyone who would listen that Brady was chicken. Tunstall had plenty of opportunity to spread rumors, since his store was open and doing fabulous business. It was perfectly natural for the storekeeper to pass the time of day with his customers by airing his opinions on the county's recent sensational events. But it must have galled Brady. McSween continued:

> Mr. Tunstall told him, "You know their shackles are filed & there are holes cut in the logs and take no pains to secure them, and do you dare accuse me who have aided in the arrest of these persons, who have threatened my life with assisting them to escape?" Sheriff

Brady thereupon put his hand upon his revolver as though he was going to draw it, and I stepped between them and plac[ed] my hand on his shoulder and said, "It ill becomes you, as a peace officer, to violate the law by shooting." Brady replied, "I won't shoot you now, you haven't long to run. I ain't always going to be Sheriff."[4]

This passage may prove nothing except that McSween had a tin ear for dialogue. The only speech of the three that rings true is Brady's parting shot, but it was transparently McSween's intent to contrast the sheriff's use of "ain't" with his and Tunstall's highfalutin speeches. Yet it seems to be true that the argument suddenly turned tense with the very real threat of violence, for Tunstall's account, written for his parents, corroborates McSween's in important aspects. Tunstall wrote that Brady

called me "a fool"; I affixed a couple of adjectives & raised my voice one note louder than his & returned the compliment. He reached around to his left hip for his Colt's revolver, but did not get his hand on it; & I would think for his sake it was as well he did not, for I had him covered with my pocket pistol that carried a half inch ball & I should have turned loose had his hand once touched the butt of his pistol.[5]

It's a long way from Belsize Terrace to the contemplated slaying of a peace officer. Tunstall was tough, but he was too proud of his toughness. Humiliating the local sheriff is never a wise move for any newcomer. Tunstall's sense of petty triumph helps to explain how he evaded the House's machinations as long as he did. Almost alone among the county's residents, he never gave the House an inch, and he regarded Brady as the House's agent. But his victory in the shouting match earned him a lifelong enemy.

Brady's accusation that Tunstall wanted to help the Boys escape was based on Tunstall's jailhouse visits. It was as obvious to Brady as to Evans that Tunstall kept coming around because he wanted his horses and mules back. Wasn't it possible that Tunstall had struck a deal whereby he would help free the Boys in exchange for the return of the animals?[6]

Brady's accusation rests on the assumption that because Tunstall was prepared to do some things to soften up the Boys, he was prepared to do anything. This overlooks the perfectly reasonable fear Tunstall had of the Boys and their unincarcerated friends. He repeated to his parents the rumor that the Boys' friends were massing for a raid on the jail. During the same period, he found himself riding along an isolated trail when suddenly his horse Mormon Pussy "threw back an ear & seemed to hear something. The next moment I heard it too, swung her around & threw up my carbine. I had not much time to waste as the horse I heard was coming on a keen run; my heart was in my mouth, for the rascals had sworn to kill 'that Englishman' on sight."[7]

Tunstall's letter reads like the cliffhanger ending of a serial episode. Like most cliffhangers, it was resolved in anticlimax, for the rider proved to be a neighbor in a hurry. But unless the incident was a complete fabrication, it shows Tunstall thought his life was in danger. Why would he free prisoners who wanted to kill him? Besides, Brady was drunk when he made the accusation and furious at Tunstall for questioning his courage. People in a drunken temper say things that shouldn't be taken seriously at the time, much less a century later.

Brewer predicted the day after the capture that the Boys would escape because they had more friends than enemies in the county. Juan Patrón likewise testified that he believed that Murphy, Dolan, Riley, and the sheriff "were friendly with [the Boys] and assisted them."[8]

Dolan's and Riley's friendship with the Boys might in itself have given them sufficient motive to aid the jailbreak. But that friendliness also meant they had reason to fear the Boys. What if the Boys were put on trial and testified that they had been put up to the job by Jimmy Dolan? Dolan also had need of the Boys' services – that's why he first associated with them. It was a mutually profitable business arrangement, and Dolan's need for profits was greater in November than in September, since Tunstall's store was sucking the lifeblood from the House.

All in all, it seems most probable that the Boys' escape was arranged by Dolan, who had the most to gain. It is equally likely that the planned jailbreak was winked at by the sheriff. Brady's accusation that Tunstall had a hand in the plot is damning: he made the accusation several days *before* the escape.

Tunstall learned of the jailbreak the day after it happened. Just as he was hearing the details from a man on the street, Justice of the Peace Wilson rode into town "in a great state of excitement" and reported that the Boys, with all of their confederates, had laid siege to Brewer's place on the Ruidoso and "had been firing there since daybreak."[9] Tunstall resolved to ride at once to Brewer's rescue. Not too surprisingly, no one wanted to accompany him.

McSween joined in Tunstall's efforts to round up an impromptu posse, but significantly did not ride with him. Tunstall did not expect him to; McSween never pretended to be a man of action. Sheriff Brady, according to Tunstall, sullenly demurred, saying, "I arrested them once and I will be damned if I am agoing to do it again. Hereafter I will look after Brady's interests."

Tunstall pressed on alone, pushing his mare hard. When he neared Brewer's house, he saw that "smoke was crawling over the flat roof & smoke was rising from the corner of the corral where the hay stack had stood." Unfortunately, it was not possible to approach the house without crossing a large open area. Tunstall spurred the mare and sped forward, expecting a barrage of bullets.

Instead, he was calmly greeted by three of Brewer's hands, who reported that Dick was up the river attending to his farm. Tunstall exploded, "Confound you, ain't any of you killed & I have got up all this agony for nothing. Where's Jesse Evans & the boys?"

As it turned out, the smoke lay on the roof because the chimney was broken, and the smoke by the corral was where the Boys had prepared their breakfast. Nonetheless, the J.P.'s excited story was partly correct: the Boys had shown up at Brewer's farm with some friends and had "ordered breakfast & sat around the fire as cozy as could be."

The Boys' visit is sometimes taken as proof of Brewer's complicity in the escape. But when the escaped prisoners showed up at daybreak, armed, accompanied by friends and demanding breakfast, Brewer didn't have the option of phoning the police. Even if one man could get away and ride into town, it would be hours before help arrived. Armed resistance was always possible, but the Boys were more experienced than the farmhands at that sort of thing.

The Boys took eight horses from Brewer's corral – not a friendly gesture. But, Tunstall reported, they apologized for taking them, saying, "We are on foot & need them more than he does." Not only that, but the Boys promised to return the horses to Tunstall "& every hoof we ever took from him; we were put up to do that job on Dick & him, but we see the stuff they are made of & we will never take a thing of theirs again." Even if they didn't make the speech quite as reported, the Boys apparently did return all but one of the horses they took that day (though not the animals they had stolen previously). The returned horses were worn out from hard riding, but still this seems extraordinary, the only real evidence of some sort of understanding. (But what was in it for Tunstall and Brewer? Why give up a second group of horses for the return of the first group?)

Perhaps, as Tunstall chose to believe, the Boys had learned a grudging respect, and their apology was sincere.

More likely, they realized they could beat the horse theft rap by returning the animals as soon as their immediate usefulness was at an end: horse stealing was a crime but horse borrowing was not, and the Boys didn't reach their pinnacle of success by pressing their luck.

Catron's Trap

8

On December 7, 1877, Charles Fritz, as administrator of the Emil Fritz estate, filed a petition with the Lincoln County Probate Court asking that Alexander McSween be ordered to pay the insurance proceeds into court, subject to the court's order. McSween probably shrugged this off. It was to be expected that Fritz would make a formal request for the money.[1]

In fact, the Fritz petition was the first step in an elaborate trap set not for McSween but for John Tunstall. The trap was the brainchild of Thomas Benton Catron, the United States attorney for New Mexico and political boss of the territory.[2]

A roly-poly man with a thick black mustache and bulging eyes, Catron was wealthy beyond the dreams of all save the true robber barons. In the course of his spectacular career he acquired over three million acres of New Mexico – an area the size of Connecticut – at a time when most of New Mexico was public domain.

Catron was the leader of the celebrated Santa Fe Ring. The word "ring" had acquired a certain glamour in New Mexico in the 1870s. Tunstall told his parents, "*Everything* in New Mexico that pays *at all* . . . is worked by a 'ring,'" adding that he intended to create his own ring.[3]

In his 1878 governor's message, Governor Samuel Axtell denied the existence of the Santa Fe Ring. *The Albuquerque Review* commented: "The poor man seems to think that he is charged with being in this 'ring.' . . . Why bless your simple heart Sammy dear! They wouldn't trust you to enter the first grade of apprenticeship in their systematized organization of rascality, because they do not need you."[4]

The word "ring" conjures up images of Tammany Hall – of an efficiently oiled political machine dispensing favors, extorting bribes, and swiftly punishing honesty and other treachery. The *Review*'s sarcasm notwithstanding, to imply that the Santa Fe Ring ever worked with such efficiency is to give it too much credit. The Ring is best understood as an informal confederation of businessmen/politicians swapping favors and telling no tales.

Catron's job as federal prosecutor gave him an ideal position from which to enforce discipline within the Ring. The distinguishing feature of Catron's career as prosecutor was the huge discrepancy between indictments and convictions. Many were charged but few served time.[5] Between grand jury and trial was plenty of time to cut a deal, and Catron was always on the lookout for a good deal.

In 1872 S. H. Newman, a territorial newspaperman and founder of the paper that became *The Las Vegas Gazette,* spent sixty-four days in jail on a charge of criminal libel (to which truth was no defense) for publishing an affidavit sworn out by a citizen of Santa Fe attacking Catron. The experience of being prosecuted by the target of his exposé taught Newman a thing or two about the Santa Fe Ring. He moved to Colorado.[6]

Catron (CATron, from the German *Kettenring*) was born in Missouri. He was named for Missouri's legendary Senator Thomas Hart Benton, but when Benton came out for the Union, his father renamed him Thomas Jefferson Catron. After the war, Tom found it expedient to resume his former middle name, thus drawing around his shoulders the cloak of Missouri pro-Unionism.

In 1861, when the South liked its chances, it was less obvious to twenty-year-old Tom, then a student at the University of Missouri, that his fortunes were best served by joining Abe Lincoln's cause. He was commissioned a lieutenant in the Confederate Missouri Brigade just two months after the shelling of Fort Sumter and served until Appomattox.

Returned to civilian life, Catron took up the study of law. Then the first Reconstruction legislature passed a law prohibiting rebels from practicing law in Missouri. At this crossroads Catron met his old college roommate, Stephen Benton Elkins, also a namesake of the senator. Elkins fought on the Union side, but by 1863 he had seen enough and lit out for the territories where no one (except maybe the Apaches) wanted to kill him. He landed in Mesilla, New Mexico, where he set up shop as a lawyer.

Little had changed in New Mexico since General Stephen Watts Kearny's 1846 invasion. The territory that had been at the northern extreme of the Mexican Republic found itself at the southwestern extreme of the United States, and both central governments tended to leave the outpost alone. The net effect was that in 1863 New Mexico remained at zero hour. No effective civilian American administration had ever been put in place, and after the Texans were routed at Glorieta, only Republicans needed apply for government positions. There was a shortage of talented Republicans to fill such posts as district attorney. At this opportune moment Stephen Elkins, with his gladhanding manner and Republican credentials, shook the trail dust from his clothes.

Elkins immediately became district attorney for the third district and by the following year was also serving in the territorial House of Representatives. A year later he moved his base of operations to Santa Fe. On a vacation to Missouri, he convinced Catron that the future was in New Mexico. Catron studied Spanish during the long journey across the plains, began calling himself a Republican, and succeeded to Elkins's position as district attorney in Mesilla even before joining the bar. He later inherited Elkins's seat in the territorial House, and then the two became partners in a law office in Santa Fe.

Elkins went on to great things. As New Mexico's congressional delegate, he met and married the daughter of Henry Gassaway Davis, a (Democratic) West Virginia senator. The two men dominated their respective state party organizations and together built twin fortunes, eventually founding Davis and Elkins College in Elkins, West Virginia. Elkins, the Republican half of the team, served as secretary of war under Benjamin Harrison. He wound up as senator and was seriously discussed as possible Republican presidential or (more realistically) vice-presidential candidate. Instead, in 1904, his octogenarian father-in-law and business partner became the Democratic nominee for vice-president. Elkins deftly combined family with party loyalty by criticizing the Democrats for placing Alton Parker at the top of the ticket over the vastly more qualified Davis.[7]

Catron and Elkins were a great team. As Catron's brother-in-law remembered:

I have often while in New Mexico heard it said that if one asked Mr. Elkins for a favor, he would shake you by the hand, smile on you, pat you on the back and ask you to come again, but he would never grant your wish; that if you asked Catron for a favor, he would bluster, take your head nearly off, but give you what you asked for if it was a reasonable request.[8]

Catron never aspired to the heights reached by Elkins, concentrating instead on the opportunities available in wide-open New Mexico to a hardworking, clever, and not overly scrupulous attorney and politician. There were those three million acres to acquire.

Catron was greedy in his legendary breakfasts of pancakes, steak and eggs, and gallons of coffee; he was equally greedy in his appetite for land. But he was always loyal to those who remained loyal to him, loaning money to get them out of trouble and giving them good patronage jobs.

Catron was a principal owner of the First National Bank of Santa Fe, which had loaned a great deal of money to the House.[9] The loans would be repaid only if the House remained in business. But, faced with competition from Tunstall, the House was rapidly going broke. And so, without knowing the first thing about it, Tunstall stood between Tom Catron and his money.

His judgment clouded by the hubris that was to (temporarily) topple him from power in less than a year, Catron resolved to nudge Tunstall to one side.

As a legal maneuver, the trap Catron set for Tunstall bordered on genius. The only reason it didn't work as planned was because Tunstall was English, but Catron can hardly be blamed for failing to foresee the significance of that fact.

McSween intended to travel to St. Louis over Christmas. Credit must be given to the legal mind that recognized McSween's travel plans – which, at first glance, had nothing to do with Tunstall – as the chink in Tunstall's armor. Later, after he had been accused of attempting to sneak out of New Mexico with the insurance money, McSween protested in a letter to the editor of a Las Cruces newspaper:

I was requested to go to St. Louis on business for Col. Hunter [the meatpacking tycoon who had purchased Chisum's entire herd]. Every man, woman, and child in the town knew I was going three weeks before I left. Before leaving I wrote Captain Crouch [the clerk of the district court], Judge Bristol, Judge Newcomb, and Mrs. Fountain of my contemplated trip, how long I expected to be absent, &c. Two or three days before leaving Mr. Fritz called at my office and asked if I would pay him a specific sum of money; I replied in the affirmative. I told him I was going; how long I expected to be absent.[10]

But there was the rub. If McSween had actually been sneaking off, Catron would not have known what to do. By giving three weeks' notice of his plans, McSween unwittingly gave his enemies three weeks to do some planning of their own. It is no coincidence that Fritz's probate court petition was filed just a few days less than three weeks before McSween's departure.

McSween left Lincoln shortly before Christmas in the company of his wife and John Chisum. Business provided the excuse for the trip, but no doubt the McSweens looked forward to a visit with family and friends back in Kansas. The cavalcade had reached Las Vegas on Christmas Eve when McSween, according to his own newspaper account, "was informed that certain parties had telegraphed to know if I were there. I told my informant to telegraph that I was."

The "certain parties" turned out to be United States Attorney Thomas B. Catron himself, as McSween revealed in later deposition testimony.[11] Catron telegraphed orders to the sheriff of San Miguel County to arrest both McSween and Chisum. The sheriff, of course, had no warrant to arrest McSween and Chisum and no probable cause to believe they had committed any crime, but he also had no reason to defy Tom Catron. He detained McSween and Chisum for as long as he could without papers. After forty-eight hours he was obliged to let them resume their trip. Just a few miles outside of Las Vegas, however, they were suddenly overtaken by the sheriff and posse.

Chisum wrote a self-glorifying, third-person account of what happened next. The sheriff, with thirty or forty men, made a "desperate charge" on the ambulance and

> Chisum was jerked out head foremost & fell upon his face on the hard road and seized by the throat . . . he still held his grip until Chisum said to the Sheriff: "Will you please be so kind as to loosen the grip of this . . . cur?" The Sheriff spoke and the man loosed his hold so Chisum breathed once more of the fresh air of New Mexico that they brag so much about. McSween was also jerked out of the ambulance and dragged off by a lot of the gang & Mrs. McSween

left sitting all alone crying in the ambulance without a driver or even a protector. The Sheriff and his party were somewhat excited; McSween was somewhat confused; Chisum laughing and cool.[12]

Cool Chisum noticed one gang member who had a clean shirt, and asked him to drive Mrs. McSween back to the hotel, which he did.

McSween Accused

9

McSween was arrested by the San Miguel County sheriff pursuant to an arrest warrant issued by Judge Warren Bristol down in Mesilla. The warrant was based on this affidavit:

> Emily Scholand, being first duly sworn on oath says that she is informed and believes and verily does believe that Alexander McSween has committed the crime of embezzlement by embezzling and converting to his own use the sum of ten thousand dollars belonging to the Estate of Emil Fritz deceased, to wit at the county of Lincoln on the tenth day of December in the year of our Lord one thousand eight hundred and seventy seven in the Territory of New Mexico and in the 3rd Jud. Dist. said Ter'y.[1]

The affidavit is a curiosity. Whoever wrote it didn't know how Emilie Scholand spelled her first name. And why the tenth of December? And what was the source of Mrs. Scholand's "information and belief"? That phrase is still used by lawyers to signal that the witness has no personal knowledge of the facts.

The Fourth Amendment to the United States Constitution says that "no warrants shall issue, but upon probable cause, supported by oath or affirmation ."[2] While Mrs. Scholand's affidavit was given under oath, the facts about the insurance money were not. Mrs. Scholand stated her conclusion without revealing its basis. In effect, she (or whoever drafted the affidavit) made the probable cause determination; Judge Bristol did nothing but sign the piece of paper placed in front of him. He must have known he was violating the Constitution when he did so.[3]

Jimmy Dolan sometimes took credit for the affidavit. In a deposition taken by Special Agent Frank Angel, Dolan testified that Probate Judge Gonzáles called a special session of court on "I think the 10th day of December 1877" (a coincidence that fails to explain quite why the affidavit claims the embezzlement occurred that day), and that McSween told the judge that "he was ready to pay over the money if Mrs. Scholand the co-administrator with Chas. Fritz was present." Dolan continued:

The result was that the court adjourned til 1st Monday in January 1878, at which time Mrs. Scholand was to be present, she being notified by the clerk of the court & the money paid over. McSween was to be present and turn over the money – he made no objection, nor did he say that he was going away or could not be present.

Before the meeting of the court McSween left for St. Louis as everyone believed never to come back. I went to Mesilla and communicated the facts to Mrs. Scholand and whereupon McSween was arrested at Las Vegas and brought back to Mesilla on the charge of embezzlement.[4]

Later in the course of his testimony Dolan changed his memory slightly, testifying:

The only object I had in going to Mesilla was to obtain legal advice and have counsel represent me before the Probate Judge at Lincoln on the 3d Monday of January 1878. That while at Mesilla word was brought to me from Lincoln by James J. Longwell that McSween had left for St. Louis as aforementioned with the intention of never returning.

I did not go expressly from Lincoln to Mesilla to communicate with Mrs. Scholand but to obtain counsel as mentioned aforesaid. I do not remember whether I called on her before I received the information of McSween's leaving, or whether I called on her after I had received the information.

There you have it, enough facts to let the investigator pick and choose his favorites. Either "everyone believed" McSween was going for good, or else Dolan had to be told by Longwell. Perhaps Dolan "communicated the facts to Mrs. Scholand," or perhaps he first heard them after he called on her. Judge Gonzáles intended to reconvene court on the first Monday in January – unless it was the third Monday.

In the same letter to the editor in which he described his arrest, McSween denied he had embezzled the money. On the contrary, he wrote:

> I told Mr. Fritz repeatedly that I was ready, anxious and willing to pay the balance in my hands over to him and Mrs. Scholand; that if Mrs. Scholand could not come in person she could authorize him or some other person to receive the money for her.[5]

McSween's professed willingness to pay over the money seems self-serving, the minimum that anyone in his position would claim. Unexpectedly, Jimmy Dolan corroborated McSween's story, needless to say, without any intention of doing so. Dolan testified:

> I did write a letter to Chas Fritz, knowing that he was in the habit of getting intoxicated, not to make any settlement with McSween before first consulting his lawyers. I never threatened him either directly or indirectly as to the same – I did this out of friendship to Fritz & his sister.[6]

The subject of a settlement could not possibly have come up between McSween and Fritz unless McSween had proposed to pay over the insurance money. In other words, Dolan told Fritz not to accept the money from McSween – and then arranged for Fritz's sister to sign an affidavit accusing McSween of embezzling it.

Dolan's actions seem inconsistent, but they were not. The money was most valuable to Dolan in McSween's hands. As long as McSween kept the money, the jaws of the trap Catron had set for Tunstall continued to close. Putting Tunstall out of business was worth far more to Catron than the few thousand dollars in McSween's bank account. The trap depended on Judge Bristol being able to find that McSween had embezzled the money. And so the last thing Catron and Dolan wanted was for McSween to surrender the money before he could be arrested for keeping it.

They had to move fast to prevent the payout in December. Dolan leaned hard on Charles Fritz not to accept the money, no doubt leaving the sodden Fritz in a state of miserable befuddlement. That bought time for Catron's telegrams to work their magic.

McSween wrote in his letter to the editor that

> it has been said that every man has his price, but ten thousand dollars and interest is not my price; for whilst I continued acting honestly and uprightly, I can easily command double that sum if necessary. In addition to all this my personal and real interests in the town of Lincoln far exceed the amount of money in my hands belonging to the Fritz estate.[7]

He was not exaggerating.

Mrs. Scholand accused McSween of embezzling ten thousand dollars, but that badly overstates the case. McSween had in his account only $7,148.46, the balance having already been paid out to the bankers and Spiegelberg Bros. Of that $7,148.46, $1,500 (10 percent of the total plus a $500 retainer) represented McSween's own fee; another chunk represented reimbursement for his expenses in traveling to New York. Moreover, McSween informed the editor of the *Eco del Rio Grande* that Murphy had hired him in 1875 to collect debts owed to the Fritz estate, and he had brought in $30,769.00.[8] McSween charged 10 percent for his collections, and so the estate owed him an additional $3,076.90, plus expenses of $538.60, for a grand total of $5,115.50. In short, when Mrs. Scholand accused McSween of embezzling the full $10,000, she was accusing him of embezzling his own money.

It wasn't all his, of course, but most of it was. Only about $2,000 remained to be embezzled. Judge Bristol knew that. When he later instructed the grand jury investigating McSween's case, he acknowledged that "there still remained $2,000 about which there was no dispute."[9]

McSween's property in Lincoln County was appraised afterwards at $7,379.50, and that was a conservative estimate. His law library was assigned a figure ($3,000) two and a half times that assigned his newly built house ($1,200).[10] The appraisal apparently did not include all of McSween's property. It did not include the income stream a busy lawyer could expect from an established practice or the future value of his interest in the Lincoln County Bank. By fleeing New Mexico as a felon, McSween would have abandoned all that. As a matter of simple economics, embezzlement of $2,000 was a losing proposition.

McSween was dragged out of the ambulance a half-mile outside of Las Vegas and bounced on the road by a sheriff's posse for an economically nonsensical crime. The sheriff seemed apologetic; he put McSween in the jailer's quarters rather than in a cell. McSween remained in custody throughout the holiday season. Sue eventually continued eastward on what must have been an anxious and uneasy vacation.

On January 5, 1878, McSween left Las Vegas for Lincoln, the first stage of a journey to Mesilla to attend a preliminary hearing before Judge Bristol.[11] He remained in custody, guarded by San Miguel County Sheriff's Deputy Adolph Barrier. Like all sheriff's deputies, Barrier was a part-timer. According to an ad he ran in the local newspaper, in real life he was a "decorative painter."[12] Dusty Las Vegas may not have been ready for a full-time housepainter. Otherwise Barrier wouldn't have needed to supplement his income by transporting prisoners across the territory, and couldn't have afforded to take a month off from work to escort McSween to Mesilla.

It would have been unlike John Tunstall to pretend nothing was happening. He may have realized he was the real target of the attacks on McSween and Chisum. He fought back.

The great advantage of Tunstall's position was that he could attack his rivals merely by telling the truth. The truth about the House's business practices was a slanderer's malicious fantasy come true. Moreover, Tunstall could make his point merely by repeating a remark made by the territory's governor, Samuel Beach Axtell, in his annual State of the Territory address to the legislature.[13] So Tunstall dashed off the following letter to *The Mesilla Valley Independent:*

January 18, 1878

"The present sheriff of Lincoln County has paid nothing during his present term of office."   *Governor's Message for 1878*

Editor of the Independent:

The above extract is a sad and unanswerable comment on the efficiency of Sheriff Brady, and cannot be charged upon "croakers." Major Brady, as the records of this County show, collected over *Twenty-five hundred dollars,* Territorial funds. Of this sum Alex. A. McSween Esq. of this place paid him over *Fifteen hundred dollars* by cheque on the First National Bank of Santa Fe, August 23, 1877.

Said cheque was presented for payment by John H. Riley Esq., of the firm of J. J. Dolan & Co., this last amount was paid by the last named gentleman to Underwood and Nash for cattle. Thus passed away over *Fifteen hundred dollars* belonging to the Territory of New Mexico.

With the exception of thirty-nine dollars, all the Taxes of Lincoln County for 1877 were promptly paid when due.

Let not Lincoln County suffer for the delinquency of one, two or three men.

By the exercise of proper vigilance the tax payer can readily ascertain what has become of what he has paid for the implied protection of the commonwealth. It is not only his privilege but his duty. A delinquent tax payer is bad; a delinquent tax collector is worse.

J. H. T.[14]

Sensational stuff, and all of it true. Everyone knew who the "one, two or three men" were. Lincoln County's 1877 taxes had indeed been collected by Sheriff Brady, as was his duty as sheriff, but had not been paid into the territorial treasury. Instead, Sheriff Brady loaned the money to the House. McSween's check (he paid on behalf of several clients as well as himself) was returned with the signature of "Jno. H. Riley" scrawled across the back for all the world to see.[15]

Tunstall was prudent enough not to come right out and say it, but then he didn't need to: the embezzler in Lincoln County was not McSween, but the county's chief law enforcement officer, Sheriff Brady.

At least Brady didn't pocket the money, so far as we know. Probably he merely deposited it with the House with the understanding that the House would pass it along to Santa Fe. But in our own day county officials have gone to jail for crimes less startling than making short-term interest-free loans from the public treasury.

Jimmy Dolan was convinced that Tunstall was fighting back in another, more insidious, perhaps more effective way, too. He complained to Special Agent Angel:

This was what started the troubles. They (McSween, Tunstall, & John Chisum & their employees), who afterwards formed a combination to ruin deponent & his partners in business, spread the reports that our checks had been protested & sent untrue reports to commercial agencies at Denver & St. Louis as to our commercial standing stating that we were not worthy of credit.[16]

Negative credit reports may well have had a devastating effect on the House. A good credit standing was, if anything, even more important in the 1870s than it is today, since the weeks it took to ship anything to New Mexico meant the supplier shipped the goods weeks in advance of receiving payment, or else the retailer had to make payment weeks before receiving any goods. One side or the other always operated on long weeks of trust.

Whether Dolan's enemies actually spread such reports is unknown. More to the point, they may not have needed to do so. In the same deposition, Dolan also testified as follows: "I was book-keeper for the firm of L. G. Murphy & Co. & examined them about the time of the death of Fritz and at that time the firm was insolvent." (So why did he buy the business?) He also testified that he had mortgaged the House to Tom Catron for "more than $20,000."[17]

The House was out of business by the time Dolan gave his deposition on June 20, 1878. So reports that the House was uncreditworthy were accurate, and many other merchants besides Tunstall might have had reason to alert the credit agencies of Denver and St. Louis. Indeed, the credit agencies may well have figured it out for themselves.

Nonetheless, there is no mistaking Dolan's tone of injury. He believed he was the victim and expected Special Agent Angel to sympathize. After all, who wouldn't be angry to discover his business rivals were spreading nasty rumors, all the nastier for being true? An abiding and deep-seated sense of injury, coupled with a fury that would have been fully understandable had it been a bit more controlled, motivated every action Jimmy Dolan took in 1878.

Dolan's immediate response to reports of his firm's credit problems was to obtain a sworn statement from the acting cashier of the First National Bank in Santa Fe attesting to the House's creditworthiness. The bank's president, Tom Catron, agreed to "endorse" or guarantee the House's obligations to suppliers, an action that may only have increased creditors' nervousness, since why was such a guarantee necessary? Given that the bank was into the House for $26,000 or more, these votes of confidence have about them more than a suggestion of self-interest.[18]

Dolan's reaction to Tunstall's letter to the editor was similar: he obtained a statement from a figure of authority casting doubt on his opponent's assertions. Dolan published the following response in *The Independent:*

To the Editor of the Independent,

Dear Sir:

In answer to a communication in reference to taxpayers of Lincoln County published in your issue of the 26th and signed J.H.T., I wish to state that everything contained therein is false.

In reference to Sheriff Brady, I will state that he deposited with our house Territorial funds amounting to nearly $2,000, subject to his order and payable on demand. Owing to sickness in the family of Sheriff Brady he was unable to be in Santa Fe in time to settle his account with the Territory. This I hope will explain satisfactorily how the Governor in his message had our county delinquent.

If Mr. J.H.T. was recognized as a gentleman and could be admitted into respectable circles in our community, he might be better posted on public affairs. For my part I can't see the object of Mr. J.H.T.'s letter, unless it is to have the public believe that Alexander A. McSween is one of the largest taxpayers in our county, which in fact he is one of the smallest.

Sheriff Brady is ready at any time to show uneasy taxpayers what disposition he has made of the money paid by them; he can also show clean receipts for the Territorial treasure for his account.

Respectfully, J. J. Dolan[19]

Dolan obtained a statement from the territorial treasurer's office stating that Sheriff Brady's accounts were in order. The statement did not mention that they were in order only because the House made the payment in response to the governor's scathing message. Beneath the spirited insults and vehement denials (and it must have been satisfying for the Irishman to write the bit about the Englishman not being a gentleman), Dolan's letter was really saying that the House paid back what it had borrowed after being found out – not, perhaps, the most convincing defense. The fact that Dolan spoke for the sheriff could only have confirmed suspicions that Brady worked for the House.

The House was now so deep in the quagmire it had no realistic possibility of ever getting out, and the tax incident must have brought that fact home to Catron. Tunstall's letter very efficiently served the dual purpose of embarrassing the House and advancing its day of reckoning.

On January 28, 1878, the accused, Alexander McSween, left Lincoln for Mesilla in the custody of Deputy Barrier.[20] At the preliminary hearing before Judge Bristol, McSween would hear the evidence against him and bail would be set.

McSween and Barrier were accompanied on the four-day trip to Mesilla by John Tunstall, who came along in a show of solidarity, and by Sue McSween's brother-in-law David Shield, an attorney who had recently arrived in Lincoln with his family to practice law in partnership with McSween. Shield would represent McSween at the hearing.[21]

Also traveling with the group was Justice of the Peace John B. Wilson. Wilson happened to have business in Mesilla, and because it was a long and sometimes dangerous journey across the desert, he joined the caravan. The coincidence of the J.P. joining the group loomed large in subsequent events.

The group reached Mesilla on February 1, 1878. McSween's preliminary hearing didn't get underway until the following day, a Saturday, and it was held at Judge Bristol's house rather than in court. McSween's arrest had become a cause célèbre in New Mexico, a scandal of the first rank, and the subject of much newspaper speculation.[22] The preliminary hearing was held in private on a weekend to keep it secret. As if to provide a civics lesson in the dangers of secret courts, the various participants all had divergent recollections of what had occurred.

Deputy Barrier was deeply disturbed by what he saw and expressed his indignation to Special Agent Angel:

> I was present during the entire examination and had McSween in my charge. . . . William L. Rynerson, the District Attorney, while the examination was in progress, frequently used insulting language towards McSween while he was a prisoner, which I regarded as unbecoming in an officer.
>
> At the suggestion of Judge Bristol the examination was continued to [the regular term of] District Court on account of the absence of Juan B. Patrón & Florencio Gonzáles, two witnesses whom McSween wished subpoenaed. The conduct of Judge Bristol during the examination convinced me that he was very much prejudiced against McSween. After the examination was continued & the amount of bail fixed, the Judge delivered a lecture to McSween which was very unbecoming and showed himself to be a bitter partisan.[23]

Oddly, McSween himself did not mention being insulted by District Attorney Rynerson or being harangued by Judge Bristol. These indignities were, perhaps, of small concern to him as long as he remained a prisoner.

Judge Bristol is the cipher of the Lincoln County War. A small, unprepossessing man with a full gray beard and a cadaverous look about his eyes, he has been described by the historian Robert Utley as a "timid, easily frightened man,"[24] but it couldn't have been easy to tease even that assessment out of the record. For thirteen years Bristol served simultaneously as a trial judge and justice of the New Mexico Supreme Court, but were it not for the troubles in Lincoln County (he sentenced Billy the Kid to hang) he would have died with hardly a trace that he had ever been alive.[25]

Bristol was a Republican hack, of course – that was the only route to federal judgeships in those days. But even as a politician he was undistinguished, having served two terms in the Minnesota legislature. Why President Grant chose to pluck him from his Minnesota seat and deposit him in remotest New Mexico is a mystery.

When McSween's case was brought before the Lincoln County grand jury in April, Bristol declared in open court that Tunstall and McSween had testified under oath during the secret hearing that they were partners.[26] Deputy Barrier and David Shield swore out a joint affidavit on this issue, stating:

> We were present at Mesilla N.M. at the residence of Judge Bristol on the 2nd and 4th days of February last at the time of the investigation of the charges against A. A. McSween. We were present during the entire examination and know all the evidence. A. A. McSween was not sworn as a witness nor did he make in person a statement of his defense. Mr. Tunstall made oath that no articles of copartnership was ever executed by and between him and said McSween.[27]

Barrier and Shield added that Bristol's statements to the contrary were "false and untrue."

Shield, an attorney, was risking his legal career to accuse a sitting judge of lying. And Barrier, the housepainter, had no reason to perjure himself. Their joint affidavit must be considered credible.

As to the underlying question, it seems true that no partnership agreement had ever been signed, although McSween told Special Agent Angel that he and Tunstall planned to sign such an agreement in the future.[28] There was no reason for Tunstall and McSween to swear they were partners when they were not. Tunstall was combative and loyal, but he was far too clever to yoke himself needlessly to an accused embezzler.

Unfortunately for Tunstall, "proof" that he and McSween were partners was the crucial second step in Catron's elaborate, ingenious plan to destroy Tunstall. To Warren Bristol, the colorless small-time politician, fell the unenviable task of establishing that proof. No doubt Bristol hoped Tunstall and McSween would cooperate by testifying as to their partnership. When they failed to do so, the less desirable alternative of making up testimony was forced upon him.

One way or another, though, Bristol needed that proof. The next step – the springing of the trap – would have been illegal without it. And like many other judges both before and after him, Bristol would sooner do something dishonest than something illegal.

The Attachment

10

On January 19, 1878, Jesse Evans took a few horses from a rancher in the scrubland of the lower Mimbres Valley. The rancher took exception, and in the subsequent chase a bullet entered Evans's left thigh just below the cheek of his buttocks (the precise location of the scar was memorialized by Texas prison authorities a few years later). The bullet exited Evans's thigh without killing him or wounding his horse, and he somehow managed to ride back to Shedd's Ranch and safety.[1]

On February 5, McSween, Tunstall, Shield, and Wilson began the journey back to Lincoln. Deputy Barrier remained with the group: Judge Bristol had ordered him to deliver McSween into the custody of Sheriff Brady and the underground Lincoln jail. Bail was $8,000, conditioned on the approval of District Attorney William Rynerson.[2]

Together the five men rode out of Mesilla and across the Organ Mountains that separate the fertile Rio Grande Valley from the desert. The only route over the mountains led across San Augustin Pass. Nestled high on the pass was Shedd's Ranch, less a working ranch than a hostel where the five travelers prepared to spend the night camped in a corral with their animals. As they were bedding down for the night, they received three visitors. One of the visitors walked with a decided limp.

The visit was pure mischief-making. One of the Boys – either Frank Baker or Frank Rivers – asked whether they had passed Dolan on the road. David Shield said they had not, and added that he didn't think Dolan would leave Mesilla until the following day. According to McSween, "Baker said that they had found Jimmie very punctual in [his] engagements with them and that Dolan had made an appointment with them to meet them here and that they believed that he would come."

A century later one can almost hear the outlaws snigger as they leave the corral, pleased to have spooked their victims.

The following morning, before breakfast, McSween watched Dolan step out of Shedd's house in the company of a limping man. The house was some seventy or eighty yards from the campsite. Dolan and Evans took a circuitous route behind some outbuildings, hoping not to be noticed.

Or at least that was McSween's version. In his deposition testimony, Dolan indignantly denied sneaking up on anyone. His agitation is reflected in the court reporter's disjointed transcription, given here as in the original:

> I went to their camp the next morning. I went to see Tunstall. I heard about a letter he had written to the *Independent* it was untruthful & as to his attempt to injure us and these facts made me very angry I was armed. I talked to Mr. Tunstall in a very severe manner he acted in a very childish manner I tried in every way to see if he was a man, he made no resistance although he was armed.[3]

McSween's account provides some detail:

> In a few minutes J. J. Dolan and Jesse Evans came around the southeast corner of [the] corral. Mr. Dolan drew his Winchester's carbine on Mr. Tunstall and asked him if he was ready to fight and settle their difficulties. Mr. Tunstall asked him if he asked him to fight a duel. Mr. Dolan replied, "You damned coward, I want you to fight and settle our difficulties." Dolan drew his gun, cocked, on Mr. Tunstall three times. Mr. Barrier placed himself between or in line with Dolan & Evans and saved as I believe the lives of Tunstall and myself.[4]

Where did the housepainter Adolph Barrier find the courage to put himself in the line of fire? This part-time sheriff's deputy, hundreds of miles from home, tried on the mantle of heroism. Almost absurdly, it fit.

Barrier's bravery broke the tension and the moment of crisis passed. But, McSween reported, when Mr. Dolan was leaving he used these words, "You won't fight this morning, you damned coward but I'll get you soon." After he had gone off about 20 yards he turned around and said to Tunstall, "When you write the 'Independent' again say that I am with 'The Boys.'"[5]

This was an effective way of letting Tunstall know how dangerous it was to be an enemy of Jimmy Dolan. Not surprisingly, Dolan later denied it all:

I did not drop my carbine on him, I threw it over my shoulder with the butt towards him. I told him that I was ready to give him any satisfaction he wanted. I made no threats against him, I never said that when you write to the Independent say I am with the "boys" or any words to that effect. I did not say I won't shoot you now but I will get you soon nor any words to that effect. Any assertions to the contrary by anyone are absolutely false and untrue. I went there to take no advantage of him, my gun was neither loaded nor cocked, nor did I sneak up to them.[6]

Dolan didn't deny that he was with Evans. He said, "Jesse Evans was standing at the corner of the stable near McSween's party's camp, he evidently saw that I was excited and followed after me, he did not follow me by my request either directly or indirectly." Moreover, Dolan added, "I had no appointment or engagement with either Baker, Evans or Rivers to meet me at San Augustine or anywhere on the road, and any assertions made by them are absolutely false and untrue."[7]

Someone was lying, but the lies were in the details. The main points of McSween's story were not disputed. Dolan was armed with a Winchester, a technologically advanced carbine, accurate at a distance and deadly at close range. Dolan described himself as "excited"; he must have been in a white-hot fury. Standing beside him — and it goes without saying that Jesse Evans was armed to the teeth — was the territory's most notorious thief and killer, an outlaw who had been jailed by Tunstall's own men for stealing Tunstall's horses.

Perhaps Deputy Barrier didn't know who Evans was. There is almost no other way to explain his reckless bravery.

Tunstall, McSween, Barrier, Shield, and Wilson wasted no time leaving Shedd's Ranch. But in the early afternoon, about twenty miles down the road, they were overtaken by a horse-drawn "ambulance," a term then used to designate any four-wheeled wagon. The ambulance was racing across the desert floor, accompanied by two horsemen. Riding inside were Jimmy Dolan and Jesse Evans. Baker and Rivers followed on horseback.

There must have been evil looks exchanged, half-involuntary checks of firearms. The sighting makes it unimportant whether Dolan actually said "Tell them I'm with the Boys." Whether he said it or not, he was.

Dolan's threats over breakfast at Shedd's Ranch could be excused as temper, but his decision to ride with the Boys was calculated, a calculation that sheds light on the earlier mystery of who helped the Boys to escape from jail. Dolan's violent temper forced the Boys to declare whose side they were on. There was never any doubt.

Dolan could explain how he happened to be traveling with the Boys:

> The way Evans came to be riding with me in the ambulance from San Augustine was as follows. Evans could not ride in a saddle on account of his being wounded. I am not positive whether I asked him or he me, at any rate I allowed him out of charity to ride with me in the ambulance. Baker and Rivers followed behind on horseback. I must confess that I was afraid that I would be killed on the road and I did not object to their following after us for that reason.[8]

The Boys did not ride with Dolan all the way to Lincoln. There were limits to even their chutzpah. They peeled off at the Mescalero Apache Agency, high on the pass separating the volcano from the Sacramento Mountains, where McSween's party bumped into them again. As McSween noted with some asperity, "they appeared to be quite familiar with Major [Frederick] Godfroy the agent."[9]

Godfroy's familiarity with the Boys incensed McSween. Soon after he arrived home he wrote to Secretary of the Interior Carl Schurz, informing him that Godfroy bought "sprouted half-rotten wheat" from the House as first-rate flour. The House also sold cattle that had to be butchered on the range because the animals were too poor to walk to the issue house. The Apaches' coffee, sugar, and blankets were sold by the House. McSween concluded, "I suggest that you send a detective here who will ferret this matter; he'll find things as I have stated them. . . . A thorough search will disclose fearful villainy on the part of all concerned."[10]

McSween's letter was shrewdly timed, or maybe it was just a lucky hit: congressional Democrats were agitating to relieve the Department of Interior of responsibilities over Indian affairs. Kentucky Congressman Andrew Boone explained why he wanted to dismember the department:

> We have had no fixed and settled policy in regard to the management of Indian affairs, except perhaps in one regard, and that is to make treaties and violate them whenever it seemed to be in our interest to do so, to appropriate money to support the Indians and send out agents to squander and consume it.[11]

A Colorado congressman blamed Indian attacks on the "rapacity, treachery, neglectfulness, and heartless frauds" committed by Indian agents. An Ohio senator avowed that "the Indians do not get one-fourth of what we vote them." The entire system was "of the very worst character."[12] Representative Boone hammered the administration for the substandard flour and beef foisted on Indians by crooked agents — the very charges McSween made against Godfroy.

Threatened with the loss of power, prestige, patronage, and appropriations, the Interior Department's bureaucrats were desperate to demonstrate they could rouse themselves to forceful remedial action. The department dispatched Frank Warner Angel as special agent. Angel went to the Mescalero reservation to see if Godfroy were padding the rolls and counted only 375 Apaches, although Godfroy drew rations for 901.[13]

After two witnesses revealed that they routinely hauled goods *from* the agency to the House, Dolan and Riley admitted that they sometimes borrowed a few items. But, they assured Angel, the goods were always paid back in kind. Regrettably, the records of those transactions were incomplete.[14]

McSween and Tunstall received a nasty surprise when they reached Lincoln. Sheriff Brady had seized McSween's house. He had also seized Tunstall's store and closed it down.

This was the trap Tom Catron had laid for Tunstall, and it worked like a charm. Immediately after McSween left Mesilla on the journey back to Lincoln, Emilie Scholand and Charles Fritz had filed a civil suit accusing him of embezzling the insurance money. They asked Judge Bristol to issue a writ of attachment and the judge complied.[15]

Attachment is a peculiar legal process by which a person's property can be seized before trial. The plaintiff in an attachment action must post a bond with the court, and in theory the bond assures the defendant of being compensated in case the attachment proves unwarranted. Emilie Scholand's and Charles Fritz's bondsmen were Jimmy Dolan and District Attorney William Rynerson; the bond was dated February 6.[16]

Under New Mexico law, attachment was available only in a handful of strictly limited situations, which were listed in the statute.[17] Scholand and Fritz picked two items off the list. First they said McSween obtained the money by "false pretenses." But that was obviously untrue. McSween obtained the money by virtue of being the estate's attorney, and there was nothing false about that.

Fritz and Scholand also alleged that "the said Alexander McSween is about to remove his property and effects out of this Territory." They had evidence to back this up: McSween had just been nabbed in Las Vegas trying to sneak out of the territory. The arrest, arranged by Catron, formed the only legal basis for the writ of attachment. It was the key maneuver in the campaign to close down Tunstall's store and revive the House as a profitable concern.

McSween testified that the writ "was dated the 7th of February 1878 and the sheriff commenced to attach thereunder on the 8th, it having been sent a distance of about 154 miles in an almost unprecedented short time for this territory."[18] McSween's sardonic understatement is the only moment of intentional humor in all the hundreds of pages of testimony in the Angel Report.

Dolan testified that he brought the attachment papers from Mesilla, which is probably true (that's why he hurried so), and that he left Mesilla on February 5, which we know to have been the case.[19] This means, as McSween hinted, that Bristol issued the writ on February 5, but postdated it February 7. Apparently the judge wanted to disguise the fact that he issued the writ the day before Fritz and Scholand posted the bond required by the attachment statute.

Tunstall's store was invaded and occupied by Sheriff Brady and four armed deputies. Brady was following the common law rule that partners own all partnership assets in common, so that if the sheriff wants to seize the property of one partner he has to seize everything.[20] This is why it was so important that Judge Bristol "hear" Tunstall and McSween testify they were partners.

Tunstall's best friend in New Mexico, Rob Widenmann, was minding the store at the time. Widenmann was twenty-four, slender and pale with thin features and a long nose. Widenmann and Tunstall had more in common than their age. Widenmann's father was German and Widenmann himself, although born in Michigan, was educated in Germany.[21] His European, outsider's outlook was highly sympathetic to Tunstall's own.

Widenmann also shared with Tunstall the experience of the Wild West as spectacle. While living on the outskirts of New York City, his daughter recalled, the middle-aged Widenmann "used to practice the quick draw and shooting at the shape of a man."[22] Widenmann never drew a gun in anger in Lincoln County, but the idea of the quick draw and all the other practices of the idealized West fascinated him his whole life.

In his deposition testimony, Widenmann listed his occupation as merchant. This was something else he had in common with Tunstall: he wasn't a cowboy. As a Victorian Englishman, Tunstall was conscious of subtle distinctions of class. Dick Brewer was a fine man, but he was Tunstall's bailiff. Alexander and Sue McSween might have belonged to the professional class, but they were chapel-going dissenters.

Widenmann, on the other hand, was cultured and young and touring New Mexico for kicks. His father left Germany in the wake of the failed Republican revolution of 1848. He maintained a friendship with Carl Schurz, one of the great leaders of the revolution. Schurz, remembered to this day in Germany for his fiery speeches from the steps of the pastel-pink Rathaus in Bonn, fled to America as the Prussians closed in, and by dint of sheer ability rose to become a Union general and later Secretary of the Interior.[23] Thanks to the family connection, *der junge* Widenmann had Secretary Schurz's ear, and his importunities probably influenced Schurz's decision to send Special Agent Angel to Lincoln County.

Widenmann told Angel:

On or about the 9 day of February, 1878, Sheriff Brady entered the business house of J. H. Tunstall of which I was then in charge and read to me a writ of attachment attaching the property of A. A. McSween. . . . I told him that the property belonged to J. H. Tunstall [&] that I protested against any attachment & would hold him and his bondsmen responsible for any loss or damages. Sheriff Brady said that he knew better, that the property belonged to A. A. McSween & he would attach it as such.[24]

New Mexico banks valued the House at more than $27,000. Tom Catron's First National Bank had made loans and guarantees worth more than $26,000, and the Lincoln County Bank kicked in an additional $1,000. Assuming Tunstall's thriving business was as valuable as the failing House, McSween's supposed half-interest in the store was worth at least $13,500. But Judge Bristol's writ authorized the sheriff to attach only $8,000 worth of property. No wonder, as Widenmann testified, Sheriff Brady's inventory neglected to place a value on the seized property.[25]

Widenmann continued:

[Sheriff Brady] demanded the keys of different doors leading from the store and upon my refusal to deliver the same had me arrested and searched without warrant or legal process and forcibly took the keys from me. He was at the time accompanied by G. W. Peppin, Jack Long, James Longwell, and F. G. Christie.[26]

Stout-hearted Widenmann, outnumbered five to one and still refusing to surrender the keys! Widenmann's flair for the futile gesture came close to costing him his life more than once.

Brady's deputies, F. G. Christie and James Longwell, were employees of J. J. Dolan & Co. The bricklayer George Peppin was, according to Special Agent Angel, "a leader of the Murphy & Co. faction."[27] Taylor Ealy, the Presbyterian missionary sent to Lincoln at McSween's request, recounted this encounter with the fourth member of the posse:

A man who went by the name of Jack Long met me as I was going down to Mr. Ellis's store . . . seemed to be under the influence of liquor. Had a revolver in his belt. I told him that I was going to the store for my wife and must hurry. On the way down he had my arm. He said, "I helped hang a Methodist Preacher in Arizona, but I won't help hang you."[28]

After their takeover, the deputies lived in the store, preventing Tunstall from doing business. Deputy Longwell's deposition is riddled with foolish inconsistencies and outright lies, but he may have been telling the truth when he testified:

> Tunstall . . . came into the store while we were making the inventory with a man called Widenmann and made threats against the Sheriff, telling the Sheriff that he was taking his property for McSween's debts, that he would make all of the party suffer for it hereafter and that they had better look out. Both Tunstall and Widenmann were armed with revolvers, and two of Tunstall's party called "Kid" & "Waite" came up to the door with them and stood there with Winchester rifles and pistols and acted in a threatening manner.[29]

Widenmann gave his own version of the encounter in Tunstall's store, playing down the very aspects of the story played up by Longwell:

> On the 11th of February Mr Tunstall & I came to the store which was then in the possession of the sheriff and again protested against the attachment. We succeeded in getting all the horses released (2 mules and six horses) and at once started a man named G. Gauss with three horses for the ranch and on the afternoon of the same day started William McCloskey & John Middleton for the ranch on two other horses. Subsequently I followed in company with F. J. Waite and William Bonney and arrived at the ranch on the morning of the 12th. R. M. Brewer was there in charge of the ranch.[30]

Gauss was the German who had lost four hundred barrels of beer to Murphy. He was Tunstall's cook.

The release of the horses suggests that Tunstall's talk with the sheriff was less confrontational than Longwell claimed. Brady was only being reasonable: even if McSween owned a half-interest in the store, there was no reason to believe he owned a half-interest in Tunstall's horses.

On the Felix

11

District Attorney Rynerson, a veteran of Carleton's California Column, had an unusual start in law enforcement: in 1867 he murdered John P. Slough, Jr., chief justice of the New Mexico Supreme Court and commander of the Colorado troops who defeated the Confederates at the Battle of Glorieta.[1]

At the time of the murder, Rynerson was a brand-new member of the upper house of the territorial legislature, the Council (and its only Anglo member). Rynerson owed his position to the territorial secretary, who had certified his election despite the minor technicality that Rynerson's opponent received a majority of the votes cast. To repay the favor, Rynerson sponsored a memorial condemning Slough, the secretary's mortal enemy but a near stranger to Rynerson. Slough told the new councillor exactly what he thought about him. Rynerson pretended not to hear but apparently gave the matter some thought overnight: the next evening he positioned himself in the lobby of the Exchange Hotel (the present La Fonda), armed with a six-gun. When Slough responded to the dinner gong, Rynerson requested an apology. None was immediately forthcoming, so Rynerson shot. Somehow he was acquitted of murder, and the killer became a prosecutor.

Judge Bristol conditioned bail for McSween on Rynerson's approval. McSween secured bail bonds from Tunstall, James West, Isaac Ellis, John Copeland, Refugio Valencia, and José Montaño. He also solicited Joseph Blazer. But, according to McSween:

> J. J. Dolan & Co. . . . threatened that if he became one of my bondsmen they would have him prosecuted for cutting timber on the

public lands as I understand in U.S. Courts by T. B. Catron, U.S. District Attorney at Santa Fe.[2]

Blazer, the owner of a sawmill, was peculiarly vulnerable to the threat. He decided against becoming one of McSween's bondsmen.

Rynerson refused to accept bonds totaling $34,500 for the $8,000 bail, which meant McSween had to go to jail. McSween realized he might not survive jail. He told Special Agent Angel that, upon arriving in Lincoln, he heard

> that Riley, Dolan and Murphy and Sheriff Brady were in ecstasy over my prospective confinement in the county jail and . . . that Riley had swept out the jail in order that he might in the future have it to say that he swept out the room in which I was incarcerated. Brady expressed himself in the presence of E. A. Dow and others to the effect that . . . he may have allowed Baker, Evans and Hill to escape but that he would not allow me to do so.[3]

It was Deputy Barrier's duty to obey Judge Bristol, but it was also his duty to save his prisoner from harm. He did so at Shedd's Ranch when he stepped between Dolan and Tunstall. But now he had reason to believe McSween would not be safe in the Lincoln County jail.

Once more Barrier protected his prisoner by putting himself in danger. He and McSween slipped out of Lincoln and traveled secretly to Chisum's ranch on the Pecos.[4] Barrier didn't free McSween — he guarded him until April, when the embezzlement charge was heard by the Lincoln County grand jury. But he must have known he put himself in harm's way when he disobeyed the judge's order: on April 23, District Attorney Rynerson filed charges against him for refusal to serve process.[5]

Widenmann testified that he, Middleton, Waite, and Bonney rode from Lincoln to Tunstall's Rio Felix ranch, joining Dick Brewer and a cowboy named William McCloskey who were already there. Godfrey Gauss arrived later with the horses Sheriff Brady had agreed not to attach.

The men knew they might have to fight. Bonney told Special Agent Angel that they "cut portholes into the walls of the house and filled sacks with earth" to build breastworks. He continued:

On the 13th day of February A.D. 1878 one J. B. Mathews, claiming to be Deputy Sheriff, came to the ranch of J. H. Tunstall in company with Jesse Evans, Frank Baker, Tom Hill and —— Rivers, known outlaws who had been confined in the Lincoln County jail and had succeeded in making their escape, John Hurley, George Hindemann, [Andrew] Roberts and an Indian and Ponciano, the latter said to be the murderer of Benito Cruz, for the arrest of the murderers of whom the Governor of this Territory offers a award of $500.[6]

The deputy, Jacob B. "Billy" Mathews, was born in Tennessee and fought for the Confederacy as a teenager. After Appomattox he drifted to Elizabethtown, near Taos, the site of a minor gold rush in the 1860s. Failing to make his fortune, he drifted south to Lincoln County and was hired by Murphy in 1873. He had worked for the House ever since, and had even invested a little bit of his own money in the business, so that in a small way he was a partner of Dolan and Riley.[7]

Brady's decision to deputize Billy Mathews and assign him the task of seizing Tunstall's ranch sent a message: Brady was the sheriff but the House called the shots. There was nothing subtle about it.

Mathews claimed his posse was formed from two different groups of men. First there was the posse proper, which he headed. Then there was that other group of four men. Special Agent Angel asked about them:

Q. Were Baker, Evans, Hill & Rivers a part of your posse or were they with you or [did they] accompany you to the Felix?

A. They were not part of the posse – Evans & Rivers I think met us at the [Mescalero Apache] agency. They did not leave with us – but caught up to us about five miles from the agency, this side. Baker & Hill came to us at the Peñasco. They did not meet us at our request either directly or indirectly. We did not know they were there. They said that they were going to the Felix after some horses.[8]

So there is no question that Evans, Baker, Hill, and Rivers (who was also known as Davis) were with the posse; the only question is what they were doing. The party line, given by Mathews and elaborated on by others, was that the Boys were after some horses. In court testimony given some months later, Jesse Evans testified that he was trying to recover horses he had loaned to "Widenmann's man 'The Kid.' "[9] But Angel questioned Mathews at length about this point, and Mathews had to admit that once they reached Tunstall's ranch the Boys never spoke a word about horses.[10]

Bonney, Brewer, Widenmann, Middleton, and the rest had no doubt why the Boys were there. That's why they dug those portholes and filled those sandbags.

Bonney continued the story of the posse's visit:

Mathews, when about 50 yards of the house, was called to stop and advance alone and state his business. Mathews after arriving at the ranch said that he had come to attach the cattle and property of A. A. McSween.[11]

The various accounts agree that two men stepped forward from Tunstall's house to confront Mathews — Brewer by virtue of being foreman and leader of the men, Widenmann because he was brash and pushy and Tunstall's pal. They met Mathews on the frozen dirt road halfway between the two groups of heavily armed men. Godfrey Gauss explained why the posse was not allowed to draw closer: "It was reported by Alex Rudders that the posse was going to kill us, and that is the reason why we did not want them to come up, and I believed this because Evans, Baker, Hill & Davis, who were notorious thieves and murderers, were with them."[12] But Tunstall's men must have shown they, too, were ready to fight; otherwise the posse would not have hung back.

In Widenmann's recollections, the narrator always fills the role of bold hero (Angel later wrote of Widenmann: "given to boasting; veracity doubtful when he speaks of himself").[13] This is how Widenmann remembered that tense parley:

Seeing [Evans, Baker, and Hill] in the party and knowing that they had threatened to kill me on sight, I stepped out and asked the party to stop where they were (which was about 50 yards from the house) and asked Mathews to come forward and state his business. Mathews said he was Deputy Sheriff and had come to attach the cattle of A. A. McSween, to which I answered that McSween had no cattle there but if there were any he might take them. I offered no resistance nor did the people with me — nor did we make any threats.[14]

Bonney testified:

Mathews was informed that A. A. McSween had no cattle or property there, but that if he had he could attach it. Mathews said that he thought some of the cattle belonging to R. M. Brewer, whose cattle were also at the ranch, belonged to A. A. McSween. Mathews was told by Brewer that he, Mathews, could round up the cattle and that he, Brewer, would help him.[15]

Mathews remembered a slightly different scene:

I had considerable talk with Widenmann & Brewer as to attaching the property. Brewer was willing that I should attach, leaving the question to the courts as to the title to the same. But Widenmann positively refused to allow me to attach the cattle. I told Brewer privately that if he would allow me to attach the cattle I would come to the ranch with only one man. I never told this to Widenmann and after Widenmann's refusal to allow me to attach we left for Lincoln to obtain instructions.[16]

Both John Middleton and Godfrey Gauss remembered Mathews saying he would go back to Lincoln for instructions, and that when he returned he would bring just one or two men, since that was all he needed to round up the herd.[17]

Special Agent Angel synthesized the conflicting accounts in his report:

The Sheriff in order to attach certain property, viz., stock and horses, alleged to belong to McSween and Tunstall sent his deputy to Tunstall's ranch to attach the same. When the deputy visited the ranch and was informed that he could attach the stock and leave a person with it until the Courts could adjudicate to whom the stock belonged, he left without attaching the property.[18]

Why not? It is impossible to avoid the conclusion that the posse was not seriously after the cattle. Their orders were to shut down Tunstall's ranching operations and drive away the herd. They arrived at the ranch expecting to fight – that's why they brought the Boys along. But by agreeing to allow the attachment, Brewer put Mathews in a terrible bind. Mathews couldn't argue with a man who agreed with him. He couldn't fight a man who gave him what he demanded. But if he allowed Brewer to agree to his demands, he would have failed his task. Defeated and confused, he withdrew for "further instructions." But only after joining Tunstall's men for breakfast.

It seems astonishing that two groups of men, each heavily armed and expecting violence, should sit down to eat together. But it was all part of Brewer's strategy of assertive reasonableness: he treated the posse members like any other early-morning visitors to the ranch.

The breakfast itself later became a subject of disagreement. One of Mathews's men, John Hurley, claimed that only the Boys accepted the invitation to eat and that the rest of the posse rode home with empty stomachs. But he added, "when we left [Tunstall's ranch, the Boys] were shoeing their horses."[19] Since a man cannot eat breakfast and shoe his horse simultaneously, time must have passed between the two events – which means Hurley was still hanging around when breakfast was cleared away.

Widenmann testified that he rode back to Lincoln to inform Tunstall of the morning's events. He mentioned in passing, "On the way to town I rode with them several miles (I mean by them Mathews, Hurley & the Indian)."[20] There was no reason for Widenmann to make up this detail, meaningless in itself. But if Widenmann left the ranch with Hurley, it can only mean Hurley stayed for breakfast.

Whether or not Hurley ate breakfast is trivial, but his reason for lying about it is anything but: he wanted to convince Angel that the Boys were not part of the sheriff's posse.

The Pursuit

12

John Sherman, Jr.'s two uncles were the general who burned Atlanta and the senator who sponsored the nation's first antitrust law. His brother-in-law was U.S. senator from Pennsylvania. He once formed a banking partnership with President Grant's son. In short, no one in Washington had more glittering connections than young John Sherman.[1]

Unfortunately, few in Washington drank quite as much as he did either. When his partner's father ceased being president, the Sherman family saw to it that John, Jr. was buried in the dustiest, most remote posting they could find. He was appointed U.S. marshal for New Mexico, where Governor Axtell pronounced him "an imbecile – drunken fraud with no ability."[2]

Marshal Sherman was not a man of outstanding practical judgment. This was never clearer than in his choice of a deputy marshal for southeastern New Mexico. Federal warrants were issued for the arrest of Jesse Evans and the Boys in early 1878 after they stole some government mules. Sherman needed someone to execute the warrants, someone bold and fearless, a leader of men, a tireless tracker through desert wastes. He needed all that, but he settled for Rob Widenmann.

Most writers on the Lincoln County War, feeling a need to explain Sherman's choice, credit Widenmann's pull with Carl Schurz. But Sherman was a presidential appointee, not answerable to the Secretary of Interior. Besides, it is unlikely a cabinet secretary would involve himself in the hunt for mule thieves. More likely Widenmann volunteered for the job and Sherman was only too glad to make the warrants someone else's problem.[3]

Being a deputy U.S. marshal would have appealed to that side of Widenmann that later made him practice the quick draw in Haverstraw, New York. It was part of the West as spectacle, the West as western with young Rob its hero. It made for a satisfying fantasy.

But Widenmann's greenness was comically apparent in his attempts to arrest the Boys. He told Special Agent Angel that he once tracked the Boys to Murphy's ranch on the Tularosa, but "I was informed by Mr. Murphy personally that they were not at his ranch."[4] This calls to mind the absurd but probably accurate image of the deputy U.S. marshal knocking at the front door of the house and inquiring politely, in a faint German accent, whether any known outlaws and murderers are at home. The master of the house responds with equal gravity and courtesy in his soft Irish brogue that they are not, at which the deputy remounts his horse and trots off, his duty done.

Over breakfast at Tunstall's ranch on the Rio Felix, Evans revealed to Widenmann that he watched him ride away from Murphy's house. Evans was sleeping in the hills near the ranch and enjoying Murphy's hospitality during the day.[5]

During that breakfast, Widenmann demonstrated those personality characteristics that made him so peculiarly unsuited to the responsibilities of deputy marshal. After Brewer had negotiated his uneasy compromise with Billy Mathews, Widenmann took Brewer aside and announced that he intended to arrest the Boys. Bonney testified that "Widenmann was told by Brewer and the others at the ranch that the arrest could not be made, because if it was made they . . . would be killed and murdered." Widenmann complained to Angel that Brewer and the rest "positively refused to aid me in the arrest."[6]

Brewer sensibly pointed out to Widenmann that they were all "ranch men" and their isolation at home made them vulnerable. This was tactfully said, since it was unlikely Widenmann could succeed in arresting the Boys in the first place. Mathews's men rode up the ranch road looking for trouble, and the sole object of Brewer's diplomacy was to frustrate them. By trying to arrest the Boys, Widenmann would have given them the opportunity to do what they did best.

Bonney picks up the story of the breakfast:

Jesse Evans advanced upon Widenmann, Evans swinging his gun and catching it cocked and pointed directly at Widenmann. Jesse Evans asked Widenmann whether he was hunting for him, to which Widenmann answered that if he was looking for him, he would find it out. Evans also asked Widenmann whether he had a warrant for him. Widenmann answered that was his, Widenmann's, business. Evans told Widenmann that if he ever came to arrest him, he would pick Widenmann as the first man to shoot at, to which Widenmann answered that was all right, two could play at that game.[7]

It was a classic schoolyard scene, the bully and the nerd. Widenmann could hold his own in the verbal parrying, but the difference was that Evans meant what he said, and everyone knew it. Bonney added, "During the talking Frank Baker stood near Widenmann, swinging his pistol on his finger and catching it full cocked pointed at Widenmann."[8]

Widenmann perceived Baker's little trick slightly differently, and it's even more sadistic in his telling. "Baker walked up in front of me with a pistol in his hand as though handing it to me, swung it on one finger, cocking it at the same time, pointing the muzzle towards me." He added, "I heard Baker say to Roberts, 'What the hell's the use of talking. Pitch in and fight and kill the sons of bitches.'"[9]

After breakfast, after the Boys had their fun with Widenmann, most of the posse rode eastward down the Felix to Seven Rivers. Mathews, Hurley, and Miguel Segovia traveled north to Lincoln to get further instructions from Sheriff Brady. Widenmann, Bonney, and Waite rode with them, on their way to report the morning's news to Tunstall.

The trail from Tunstall's ranch to Lincoln took the riders across the wide wooded ridge that separates the Rio Felix from the Rio Ruidoso. Nearing the Ruidoso, where the trail drops precipitously downhill, a man could pause and admire clear views of the snow-covered volcano on his left hand and the rounded massive eminence of Capitan Peak on his right. As the trail winds down to the river, the red-barked Ponderosa gives way to scrubbier stands of juniper and piñon. The trail reaches the Ruidoso at the present-day hamlet of Glencoe, on the Coe ranch. From there it is a relatively short ride across a much narrower ridge to the next valley scoring the flanks of the volcano, that of the Bonito.

Widenmann, Bonney, and Waite had plenty of time to admire the spectacular scenery – they rode the trail four times that week. They arrived back in town the evening of February 13. According to McSween, who was there, Widenmann told Tunstall

that he was satisfied that Mathews intended to raise a large posse and take the cattle by force, that for that purpose Baker had gone down to Dolan & Company's cow camp on the Pecos with instructions to William Morton, their foreman, to raise all the men he could and meet Mathews with his posse at Turkey Springs a few miles from Tunstall's cattle ranch on the evening of the 16th of February, 1878.[10]

Tunstall was in the position of a general far behind the lines, receiving urgent dispatches from the front, forced to rely on others to be his eyes and ears. He sent Widenmann, Bonney, and Waite back to the ranch the following morning, February 14, to keep an eye on things.[11]

Two days later, Tunstall's anxieties were compounded by a rumor borne by George Washington, one of the black cavalrymen who had stayed in Lincoln after his tour of duty expired. Washington told Tunstall in McSween's presence that

Murphy, Riley, & Dolan had helped Mathews to raise a force to the number of 43 men. Riley informed him (Washington) that there was no use in McSween's and Tunstall's trying to get away from them this time as they had them completely in their power. They could not possibly be beat as they had the District Attorney (meaning Rynerson), the court and all the power in Santa Fe to back them. Their plan was to take the cattle from Tunstall's ranch by sending two Mexicans they had in the posse to make a sham round-up of the cattle and horses so as to draw the men in Tunstall's house out of it, then the balance of the posse was to take possession of the house and *"get"* Tunstall's men.[12]

As soon as he heard Washington's story, according to McSween, "Mr. Tunstall concluded to go to the ranch and induce his men to leave and allow Mathews and posse to take the property and seek his remedy in the courts."[13] Tunstall took a risk riding to his ranch alone, but he was determined to arrive before the posse returned.

He arrived after dark on February 17. A council of war convened and discussions were held until early in the morning. As reported by Widenmann, a decision was reached:

Rather than risk the lives of the men, we would leave everything as it was, send McCloskey over to the Peñasco to inform Mathews and his posse that they could take the cattle and that we would seek our remedy by the law. We did this because we did not wish trouble & to show them that no resistance would be made. We sent McCloskey because he was a friend of a great number of the party that was reported to be with Mathews.

McCloskey left the ranch at three o'clock in the morning and he had orders to tell Mr. Martin on the Peñasco to come over and stay at Tunstall's ranch to count the cattle with the Deputy Sheriff.[14]

"Mr. Martin" was Dutch Martin, whose real name was Martin Mertz. Mertz was Tunstall's neighbor. The fact that even the German-American Widenmann couldn't remember his name confirms his neutrality.

Gauss, fifty-two at the time, was left behind. He testified:

On the 17th of February, 1878, Mr. Tunstall came to the ranch. He told Widenmann that there must be no blood shed. We must not remain, let them attach what cattle they please. We will leave Gauss here. He is an old man, they won't touch him.[15]

Theoretically Tunstall could seek redress against Brady's bondsmen, Rynerson and Dolan. It was a slim reed, but it was all he had.[16]

The next morning, around eight o'clock, Tunstall and his men left for Lincoln. Fred Waite was driving a wagon; the others – Brewer, Widenmann, Bonney, and Middleton – were on horseback. They drove a small herd of eight horses, five of which belonged to Tunstall.

Widenmann described the horses:

The horses were the property of J. H. Tunstall, R. M. Brewer and myself. None of the horses then or ever belonged to A. A. McSween – and all but three had been released by the Sheriff and of those three horses one belonged to Brewer, one to Bonney and the third was traded by Brewer to Tunstall for one of the horses which the sheriff had not attached here.[17]

So which one was the property of Rob Widenmann?

Two hours after Tunstall and his men left, the posse arrived. Mathews testified, "We went to the ranch carefully, one party in front of the house & the other from the rear – myself and Roberts being the party in front."[18] That is, Mathews pretended he was returning to the ranch with just one man to round up the cattle, as he had promised Dick Brewer he would do. Meanwhile, the second party of men approached from the rear – no fewer than twenty-five of them, including the Boys.

The plan was unfolding exactly as predicted by ex-trooper Washington. Mathews hoped that he and Andrew Roberts (called Buckshot Roberts in many books but not in any contemporary account) would be able to draw Brewer and his men out of the house to participate in a roundup of the cattle.

Jimmy Dolan testified that everyone expected a fight, but all the tense waiting proved anticlimactic. "Hearing no shots we also came to the house, and found cattle over the range. Gauss informed us that the horses and party had left about two hours ago for either Lincoln or Brewer's ranch."[19] Dolan immediately resolved to send a party after them.

Gauss, the welcoming committee, testified, "I gave them something to eat, or rather they helped themselves to what they wanted." After grabbing a quick bite, Dolan

> picked out the men to follow after Tunstall's party, to bring them back if they caught them before they reached the Plaza. . . . P. Gallegos started to make a list of the posse and started to put down the parties who were with them and had started to write Davis's name when Mathews stopped him and said don't put the "boys" down at all, meaning Baker, Evans, Hill, & "Davis." . . .
>
> I am positive that Mathews and Dolan picked out the men. They would say "you go," "you go" & so on [&] point out each person, and these persons commenced to examine their arms & horses. I saw Baker, Evans, Hill & Davis at this time getting ready with the rest of the party. I heard no one make any objections to their going.[20]

Gauss was honest enough to admit that objections may have been made out of his earshot, since he was cooking in the "shanty" or summer kitchen. But he insisted he heard most of what went on, since "I was in and out [of] the house, the door was open all the time, and the party were coming in and out of the house shouting a great deal."[21]

Pantelón Gallegos, a teenaged clerk in Dolan's store and one of the very few Hispanics to side with the House, reported that Mathews specifically ordered the Boys not to ride with the posse, but the Boys insisted they were only interested in retrieving the horses they had loaned to Bill Bonney. So, according to Gallegos, they left the ranch with the posse over Mathews's objections.[22]

Charlie Kruling, another posse member, flatly contradicted Gallegos: he testified that the Boys were not at Tunstall's ranch at all, but only met the posse some twenty miles down the road.[23] This is one of many minor but telling discrepancies in the testimony of the posse members. They had coordinated the main outlines of their story, but Special Agent Angel's seemingly trivial questions exposed the absence of any agreement on the details.

Mathews, the sheriff's deputy, didn't lead the posse himself. Dolan put William Morton in charge. As foreman of Dolan's Seven Rivers cow camp, Morton was used to supervising others. He was very bright and had a reputation as a tough guy. Most important, from Dolan's point of view, he was unlikely to be buffaloed by Dick Brewer. After the previous week's fiasco, Mathews simply couldn't be trusted to get the job done. The four Boys and fourteen other men were picked to go with Morton after Tunstall.

Gauss said, "I heard I think it was Morton cry out, 'Hurry up, boys, my knife is sharp and I feel like scalping someone.' They were all excited and seemed as though they were going to kill some one."[24]

Before leaving, three or four of the men "commenced to shoeing their horses out of Tunstall's property," according to Gauss.[25] The petty theft was considered bad form enough that John Hurley claimed the incident occurred on the posse's prior visit, when the Boys supposedly were invited to help themselves.

The eight men who were left behind on Tunstall's ranch rounded up the cattle, some three hundred head.[26] Since the market rate for each animal was somewhere between ten and twenty dollars, the herd had a minimal value of some $3,000, half of which could be attributed to McSween's supposed partnership share. McSween's own property was eventually appraised at $6,379.50, which almost certainly was low. McSween's spurious one-half interest in Tunstall's store was valued at $1,000, which was ludicrously low. The real value of the property attached was probably over $30,000,[27] but even the minimum value of $8,879.50 already exceeded $8,000, the amount of property Brady was authorized to attach.

Listed on the sheriff's appraisal were four saddle horses belonging to McSween valued at $200, or an average of $50 each. This figure, too, was on the low side, but it puts the pursuit of Tunstall into perspective:

after attaching property worth at a minimum $8,879.50, the posse chased Tunstall for an additional five horses valued at $250.

Some ten miles from Tunstall's ranch, the horse trail branched off from the main road. Fred Waite, driving the wagon, took the road, the longer and more roundabout route. Tunstall, Widenmann, Brewer, Middleton, and Bonney continued on the trail, angling north by west through rugged country in the direction of the volcano.

Around five o'clock in the evening, some thirty miles from the ranch and just ten miles from Lincoln, at the spot where the trail drops precipitously down to the Rio Ruidoso, the riders startled a flock of wild turkeys. Widenmann described the scene:

Brewer, Tunstall and I were riding along driving the horses, Middleton and Bonney being about 500 yards in the rear, and we three had just come over the brow of the hill when a flock of turkeys rose to the left of the trail. I offered Tunstall my gun, he having none with him, to shoot some of them but he declined the use of it saying that I was a better shot than he was. [Vintage Widenmann!] Brewer and I started off for the turkeys leaving Tunstall with the horses.[28]

The division of the men was probably not happenstance: Tunstall, Widenmann and Brewer – the general and his lieutenants – rode in front while Bonney and Middleton brought up the rear. The horses were strung between the two groups of men.

At five on a February evening, at an altitude of 6,500 feet, with the light failing, it was cold. The exposed highlands between the rivers would have had snow, which must have slowed the party's pace along the narrow trail through the trees. Ordinary winter trail garb for the men included long greatcoats with flat-brimmed hats pulled low, but still the cold must have seeped into their bones. The turkeys, besides representing fresh meat and a change from the all-beef winter diet, were probably the first real excitement on an all-day ride.

Riding in the rear, Middleton and Bonney crested the hill and, looking back, saw the pursuing posse. Bonney described what happened next:

When the party and I had traveled to within about 1 mile from the Rio Ruidoso, John Middleton and I were riding in the rear of the balance of the party and just upon reaching the brow of a hill we saw a large party of men coming towards us from the rear at full speed. Middleton and I at once rode forward to inform the balance of the party of the fact. I had not more than barely reached Brewer and Widenmann, who were some 200 or 300 yards to the left of the trail, when the attacking party cleared the brow of the hill and commenced firing at me, Widenmann and Brewer. Widenmann, Brewer and I rode over a hill towards another [hill] which was covered with large rocks and trees in order to defend ourselves and make a stand.[29]

Middleton, meanwhile, raced forward to warn Tunstall. Tunstall had apparently stopped on the trail to watch the turkey shoot. Middleton testified, "I sung out to Tunstall to follow me. He was on a good horse. He appeared to be very much excited and confused. I kept singing out to him for God's sake to follow me. His last word was 'What, John! What, John!'"[30]

With the posse now very close and bullets flying around their heads, Middleton plunged into the woods after the others. After a moment's confused hesitation, Tunstall followed. Since he had been riding at the head of the party, he was the last to know they were being pursued, and the last to seek shelter on the hill.

When Bonney raced ahead to warn Brewer and Widenmann, he was initially followed by the posse. The posse shot at him; Widenmann testified that he first understood what was happening "when a ball whizzed between me and Brewer." However, Bonney related, "the attacking party, undoubtedly seeing Tunstall, left off pursuing me and the two with me and turned back to the cañon in which the trail was."[31]

As the exposed last rider in the column, Tunstall spurred his horse uphill at a right angle to the trail. The trail and his path formed the side and base of a right triangle; the posse described the hypotenuse. At the vanguard of the posse were William Morton, Jesse Evans, and Tom Hill.[32]

Bonney, Middleton, Widenmann, and Brewer made it to the top of the hill. The entire chase did not last more than a few minutes. Suddenly, they were left alone in the cold dusk, straining to hear above their pounding heartbeats and the panting of their horses. Then, Bonney testified, "We heard two or three separate and distinct shots."

Middleton said to the others: "They've killed Tunstall."[33]

Part Two

THE REGULATORS

*There are two
parties in arms
and violence
expected.*
William Morton,
March 8, 1878

Postmortem

13

Pantelón Gallegos, a member of Morton's posse, was as young as Bonney. His loyalty to his employer, Jimmy Dolan, shines through every word of his testimony to Special Agent Angel describing the circumstances of Tunstall's death:

> We rode about thirty miles before we came up to Tunstall and his party with the horses. Morton was ahead and the rest of us were riding behind as near as possible; there was only a trail through the mountains and it would not permit of our riding close together. Billy Morton and I first saw a man ahead riding a grey horse, who upon seeing us, called out to the men driving the horses ahead of him. It was too far to distinguish what he said.[1]

Elsewhere, Widenmann testified, "Bonney was riding a gray" while the others rode horses of different color, so Billy the Kid himself gave the first warning.[2] Gallegos continued:

> Thereupon Tunstall and his men left, the horses ran and scattered. Morton and John Hurley followed after them. Myself, Robert Beckwith, [George] Kitt and Thomas Green went after the horses. I do not now remember sufficiently to name any other persons that were with either me or Morton. The next thing that occurred was my hearing shots fired in quick succession. I did not see the shooting because it took place in the bushes. It was all over in a moment. There might have been others with me or Morton. There was so

much excitement at the time I cannot tell exactly who was with me or who was with Morton.

Afterwards Morton returned and said that a man had been shot and killed. I asked who, and he said Tunstall. I asked how it occurred. He said, "I rode after Tunstall calling to him to halt and waving at him the attachment. Suddenly Tunstall wheeled his horse around and came towards me on a jog trot with his hand on his revolver. I asked him to halt again, as I desired to serve a writ and to throw up his hands and he would not be hurt. In place of which he, Tunstall, pulled out his six shooter and fired at me. Whereupon I and those with me returned the fire. The rest of Tunstall's party were not near him at the time he was shot. Tunstall was shot about one hundred yards off the trail just upon the top of the hill." All this was told me by Morton. Hurley at the same time told me and the rest of our party the same story.[3]

The story Gallegos repeated was the party line adopted by the Dolan faction: Tunstall, after surrendering his store, bank, ranch, home, and three hundred head of cattle suddenly, in defense of a few horses, decided to do single-handed battle with the county's most notorious bandits, backed as they were by an entire sheriff's posse, and so gave Jimmy Dolan what he most wanted – a justifiable homicide.

The story has its weaknesses. According to Gallegos, Tunstall and his men "left," and the shooting took place in the bushes. Would a man intent on a gun battle first run away? Gallegos also said that Tunstall died one hundred yards from the trail. Special Agent Angel, after visiting the murder site, was more specific. Tunstall died "some hundred yards or more from his horses." The significance of those hundred yards is explained in Angel's report: "There was no object for following after Tunstall except to murder him, for they had the horses which they desired to attach before they commenced to chase him and his party."[4]

Extrinsic evidence is even more damaging to Gallegos's story. Gallegos put John Hurley with William Morton at the head of the party and claimed to hear the story directly from Hurley. But Hurley testified:

I was about the center of the party. We followed up and after the horses we were after. I did not follow after the men but looked after the horses. Just before I got up to the horses I heard some shots, how many I cannot tell. I was not present when Tunstall was shot. I did not see him shot, nor did I see any one shoot at him — it was scrub timber & a person could not see.

Hurley added that anyone who said otherwise was mistaken.[5]

Once again, Angel had forced a witness to improvise. Gallegos couldn't very well pretend Morton rode up to Tunstall alone — that just wasn't believable. But he also didn't feel he could admit that Morton was accompanied by the jailbreakers Tom Hill and Jesse Evans. So he caught himself in a foolish lie.

The Olinger family name has gone down in Lincoln County history thanks to Robert Olinger, who had the honor of guarding the Lincoln County jail from which Billy Bonney made his most flamboyant escape. Bob's brother Wallace served in Morton's posse. Wallace Olinger reported that, after the shooting, he examined Tunstall's pistol

and found two loads out of it. It was reported that he had shot it off at Morton. . . . I heard I think two shots fired about this time. I heard the shots before I examined the revolver. I think that Hill fired those two shots. I do not know positively whether he did or not or whether they were fired out of a pistol or a carbine. There might have been three shots. I thought at first that perhaps the Tunstall party had fired at us, then I thought the shots were fired to collect our party.[6]

Sam Perry, another posse member, also heard those shots:

While I was laying out Tunstall I heard two or three shots. I will not be positive. I enquired what they were shooting about and they said they were shooting at *that* tree. There was some talk at this time that either Hill or Morton or Evans had fired off Tunstall's pistol. I thought it a little strange that they were shooting at a mark. I did not think it was an appropriate time to be shooting at a mark. I do not know who were shooting at the mark. I was busy laying Tunstall out.[7]

Olinger and Perry knew what they were saying, of course. They were being as honest as they dared. For obvious reasons, they were reluctant to come right out and say that Jesse Evans, Tom Hill, and William Morton murdered a man and then coolly discharged his gun to make the murder look like self-defense. So they recounted exactly what they heard and saw, then left it to Angel to draw whatever conclusions he wished.

Albert H. Howe was a resident of Lincoln County with the good sense not to get involved in the fighting, and consequently little is known about him. Howe repeated for Special Agent Angel a conversation he had with George Kitt, a member of Morton's posse. Kitt, according to Howe,

> did not see the shooting but was informed how Tunstall was killed by the boys. Tunstall was some distance off from the road, and when he found he had been deserted by his party he turned and rode towards Hill & Morton. When he came in sight of them he seemed very much surprised and hesitated. Hill called to him to come up and that he would not be hurt. At the same time both Hill & Morton threw up their guns resting the stocks on their knees. After Tunstall came nearer Morton fired and shot Tunstall through the breast and then Hill fired & shot Tunstall through the head. Someone else fired and wounded or killed Tunstall's horse at the time Tunstall was shot through the head by Hill. Two barrels of Tunstall's revolver were emptied after he was killed. Tunstall fired no shots and Tunstall was killed in cold blood.[8]

Olinger put the murder in a certain perspective when he said, "I never saw Tunstall to know who he was until after I saw him dead."[9] Until Tunstall's murder, the rivalry with Dolan was largely a personal matter, emotionally involving only a handful of adherents on either side. For most of the people in the region, the opening of Tunstall's store meant no more than another place to shop. It was the store's abrupt closing that first involved the whole countryside.

McSween repeated a rumor that "Tunstall's hat was lying under the head of [his] dead horse." The suggestion was that the killers put Tunstall's hat on the horse as a joke before killing it. Angel considered this strange rumor important enough to pursue, and both Olinger and Sam Perry denied it. ("We thought it was a very serious matter," Olinger said.)[10] But how does a rumor like that get started?

An autopsy was performed on Tunstall's body by the assistant post surgeon from Fort Stanton, Lieutenant Daniel M. Appel. Dr. Appel concluded that both shots were fired from carbines while Tunstall was on horseback.[11] This portion of his autopsy report is contradicted by Judge

Gonzáles, who testified: "On examination we found . . . that a rifle or carbine bullet had entered his breast and a pistol bullet entered the back of his head coming out of the forehead."[12] In other words, after Tunstall pitched forward from his horse, Morton or one of the Boys pressed a pistol to the back of his head, and fired.

Around 10:00 P.M. on Monday, February 18, 1878, Bonney and Widenmann rode into Lincoln town with the news of Tunstall's death. It is probably not coincidence that the members of the party who seem to have been shortest on common sense were the ones who brought the news to town.[13]

McSween's house filled with mourners who gathered in response to news of Tunstall's death.[14] Around midnight, a very strange thing happened. McSween described the incident in an affidavit:

On the night of the 18th day of February, 1878, one John H. Riley, a member of the firm of J. J. Dolan & Co. of the town of Lincoln, came to my house. He was bareheaded and seemed very badly scared and was also intoxicated. In order to convince those present that he had no concealed weapons he emptied his pockets of their contents. In so doing he took out of one of his pockets a memorandum book containing some letters, etc. He left the same on the table.[15]

Why did Riley come? He was drunk, for one thing. Then there were motives of self-interest. Riley may well have been scared that the crowd gathering in McSween's house meant him harm and wanted to demonstrate his friendly intentions. He may have realized that the murder was a blunder, that it would likely provoke Tunstall's friends to exact revenge. Or maybe he was sorry.

He left town the next day, hustled away by friends alarmed at his lapse in judgment. And then John Riley largely fades from the story. He did not earn the enmity of Tunstall's friends as thoroughly as did his partners Murphy and Dolan. His sorrow at Tunstall's death stank of hypocrisy as well as whiskey, but it may have been genuine.

Also genuine was the letter from District Attorney Rynerson he left on McSween's table. It read:

La Cruces, N.M. Feb'y 14th, 1878

Friends Riley & Dolan
Lincoln N.M.

I have just received letters from you mailed 10th inst. Glad to know that you got home OK and the business was going on OK. If Mr. Weidman [*sic*] interfered with or resisted the Sheriff in discharge of his duty Brady did right in arresting him and any one else who does so must receive the same attention. Brady goes into the store in McS' place and takes his interest. Tunstall will have same right then he had heretofore but he neither must not obstruct the Sheriff or resist him in the discharge of his duties. If he tries to make trouble the Sheriff must meet the occasion *firmly* and legally. I believe Tunstall is in with the swindles with the rogue McSween. They have the money belonging to the Fritz estate and they must be made to give it up. It must be made hot for them all the hotter the better. Especially is this necessary now that it has been discovered that there is no hell. It may be that the villain Green "Juan Bautista" Wilson will play into their hands as Alcalde. If so he should be moved around a little. Shake that McSween outfit up till it shells out and squares up and then shake it out of Lincoln. I will aid to punish the scoundrels all I can. Get the people with you. Control Juan Patrón if possible. You know how to do it. Have good men about to aid Brady and be assured I shall help you all I can for I believe there was never found a more scoundrelly set than that outfit.

Yours &tc
W. L. Rynerson[16]

The House forces later claimed that Rob Widenmann stole this letter while Governor Axtell asserted Rynerson could stand on every word. Without such implicit assurances that the letter was genuine, it would be easy to conclude it was a forgery.[17] But District Attorney Rynerson, the man who gunned down the chief justice, was not a subtle personality. He did what he could to help his friends.

The letter was enough to convince McSween, if he didn't know already, that Rynerson would never approve bail. And Rynerson would never prosecute his friends for taking his advice to make it hot for Tunstall.

Widenmann's Raid

14

On the night of the February 18, McSween "wrote a note to John Newcomb requesting him to go to where Tunstall's corpse was and bring it into Lincoln that it might have a decent burial."[1] Newcomb's farm, near the village of San Patricio, was close to the murder site. Four men accompanied him on the melancholy task of searching for the body: Judge Gonzáles, Patricio Trujillo, Lazaro Gallegos, and Roman Barragán.[2]

As Pantelón Gallegos said, the trail was narrow. Consequently Newcomb and the rest couldn't drive a wagon up to the murder site, but instead were forced to strap the body across a horse and then lead the horse back down the steep and winding trail to the river. Once they reached level ground, they were able to transfer the corpse to Newcomb's wagon. None of the members of this funeral party left a record of the condition of Tunstall's body, but it had lain exposed to frost and animals through a long winter's night.

They reached Lincoln on the evening of February 19, and Justice of the Peace John B. Wilson immediately held an inquest. District Attorney Rynerson had warned that Wilson might play into McSween's hands. The basis of Rynerson's suspicion is suggested by his reference to Wilson as "Juan Bautista" the "*alcalde*." Wilson was one of the few Anglo soldiers to remain behind after the Mexican War. He settled in New Mexico in 1849, converted to Catholicism, married a Hispanic girl, named his son Gregorio, and spoke Spanish. As Juan Patrón pointed out, with few exceptions the Hispanic population had closed ranks in hostility to the House. Dolan and Riley weren't likely to miss the broad hint found in Rynerson's use of Spanish.[3]

The office of justice of the peace was elective, but Wilson hadn't been elected. James Farmer had run in and won the previous election, but he resigned before his term was up. In 1876 the territorial legislature passed a law giving county commissioners the power to fill vacancies in county offices by appointment.[4]

In the spring of 1878, this provision was pronounced unconstitutional by Governor Axtell, the very governor who had signed it into law. Axtell's pronouncement ignited a fierce controversy concerning Wilson's right to hold office. All that was far in the future in December 1876, however, when the Lincoln County commissioners appointed him to complete Farmer's term.

The inquest conducted by Justice Wilson functioned more or less as a miniature grand jury, hearing evidence and ascertaining, in the words of the statute, "by whom the crime was committed." The statute specified that the inquest was to be held "over the body of the deceased."[5] McSween, an efficient lawyer, obtained affidavits from Brewer, Bonney, and Middleton describing the circumstances surrounding the murder.[6] It's impossible now to know what other evidence, if any, the jury considered in reaching its verdict that Tunstall

> came to his death on the 18th day of February, A.D. 1878, by means of divers bullets shot and sent forth out of and from deadly weapons, and upon the head and body of said John H. Tunstall, which said deadly weapons then and there were held by one or more of the men whose names are herewith written: Jesse Evans, Frank Baker, Thomas Hill, George Hindemann, J. J. Dolan, William Morton, and others not identified by witnesses that testified before the coroner's jury.

The verdict, dated February 18, 1878, was signed by Wilson and five jurors: George B. Barber, John Newcomb, Samuel Smith, Frank Coe, and Benjamin Ellis.[7]

The verdict reads like a mirthless satire of legal writing, but in fact was largely taken verbatim from the statute. The jury (or, probably, Wilson) filled in the blanks on the form provided by the legislature.[8]

Oddly, the date is wrong. Tunstall was killed on February 18, as the verdict recites, but the inquest was not held until the following day.

The jury had a pro-McSween slant. Future events proved Coe and Ellis to be McSween partisans, and Newcomb's hatred for the House was vividly expressed in his deposition testimony. Still, that doesn't necessarily prove their verdict was partisan, since there was relatively little to be partisan about before the necessity for the inquest arose.

As to the testimony, the verdict states the murder was committed by the six named men "and others not identified by witnesses." By implication, then, the six named suspects *were* identified by witnesses. The witnesses, so far as we know, were Brewer, Bonney, and Middleton. That means that Brewer, Bonney, and Middleton thought the murder was committed by the three Boys plus Morton, Hindemann, and Dolan.[9] The jury presumably had positive eyewitness identifications of the first five, all of whom we know were present. But who saw Dolan? He was back on the Felix, making himself at home in Tunstall's house. Perhaps Bonney, Brewer, or Middleton claimed in their testimony to have seen him at the murder site, or maybe his name was added to the list solely on the assumption that he was the brains behind the hit.[10]

On the basis of the jury's formal findings, Justice Wilson issued warrants for the arrest of Evans, Baker, Hill, Morton, Hindemann, and Dolan, delivering the warrants to Constable Atanacio Martínez to serve. Wilson also issued affidavits for other members of the posse as accessories.[11]

On the same day, February 19, Justice Wilson also heard charges that Sheriff Brady and his deputies had stolen hay from Tunstall's store. To add insult to injury, they had refused to allow Tunstall's horses to be fed from the hay. Justice Wilson duly issued a warrant for the arrest of Brady and the deputies he had stationed in the store. The warrant was given to Constable Martínez to serve.[12]

Rob Widenmann did not testify before the inquest because he had ridden directly to Fort Stanton. There, on February 20, wearing his deputy marshal's hat, he formally asked the commanding officer, Captain (Brevet Colonel) George A. Purington, for the assistance of troops to help him arrest Evans, Baker, Hill, and George Davis (who was probably the same man as Frank Rivers) for stealing government livestock. Widenmann wrote, "It is impossible to get a civil posse to execute warrants for the arrest of the above men."[13] Purington provided a detachment of troopers under Lieutenant Millard Filmore Goodwin.

Constable Martínez gave a laconic description of what happened next. In the morning, he testified, "about 4 o'clock, Robert A. Widenmann, Deputy U.S. Marshal, surrounded the house of J. J. Dolan & Co. with U.S. soldiers prepatory to searching it and the store of J. H.

Tunstall, deceased, for the purpose of arresting Jesse Evans and all others against and for whom he had warrants."[14]

Riley later claimed that Widenmann tore the place apart, overturning furniture, ransacking drawers, examining articles of clothing.[15] Widenmann denied it, of course. He was just looking for Evans, Baker, Hill, and Davis.[16] He and the "two citizens" who were assisting him also searched the Tunstall store, which was still occupied by Sheriff Brady's deputies. They didn't find the Boys in either place.

Meanwhile, Constable Martínez followed Widenmann from store to store. Both were at pains to emphasize they weren't in cahoots. Widenmann said (it sounds like a new verse to "The House that Jack Built"): "I had nothing to do with the constable and his posse who arrested the posse of the Sheriff of Lincoln County who held the store of J. H. Tunstall under a writ of attachment against one A. A. McSween. . . . I positively told the constable that he could not enter any building until I had withdrawn with the troops." Martínez's account follows Widenmann's almost word for word.[17]

In short, it was mere happenstance that Martínez was on the streets of Lincoln at four that morning, holding in his hand not just the original murder warrants against Evans, Morton, Dolan, and the rest, but also the second group of warrants against Brady and his deputies for looting Tunstall's store. And, under cover of the "withdrawn" troopers, he "searched the store of J. H. Tunstall and there arrested sundry persons."[18] The sundry included James Longwell and a man who later captained the House forces, George Peppin. From one of the sundry Martínez acquired the keys to the Tunstall store, and "the keys were never again demanded by the Sheriff or any of his deputies."[19]

In Lieutenant Goodwin's memory, the distinction between civil and military authority was less scrupulously observed.

In searching both places citizens came in with the soldiers and served civil writs on the occupants of the buildings, and arrested them. I spoke to Widenmann and told him I did not think it right to use the troops for the purpose of allowing these people to serve their writs. Widenmann said he was sorry for it and regretted that it had occurred.[20]

The citizens were Constable Martínez and his posse, Bill Bonney and Fred Waite, who almost certainly were also the unnamed "two citizens" assisting Widenmann.[21]

Goodwin added that while he "was still present with the troops, writs were attempted to be served on the Sheriff of the County, Sheriff Brady, and others. The writs were resisted."[22] Martínez described the nature of the resistance: "at the door of the House [we were] met by William Brady . . . sheriff of Lincoln County, who, with others for whose arrest I had warrants, at once covered me and Wm. Bonney and F. T. Waite with their rifles. They forcibly disarmed and took prisoners me, Bonney and Waite and then demanded of us our business."[23]

Widenmann, meanwhile, pleaded with Lieutenant Goodwin to protect the constable. Goodwin told him, "I most certainly would not interfere, writs being civil authorities."[24] Brady called Martínez's bluff, and Widenmann was powerless to help.

Martínez bravely soldiered on and, at gunpoint, began reading Justice Wilson's warrant for the arrest of Tunstall's murderers. He didn't get far. "William Brady, . . . as soon as he heard the purport of [the] warrant, told me that I could not arrest any person in the house of J. J. Dolan & Co. That the persons then in said house were his posse, and as such could not be arrested, that he did not recognize J. B. Wilson, who had issued the warrant, as justice of the peace."[25]

Not until he made that little speech did Brady irrevocably commit himself. He was not present when Tunstall was killed and could have distanced himself from the murder. He could have arrested the killers himself or, if he didn't want to go that far, he could have pointed out that he never deputized William Morton and that Morton's sub-posse was acting on its own. He could have allowed the six suspects to be arrested and then testified in their defense. In short, there was a spectrum of positions he could have taken, from A to Z, and he went straight to Z.

The fact that he did so claiming that Wilson was not a real judge suggests that already, two days after Tunstall's death, the House forces had decided on their strategy. Over the next several weeks, they maintained with perfect consistency that Wilson had acted without legal authority, since he had been appointed rather than elected to his position.

Possibly Brady thought of this legalistic argument on his own, but it's doubtful. More likely the district attorney, Rynerson, anticipating that Wilson would play into McSween's hands, supplied him with the legal ammunition.

Constable Martínez continued his account of the attempted arrest:

William Brady and the persons with him abused and cursed me, [and] I was held prisoner by Brady for several hours without warrant or legal process. Subsequently I was released and allowed to return to my home, but my arms were not returned to me. . . . Wm. Bonney and F. T. Waite were held prisoner by Wm. Brady about 30 hours and then released.[26]

Months before, Tunstall had arranged to have Jesse Evans and the Boys jailed, and the Boys evidently considered that justification for murder. Bonney and Waite, who were following a judge's orders when they were locked up, had far better justification. Bonney had already demonstrated that his was not a nature to forgive and forget.

Taylor F. Ealy was born in September 1848, so he was just twenty-nine when, together with his wife and two small daughters, he arrived in Lincoln the day after Tunstall's death. Ealy, a Pennsylvania Presbyterian, received degrees from Washington and Jefferson College, Western Theological Seminary, and the medical department of the University of Pennsylvania. He then took all this formidable learning to the Indian Territory, where he became headmaster of a school for freedmen and contended with the white racists who rode onto campus shooting guns to disrupt classes.[27]

Ealy was a bearded bear of a man with a long face and a self-confident air. His wife, Mary, was extraordinarily beautiful, with delicate cheekbones and a determined, strong chin. Doing good works on the frontier was a way to build the kingdom of heaven on earth, and the Ealys remembered their time in Indian Territory as "golden days."[28]

But the Presbyterians cut a no-compete deal with their brethren in the field, whereby the Baptists took over the Indian Territory in exchange for the Rocky Mountains, and Ealy and his family got the Baptist boot. About this time, Alexander McSween began bombarding the Presbyterian home mission board with requests for a mission to southeastern New Mexico. The Ealys heard the call.

Mrs. Ealy wrote a report of the family's journey to Lincoln for a missionary newspaper, *The Rocky Mountain Presbyterian*.[29] The transcontinental railroad took the family only as far as the Colorado border; they had to continue to Las Vegas in a stagecoach. From Las Vegas, they traveled in a four-wheeled carriage with a driver who spoke no English. The first night they slept on the floor of an adobe home in Antón Chico. The following day they drove into a storm so cold that Mrs. Ealy feared their baby daughters (one two and a half years old, the other four months) would freeze to death. After a supper of tortillas and bacon washed down with coffee made from snow water, they slept on the ground.

They slept out the next night, too, and were faced with the problem of finding firewood — not an easy task on the Llano Estacado, the western rim of the Great Plains. Mrs. Ealy wrote: "Saturday noon we reached Alkali Holes, the first dwelling since we left Anton Chico. Finding the inmates all drunk, both men and women, we did not remain over Sabbath as we first intended to do, but pushed on to the mountains, which we reached some time after dark."

The following morning they woke to find a hungry wolf prowling around their camp. No doubt the parents of the morsel-sized children thought the worst, but the wolf was probably displaying maternal instincts of her own. Mrs. Ealy wrote, "From all appearances there must have been a den beneath us, as sounds proceeded from under the ground."

They were without water that Sunday morning, and were forced to drive their thirsty mules forward, eventually melting snow for them to drink. One more night was spent outdoors, in the mountains; the next night they reached Fort Stanton.

They arrived in Lincoln the following day, February 19, where, Dr. Ealy reported, "we found ourselves in the center of a battlefield — about 40 men armed in full fighting trim — double belts of cartridges, one for the revolvers and the other for the Winchester rifles."[30] Who were the armed men? Dr. Ealy reported that "they said they were looking for a man, and thought he might be getting away in that wagon." But even that detail teases. Who were they looking for? Did Bonney and Waite (before they were arrested) think the Boys were sneaking out of town? Or were the Boys looking for McSween?

The first act of Ealy's mission was to assist in an autopsy. John Tunstall, he determined, "was run upon and shot in the back."[31]

Mrs. Ealy wrote, "Our work will be among Americans and Mexicans. We are anxious to begin. We feel hopeful."[32]

"If a Man Die . . . "

15

John Henry Tunstall was buried on the afternoon of Friday, February 22, 1878. A large crowd listened to Reverend Ealy's sermon on Job's despairing question: "If a man die shall he live again?" Justice Wilson simultaneously translated into Spanish.[1] The preacher may have been the only man in the crowd who had never seen Tunstall alive.

A detachment of soldiers also attended the funeral.

Some months after the fact, Captain (Brevet Colonel) George A. Purington addressed an official report on his command of Fort Stanton to Special Agent Angel. The report had a single overriding theme: Captain Purington should not be blamed for the Lincoln County War.[2] Purington included with his report a copy of his Order #18, dated February 22, 1878, which explained how the soldiers happened to attend Tunstall's funeral. Order #18 began, "It having been represented to the Commanding Officer of this Post, by the Sheriff of Lincoln County that a state of lawlessness beyond his control exists in Lincoln N.M."; the Order ended by ordering Lieutenant Cyrus DeLany into town "with all available men."[3]

Sheriff Brady had indeed asked Captain Purington for help. On February 18, Brady wrote the following letter, employing a bureaucratic prose style he must have learned in the army:

> Lincoln N.M. Feby 18th 1878
>
> Colonel:
>
> I have the honor to represent that I cannot find in this County a sufficient number of armed men to assist me in the execution of my duty though I have done all in my official capacity to obtain such.

I therefore respectfully request that an officer and fifteen mounted men be immediately detailed me to come to Lincoln only for the preservation of the peace.[4]

The odd thing about the whole business is that Brady's letter is dated February 18, four days before Purington's Order #18, and the very day of Tunstall's death. Did Brady request the troops before news of Tunstall's death hit town? If he did, it suggests he knew Tunstall was to be killed. Less conspiratorial explanations also suggest themselves. The date on the letter could be wrong, just as the inquest verdict bears the wrong date. Maybe Brady wrote the letter late at night after hearing the news, or maybe he believed that the mere attachment of Tunstall's ranch was provocative enough to trigger violent revenge. But why did he say that he could not find "a sufficient number of armed men to assist me" the very day (or soon after) his large posse seized Tunstall's ranch?

The story has another odd twist, for Purington visited Lincoln in person sometime between February 18 and 22. In his exculpatory report, he wrote:

A day or so after Tunstall's death I went to Lincoln with Lieutenants DeLany, Goodwin, Pague, Smith and Humphries, and saw in McSween's house from 25 to 50 armed men, a large majority of whom were men of reputed bad character – most of these men McSween said were in his employ, some of whom he was paying as much as four dollars a day.[5]

Purington's account may be no more than the unvarnished truth, but one wonders. The assumption that there were twenty-five to fifty guns to hire in all of underpopulated Lincoln County has a certain inherent improbability, as does the further assumption that McSween was not only solvent enough to hire them all but extravagant enough not to use them, for this ferocious band committed no wanton acts in the days following the murder.

When Purington drafted his report, his actions were under civilian scrutiny, an uncomfortable position for any soldier. By exaggerating the strength of McSween's forces at the beginning, he may have intended to justify the more aggressive steps he took later on, which were the subject of Angel's inquiries.

Dr. Ealy's sermon closed and the coffin was lowered into the ground. Still the mourners waited in the February sunshine. Someone said a few words, and someone else said something else, and the funeral service became a town meeting. Constable Martínez's failed effort to apprehend Tunstall's murderers was the topic of the moment. Martínez himself had been released, but his posse – Bonney and Waite – remained in jail. Meanwhile, the six men wanted for Tunstall's murder enjoyed the protection of the sheriff.

The mourners, still trusting to reason and the rule of law, sent a committee to negotiate with Sheriff Brady. Judge Florencio Gonzáles was one of the four negotiators who walked the hundred yards or so to Sheriff Brady's office in the tiny Lincoln County courthouse. He described what happened:

> I, with John Newcomb and Isaac Ellis, Merchant, and José Montaño, Merchant, of [Lincoln] town, was one of a Committee to wait upon Sheriff Brady and ascertain from him why he had taken as prisoners, without warrant, complaint or authority of law, the constable Atanacio Martínez and his *posse*. . . . Brady replied in substance that he kept them prisoners because he had the power.[6]

Gonzáles and his committee then brought up their second point, which got down to the root of the troubles. The committee offered to provide Sheriff Brady with bonds in double the value of McSween's and Tunstall's attached property.

It was no more likely that Sheriff Brady would accept bond for the attachment writ, even at twice the value, than that District Attorney Rynerson would approve bail for McSween. Brady and Rynerson had only one purpose in mind: "Shake that McSween outfit up until it shells out and squares up, and then shake it out of Lincoln." And so, inevitably, "said Sheriff refused to take bond so aforesaid."[7]

Judge Gonzáles's committee was reduced to asking Brady to assign a value to the property he had already attached. But if Brady appraised everything at its true value, the total would far exceed the $8,000 he was authorized to attach, which in turn would reveal that no honest purpose was served by sending Morton's sub-posse after the horses. If Brady appraised everything at a fraction of its true value, the numbers would come out right, but the deception would be obvious.

Brady knew all this, of course. He told Gonzáles and his committee to get lost. But he did release Bonney and Waite later that day.

Less than a week later, on February 28, Brady sent a telegram to Thomas B. Catron, reporting that McSween and Widenmann had amassed a "well armed mob of about fifty men and are still getting more to join them." Faced with this small army, he claimed, "I cannot serve any legal document or carry out the law if I am not assisted by the military." Therefore, he requested, "Please see his Excellency the Governor and ask him to obtain an order from Gen. Hatch to the Post Commander of Ft. Stanton to protect me in the discharge of my official duties."[8]

Catron knew how to get things done. Four days later, on March 4, Governor Axtell sent a telegram of his own, to President Rutherford B. Hayes, enclosing Brady's message and reporting that he was hurrying to the scene of the troubles. The following day, the commanding general of the army, William Tecumseh Sherman, telegraphed another Civil War legend, General Philip Sheridan, informing him that the secretary of war wanted troops to assist Sheriff Brady. Sheridan passed the order down the line, and soon the soldiers in Fort Stanton knew which side they were on.[9]

On Monday McSween did the prudent thing and executed a will, witnessed by Reverend Ealy, and on Wednesday he lit out for the hills. Deputy Barrier, who faithfully accompanied him, explained why they left town:

> I learned that Dolan had gone to Mesilla to obtain a warrant from Judge Bristol to take McSween from my custody and also to have me arrested for failing to turn McSween over to Sheriff Brady. . . . We received reliable information [around] midnight that Riley (Dolan's partner) had received a letter from Dolan, directing him to have the military ready to assist Brady in arresting McSween & myself, and that he should have Baker, Evans & company ready to do their part as soon as the military left, but that he should be careful and not let the military know they were about.[10]

Barrier and McSween were well advised to take this "reliable information" seriously, but who was their source? Who would have known the contents of a letter from Dolan to Riley? Perhaps it was all paranoid rumor, although it is true that Dolan obtained an alias warrant from the judge in Mesilla. But the possibility exists that Riley tipped off McSween.

Barrier's testimony points to another fact: Barrier, too, was at risk. He could have returned to Las Vegas at any time, but he remained behind with McSween "to protect and guard him, camping out most of the time." Barrier added that he did not do this "for any pecuniary or personal considerations." Indeed, he neglected his business for many months while courting violent death. The unprepossessing figure of this provincial housepainter looks ungainly beneath the cloak of heroism, but the absence of any more cynical explanation forces us to accept him at face value: "my action in regard to McSween was only for the purpose of preserving his life."[11]

Three months before, Brady had done nothing to arrest Jesse Evans and the Boys for stealing Tunstall's horses. Faced with the sheriff's passivity on that occasion, Dick Brewer calmly took the situation in hand by securing a commission for himself as deputy constable and doing Brady's job for him. The stratagem worked the first time, and by Friday, March 1, Brewer decided to employ it again. He appeared before Justice of the Peace Wilson and was once more sworn in as special deputy constable. This time, his mission was to track down Tunstall's killers.[12]

Wilson outraged the sheriff when he issued warrants for the six men fingered by the inquest, but he would have been derelict in his duty to do any less. Having issued the warrants, he had a further duty to see them enforced, and his selection of Brewer as enforcement agent was more than sensible. Brewer's arrest of the Boys, besides making him something of a folk hero, showed he had the courage of an Evans or a Bonney. But the way he divided his time between his own farm north of town and Tunstall's ranch to the south, quietly working hard at both places and generally keeping clear of the acrimony swirling around town, showed he shared the good sense of most of the county's farmers and ranchers. He was an imposing figure but not a controversial one. Besides, he had already proven himself an efficient deputy.

On the very day Brewer was deputized, just hours after Widenmann's predawn raids, Sheriff Brady struck back. He arrested Widenmann and an entire roster of Tunstall/McSween adherents, including John Middleton, Doc Scurlock, Frank MacNab, and the cousins Frank and George Coe, all soon to make names for themselves in the Lincoln

County War, as well as Ignacio González, Jesús Rodriguez, Esequio Sánchez, and Roman Barragán, whose presence tends once more to confirm Juan Patrón's statement that the county was divided along ethnic lines.[13]

The charge entered against all of the arrested men was rioting and resisting the sheriff (but resisting him from doing what?) in connection with Widenmann's raids. The constable had tried to arrest the sheriff's deputies for murder, then the sheriff arrested the constable and his posse on no charge at all, then the constable arrested the sheriff's deputies for theft, and the sheriff arrested the constable and all his friends for rioting. It was a silly game, made all the sillier as the charges and countercharges slid down the felony/misdemeanor scale from murder to riot, although "riot" was probably an apt description of the chaotic events of the morning.

Justice Wilson, a busy man, heard out Brady's story and bound the horde over to the grand jury. No one went to jail, but the battle of jurisdictions was far from over.

Three days later, Sheriff Brady wrote an extraordinary letter to District Attorney Rynerson. Copies were given to several newspapers. Brady described how, twenty days before, he had sent his deputy to Tunstall's ranch on the Rio Felix.

> He took with him four men and on his arrival he found there one Widenmann in charge of some fifteen armed men, and some men against whom the same Widenmann claims as Deputy U.S. Marshal to have warrants of arrest, these men he invited to partake of his hospitality while the posse were not allowed to approach the house.[14]

Presumably Brady obtained this information from his deputy, Billy Mathews. But while Brady had Widenmann leading fifteen men, Mathews only counted ten. (The noncombatant Godfrey Gauss said the number was just seven, himself included.)[15]

Brady wrote that Mathews found the Boys at the Tunstall ranch while Mathews admitted the Boys rode with his posse.[16] Brady wrote that the Boys were extended a hospitality denied the posse, but Mathews testified that "we were afterwards invited [to breakfast] but declined."[17]

After thus using poetic license to set the scene, Brady continued with his narrative, explaining how Mathews "wisely returned" to Lincoln upon realization that "the destruction of himself and party would speedily follow any attempt to enforce the attachment." A day or two later, Mathews returned with a larger party. While this posse was calmly engaged in attaching the horse herd, Tunstall "fired on the posse and in the return fire he was shot and killed."

Brady added:

It has been falsely averred that attached to my Deputy's posse were men against whom U.S. warrants had been issued. To disprove this, I present you a letter which reached him before he attached and in addition to my minute verbal instructions:

J. B. Mathews, Deputy Sheriff.

Lincoln N.M. Feby 15th 1878

Dear Sir

You must not by any means call on or allow to travel with your posse any person or persons who are known to be outlaws, let your Mexicans round up the cattle and protect them with the balance, be *firm* and do your duty according to law and I will be responsible for your acts.

I am sir
Respectfully yours,
William Brady, Sheriff
Lincoln Co.

The Mesilla Valley Independent reprinted Sheriff Brady's letter and asked the obvious question: "Why did Sheriff Brady find it necessary to instruct his deputy not to select 'known outlaws,' as a *posse*? Why did he permit a man to act as his Deputy to whom it was necessary to send such instructions?"[18] The obvious answer is that Brady didn't communicate with his deputies through the post. What sheriff would? The letter to Mathews was strictly for public consumption.

Brady concluded, "Anarchy is the only word which would truthfully describe the situation here for the past month, and [while] quiet and order now prevails, I fear very much that this condition will not last."

In late February, 140 head of Tunstall cattle were driven into Lincoln-town by cavalrymen from Fort Stanton. The troopers were assisting the constable for the Seven Rivers region, who found Tunstall's cattle in his district and drove them back home.[19]

The incident reveals the effective role played by the military as auxiliary police as well as what happened to the cattle attached by Sheriff Brady's posse. Brady didn't even try to keep the cattle on Tunstall's ranch to guarantee McSween's debt.

The fact that the cattle were found in Seven Rivers was of particular interest to Special Constable Dick Brewer. It gave him a clue as to the whereabouts of the men for whom he held arrest warrants.

When Sheriff Brady arrested Widenmann's posse and all of its sympathizers for rioting – eighteen men in all – he did much to define the membership of Lincoln County's two armed camps. Each man acquired with his arrest a new grudge against Brady and the interests he protected. Five of those arrested – Bonney, John Middleton, Fred Waite, Frank MacNab, and Doc Scurlock – joined Brewer on his mission to hunt down William Morton and the Boys.

Ten men altogether rode out of Lincoln with Brewer on March 4. This force of men called itself the Regulators, a name it retained through many subsequent changes in personnel.

In pre-Revolutionary South Carolina, the writ of the colonial government extended only across the rice plantations of the coastal plains. The settlers of the western hill country lived beyond the pale, so they could not rely on the government for protection against bandits. They formed themselves into a homemade militia they called the Regulators. The Regulators didn't see themselves as extralegal vigilantes, but as the region's only representatives of the law.[20]

Brewer's Regulators, too, saw themselves providing basic police protection. Dolan, Morton, Evans, Baker, Hill, and Hindemann were wanted men. Warrants for their arrest had been issued after a judicial inquest, all in accordance with the laws of the territory. Yet the sheriff refused to allow the wanted men to be arrested.

Lincoln County's Regulators did not fit the usual pattern of vigilantes in other ways as well. Richard Maxwell Brown has written, "Fundamentally, [vigilantes] took the law into their own hands for the purpose of establishing order and stability in newly settled areas. In the older settled areas, the prime values of person and property were dominant and secure, but the move to the frontier meant that it was necessary to start all over again."[21] In this sense, Brown suggests, vigilantism was essentially conservative. However, the problem in Lincoln County was not the absence of a legal system, but its corruption. Brewer's Regulators were indeed "starting all over again" in Lincoln County, but they were not the first to do so. Their conservative movement was also revolutionary.

There was a breakdown of public order, not only in the streets (or on the open range) but in the institutions of society. The only civil authority still observing the rule of law was the justice of the peace, aided by his corps of constables. And in this sense, above all, the Regulators were not vigilantes: Brewer was a special constable, authorized by law to take the law into his own hands.[22]

One of the original Regulators was William McCloskey. McCloskey had been sent as midnight emissary from the Tunstall ranch to Morton with the message, delivered on Tunstall's death day, that no resistance would be made when the posse came to attach the ranch and livestock. McCloskey was selected for the job because, although he worked part time for Tunstall, he remained on good terms with Dolan's men. After delivering his message he retraced his tracks, riding with Morton's party from their camp on the Peñasco to Tunstall's ranch; from there he even joined the pursuit after Tunstall. He rode fifteen miles from Tunstall's ranch before his exhausted horse finally pulled up lame. He wasn't present when Tunstall was killed.[23] After joining Morton's pursuit of Tunstall, he turned around and joined the Regulators' hunt for Morton.

An anonymous correspondent to *The Mesilla Valley Independent* reported matter-of-factly: "Richard Brewer and a constable's *posse,* with legal process, arrested William S. Morton and Frank Baker on the banks of the Pecos after an 8 miles chase."[24] A letter to *The Las Vegas Gazette* added some details: the capture was made "nearly opposite the crossing of the Peñasco. . . . This capture was not made until after a chase of more than six miles, in the bottom of the banks of the Pecos. No one was hurt and but a few shots were fired."[25] This letter is sometimes attributed to John Chisum, to whose ranch the prisoners were taken on the journey back to Lincoln.

In a letter he wrote to a Richmond, Virginia attorney, Morton himself said the chase lasted only "about five miles" – one would expect the pursued rather than the pursuers to exaggerate the distance – and that "they (eleven in number) fired nearly one hundred shots at us."[26]

But what were Morton and Baker doing "in the bottom of the banks of the Pecos"?

The Pecos River winds back and forth between the sheer, crumbling walls of a sandy canyon as it approaches its juncture with the Rio Grande. The canyon walls are ten to twenty feet deep. Since the landscape near Seven Rivers is otherwise relatively flat, a rider would be exposed until he guided his horse down those crumbling canyon walls to the river, when he would disappear abruptly. Most likely, Morton and Baker rode between the banks because they knew the Regulators were after them.

References to a chase of five, six, or eight miles convey nothing of what the chase must have been like. Even five miles is a very long distance for a horse to run, and because the Pecos winds back and forth between its banks the chase required many river crossings with much splashing and soaking. In early March the water must have been deathly cold. Members of the posse (if Morton is to be believed over Chisum) wasted ammunition squeezing off shots at the fleeing pair whenever a clear line of sight was obtained. The noise of the gunshots, the hoofbeats alternately thudding and splashing, horses slipping and stumbling and recovering their footing, men shouting with the wind in their ears — it must have been terrifying, above all to the horses.

While held at Chisum's ranch, Morton wrote his long letter to the Richmond attorney. After describing Tunstall's death ("Nearly all of the sheriff's party fired at him, and it is impossible for any one to say who killed him."), and the chase along the Pecos, he continued:

We ran about five miles when both of our horses fell and we made a stand, when they came up they told us if we would give up, they would not harm us; after talking awhile, we gave up our arms and were taken prisoners. There was one man in the party who wanted to kill me after I had surrendered, and was restrained with the greatest difficulty by others of the party. The constable himself said he was sorry we gave up as he had not wished to take us alive. . . .

There are two parties in arms and violence expected, the military are at the scene of disorder and trying to keep peace. I will arrive at Lincoln the night of the 10th and will write you immediately if I get through safe. Have been in the employ of Jas. J. Dolan & Co., of Lincoln for eighteen months since the 9th of March '77 and have been getting $60.00 per month. Have about six hundred dollars due me from them and some horses, etc., at their cattle camps. I hope if it becomes necessary that you will look into this affair, if anything should happen, I refer you to T. B. Catron, U.S. Attorney of Santa Fe, N.M., and Col. Rynerson, District Attorney, La Mesilla, N.M. They both know all about the affair as the writ of attachment was issued by Judge Warren Bristol, La Mesilla, N.M., and everything was legal. If I am taken safely to Lincoln I will have no trouble but [will] let you know.

If it should be as I suspect, please communicate with my brother, Quin Morton, Lewisburg, W.V. Hoping that you will attend to this affair if it becomes necessary and excuse me for troubling you if it does not,

> I remain,
> Yours respectfully,
> Wm. Morton

Morton told the attorney that he would write a second letter in four days if he reached Lincoln safely, but added, "If you do not hear from me in four days after receipt of this, I would like you to make inquiries about the affair." Morton listed by name nine of his captors, then mentioned "two others named McCloskey and Middleton who are friends."

Who was the "one man in the party" who counseled instant execution? Perhaps Bonney, as legend would have it. It was practical advice. The only alternative was to lock the prisoners in Sheriff Brady's jail while waiting for District Attorney Rynerson to prosecute them in Judge Bristol's courtroom. That's why Morton wrote, "If I am taken safely to Lincoln I will have no trouble."

Morton addressed his letter to an attorney and makes no mention of parents or relations other than one brother, which might offer a clue as to why he (like many others) found himself in remote New Mexico. No place else was home.

Morton wrote well and his stoicism is moving. He wrote the letter because he believed he was about to die, yet he wrote calmly, setting out the important points in logical order: justifying himself, fingering his probable executioners, absolving his two friends, referring the attorney to his powerful protectors (the instruments of his revenge), arranging for the disposition of his worldly goods, and devising a system to get word out without needlessly alarming his brother. (One imagines the lawyer waiting for the second letter to arrive.) Morton gave the letter to Roswell postmaster Ash Upson, who years later would achieve a type of immortality as ghostwriter of the inauthentic portions of Sheriff Pat Garrett's *Authentic Life of Billy the Kid*.

Morton never wrote the second letter. A day after the first was written, he, Frank Baker, and William McCloskey were all shot and killed in Blackwater Canyon on the trail to Lincoln.

A good road leads straight up the Hondo River valley from Roswell to Lincoln. Blackwater Canyon is far to the north of that route. The Regulators chose their circuitous route to frustrate pursuit. John Middleton testified, "We understood an effort would be made by their friends, J. J. Dolan, J. H. Riley, L. G. Murphy et al. to rescue them so we took the Black Water road."[27]

Blackwater Canyon is, even today, a landscape of great stillness, remote from everything. It's not even properly a canyon, but a pale dusty riverbed shaped by low hills dotted with juniper. The river, bounded on both sides by thin stands of desert willow, runs with rocks – large, round, white rocks, debris from the Capitan Mountains – and only rarely with water. But when the water comes, it comes in scouring floods that tumble together boulders, willows, and any living thing unfortunate enough to get in the way.

Baker and Morton weren't killed until the fourth day of captivity. Some of the Regulators must have wanted to bring them back to Lincoln to stand trial or they would not have survived as long as they did, nor would Morton have been permitted to post his letter. The time for summary execution was the first day, when Baker and Morton made their stand, resisting lawful arrest. Few juries, even today, would have any difficulty finding such killings justifiable.

But if some of the Regulators wanted to bring the men back alive, why were they killed at all? And why was McCloskey shot? Middleton gave the party-line explanation:

When within 25 miles of the town of Lincoln, Morton drew a revolver out of McCloskey's scabbard, they riding side by side . . . and shot McCloskey in the head. Baker had a pistol concealed. Morton & Baker then made every effort to escape and refusing to halt were fired upon and killed about half a mile from where McCloskey was killed.[28]

It's possible it happened that way. Morton, as we've seen, had doubts about whether he would be brought back to Lincoln alive. If he was convinced that he faced certain death, why not try to escape? Even the most desperate attempt improved his odds of survival (if only from nil to a million to one), and if the attempt failed, at least his death would be more dignified than waiting passively for the executioner's bullet.

Or maybe the Regulators simply murdered their prisoners. Maybe Morton and Baker tried to escape from their killers the same way that Tunstall fired on his. Shooting in self-defense, shooting prisoners as they tried to escape – these were the West's favorite after-the-fact excuses for cold-blooded murder.

The Albuquerque Review reported that Morton and Baker were buried by a party that included Sheriff Brady. The party found "9 balls in Morton's body and 1 in his head; and five in Baker."[29] It is gruesome even to speculate whether this information was accurate, but if so, it tends to support the Regulators' story – unless one is prepared to believe that the Regulators indulged in ritual murder, with each man adding his shot.[30]

But why did they wait until the fourth day? And why did McCloskey die? It shouldn't be forgotten that the Regulators had reason to kill Morton and Baker, two of Tunstall's murderers. There was only one punishment for first-degree murder in New Mexico Territory in 1878. Under the legal and moral standards of the day, Morton and Baker deserved to die.[31] But the same cannot be said of McCloskey.

The most likely explanation is found in Morton's letter. One Regulator advised execution from the start; probably he took his own advice. It required just one man to kill the prisoners but unanimity to keep them alive. McCloskey may have been incautious enough to counsel caution. This was the view expressed by *The Review*'s anonymous correspondent: "McCloskey, one of their party, objected to shooting them while tied, and said he'd testify to that effect . . . 'Young Kid' (Antrim) shot him."[32]

The Highest Levels

16

No fewer than five governors ruled New Mexico in the fifteen years from 1866 to 1881, and all of them took long leaves back home, remaining absent from their posts for months at a time. But while the governors came and went, the Santa Fe Ring remained. Samuel Beach Axtell, the fourth of the post–Civil War governors, understood this enduring truth. Formerly a Democratic congressman from San Francisco, he switched parties and was rewarded with the governorship of Utah, where he foolishly took sides in the unending Mormon-Gentile power struggle. Adroit local politicians drove him from office in a matter of months. He was forced to accept a demotion to New Mexico, a smaller, poorer territory with no prospect of early statehood – meaning that its governor had no chance of cajoling the legislature into naming him senator. Believing he had learned from his Salt Lake experience, Axtell spent most of his tenure in Santa Fe ingratiating himself with Tom Catron and his friends.[1]

Pushing sixty when he moved into the ramshackle adobe Palace of Governors on Santa Fe's Plaza – surely the least prepossessing building ever called a palace – Axtell was a handsome fellow with dramatic white hair, Roman nose, and a strong chin. Somewhat eccentrically for the 1870s, he was also clean-shaven. Special Agent Angel summed up his term of office with more contempt than syntactical grace: "It is seldom that history states more corruption, fraud, mismanagement, plots and murders, than New Mexico has been the theatre under the administration of Governor Axtell."[2]

On March 9, a little more than a week after Widenmann's liberation of the Tunstall store, Axtell traveled to Lincoln County. His motivation for making the eight-day round-trip is unclear. Axtell himself protested that he only wanted to ensure that order was maintained, but it was hardly necessary for the governor to journey from Santa Fe to exhort citizens to obey the law. It is tempting to speculate that Axtell may have been impelled by a growing realization that the Lincoln County troubles presented a political problem for his administration. But his actions once he arrived in Lincoln only transformed the problem into a crisis.

The most likely explanation for Axtell's flying visit (after days of uncomfortable travel, he stayed in Lincoln for just three hours) is that he viewed the Regulators as a threat to established order – which, of course, they were. The Regulators viewed the Brady-Rynerson-Bristol combine as corrupt and unreliable while Tom Catron saw the same triumvirate as the only force protecting him from a financial bath. Both were right. Axtell believed (reasonably, but mistakenly) that it was in his own interest to adopt Catron's point of view.

Catron wasn't the only person Axtell was eager to please. As Investigator Angel noted:

> The facts are that in 1876 Gov. Axtell borrowed of Mr. Riley $1,800, which sum was probably repaid in November 1877. I do not believe, however, that Gov. Axtell received the money to directly influence his action. It was some time before the troubles actually commenced in Lincoln County. However, they were brewing at the time. The only influence this transaction could have on the action of Gov. Axtell was that as Riley had befriended him, to return the compliment, and certainly his official action lays him open to serious suspicion that his friendship for Murphy, Dolan and Riley was stronger than his duty to the people and the government he represented.[3]

At the time he accepted the $1,800 loan, Axtell's annual salary was $3,500.[4]

Axtell told Angel that, while in Lincoln, "I conversed with all the citizens of Lincoln County I could meet."[5] The flavor of some of these conversations is provided by David Shield, who testified as follows:

> On the 9th day of March 1878, Gov. S. B. Axtell . . . called at the house of A. A. McSween in Lincoln. Robert A. Widenmann, Deputy U.S. Marshal, Rev. T. F. Ealy and myself were present. The Governor informed us what he proposed to do in regard to the situ-

ation. Someone present requested that he should ascertain the true situation of affairs from the citizens. The Governor's reply was: "God deliver me from such citizens as you have here in Lincoln." To which Mr. Widenmann replied: "The citizens are right, but God deliver me from such executive officers."[6]

In that snappy comeback is a clue as to why so many people disliked Rob Widenmann. But the governor's stiff rejoinder was even more revealing: "Gov. Axtell said he had all the information that he wanted and that he would act upon it."[7] Full of misplaced certitude as to where his own best interests lay, Axtell issued the following bizarre proclamation, which was posted in Lincoln town:

To the Citizens of Lincoln County.

The disturbed conditions of affairs at the County Seat brings me to Lincoln County at this time; my only object is to assist good citizens to uphold the laws and to keep the peace; to enable all to act intelligently it is important that the following facts should be clearly understood.

1st

John B. Wilson's appointment by the County Commissioners as a Justice of the Peace was illegal and void, and all processes issued by him were void, and said Wilson has no authority whatsoever to act as Justice of the Peace.

2d

The appointment of Robt. Widenmann as U.S. Marshal has been revoked and said Widenmann is not now a peace officer nor has he any power or authority whatever to act as such.

3d

The President of the United States upon an application made by me as Governor of New Mexico has directed the Post Commander Col. George A. Purington to assist territorial Civil officers in maintaining order and enforcing legal process. It follows from the above statement of facts that there is no legal process in this case to be enforced except the writs and processes issued out of the Third Judicial District Court by Judge Bristol and there are no Territorial Officers here to enforce them except Sheriff Brady and his Deputies.

Now therefore in consideration of the premises I do hereby com-

mand all persons to disarm and return to their homes and usual oc-
cupations, under penalty of being arrested and confined in Jail as
disturbers of the Public peace.

S. B. Axtell

Governor of N.M.

Lincoln March 9 1878[8]

The purpose of the proclamation was to turn the Regulators into outlaws. If Wilson's appointment was illegal and void, then (Axtell's argument ran) so was Brewer's commission as deputy constable. And that
meant that the Regulators, far from being a legitimate police force, were
vigilantes, operating outside the law. The inquest held by Justice Wilson
was void, as were the arrest warrants based on its verdict. It was criminal for the Regulators, or anyone else, to arrest Tunstall's murderers.

The arrest of Morton and Baker, lawful when made, was retroac-
tively transformed into kidnapping, and shooting them when they tried
to escape (the Regulators' explanation for the deaths) was cold-blooded
murder, punishable by death. If Baker and Morton had been brought
back to Lincoln for trial, as had been urged by the more upright and perhaps naive Regulators, Sheriff Brady would have been acting in accordance with the governor's proclamation to turn the killers loose and arrest the policemen.

All of this was well understood by McSween and the Regulators.
There was no more talk, ever, of holding prisoners for trial.

Axtell proclaimed that Wilson's appointment was illegal, although he
had signed into law the statute that permitted justices of the peace to be
appointed.[9] Asked by Special Agent Angel to explain himself, Axtell
said that Wilson's appointment "was good for nothing – that a Justice
of the Peace must be elected, could not be appointed, that it was so established by our Territorial Constitution, the Organic Act. . . . I did not
remove him from office – he was not in office."[10] In other words, Axtell
claimed that the statute he signed was unconstitutional.

Whether Wilson was lawfully in office was, in fact, a close legal question, with good arguments to be made on both sides of the issue.[11] But
even if Wilson's appointment were illegal, the governor had no power to
remove him summarily from office. That's why Axtell was so careful to
say "I did not remove him from office." The governor's powers were

carefully enumerated in the territory's Organic Act, and the power to dismiss county officials was not one of them. As McSween wrote in a letter to the editor of *The Cimarron News and Press,* "If Mr. Wilson were not a justice, as the Governor proclaims, then a proceeding should have been instituted in our courts to test that fact. But this would have been too tedious, and numerous arrests of murderers, etc. would have been made that he evidently desired to avoid."[12]

Finally, because Wilson had been appointed by the county commissioners pursuant to statute, he was at least J. P. de facto, and the actions of a judge de facto are legally valid. If this were not so, couples who had been married (or divorced) by a judge whose bona fides were later challenged would be in for a nasty surprise. Prisoners would have to be freed, creditors would have to repay debtors, and the entire handiwork of the nonjudge's term of office undone. Early on, the Anglo-American legal system pulled back from that logical cliff.

In short, Axtell was flat wrong when he proclaimed that "there is no legal process in this case to be enforced except the writs and processes issued . . . by Judge Bristol." Axtell was a lawyer; he later became chief justice of the New Mexico Supreme Court. He knew his proclamation was false. His goal was to restore order, even at the expense of law.

Axtell's proclamation also stated that Rob Widenmann's appointment as deputy U.S. marshal had been revoked. At the time it was issued, this portion of the proclamation was accurate: Widenmann's commission had indeed been revoked, at the governor's instigation. However, Marshal Sherman reinstated Widenmann as deputy almost immediately. It all had to do with a letter to Axtell from a prominent San Francisco lawyer, whom Tunstall had met during his swing through California and who probably knew Axtell from his days as San Francisco's congressman:

Hon. S. B. Axtell
Governor of New Mexico:

March 9, 1878

My dear Sir:

At this moment I write you respecting a painful matter. I here insert a copy of a letter just received by me from your territory.

To R. Guy McClellan   Office of John H. Tunstall
San Francisco, Cal.   Lincoln, Lincoln County, N.M.
                                       Feb. 26, 1878

Dear Sir:

I am under the painful necessity of informing you that my dear friend, Mr. John H. Tunstall, was murdered about 11 miles from here by a party of 18 outlaws and murderers on the 18th inst. about 5 1/2 o'clock, P.M. Three others and I, who were with Mr. Tunstall at the time, only escaped by taking a determined stand. It was a cold-blooded and premeditated murder, committed in the interests of the New Mexico ring, and as the ring controls the courts of the territory, it is difficult to bring the murderers to justice. Even our sheriff here is in the ring and refuses to allow the murderers to be arrested.

I have laid the case before the British minister at Washington and would politely request you to bring all your influence to bear with the British Minister and the authorities at Washington to have the murder thoroughly investigated.

Yours truly,
Robert A. Widenmann

The above is the letter and all that I know of the affair. That such a state of affairs can exist, as here stated, I can not believe, and therefore refer the matter to you, both as a friend, and in your high official capacity, so that no such disgrace, if true, may rest upon any section of our country.

Yours respectfully,
R. Guy McClellan[13]

The letter has come down to us for the odd reason that Governor Axtell had it published in *The Weekly New Mexican*. Axtell was furious at Widenmann for writing the letter; he arranged its publication for the opportunity it gave *The Weekly New Mexican* to swat the pest. The paper obliged, going so far as to blame Widenmann for Tunstall's death, since if Widenmann had arrested the Boys they would not have been free to kill Tunstall.[14]

Axtell demanded that Marshal Sherman remove Widenmann from his position as deputy marshal, and Sherman acceded while he looked into the matter. Shortly afterward he reappointed Widenmann.[15]

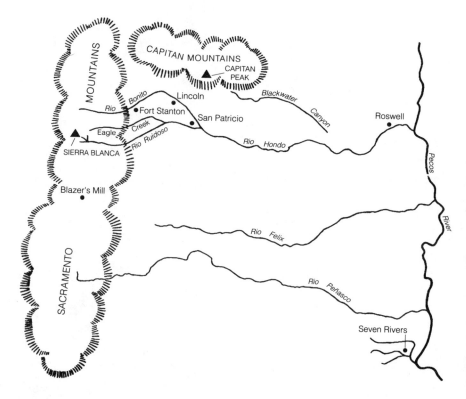

Map 1. *Overleaf* Southeastern New Mexico. Detail from an 1886 map of the New Mexico and Arizona Territories published by Wm. M. Bradley & Co. After two centuries of European settlement the lower Rio Grande valley could be mapped in some detail, but a journey to the east quickly brought a traveler to blank spaces. The map is noncommittal about unsurveyed geographic features such as the north slope of the Sacramento Mountains, which modern mapmakers place near White Oaks.

Map 2. Principal peaks, rivers and settlements of Lincoln County, 1878. Derived from modern Geological Survey maps. Map by Amy Dixon.

Figure 1. The west face of Sierra Blanca.
Nineteenth-century travelers from Mesilla to
Lincoln saw this view. New Mexico State
Tourist Bureau photograph; courtesy Center
for Southwest Research, General Library,
University of New Mexico, neg. no. 000-
299-2565.

No. 235 Bald Mountain from Fort Stanton N. M.

Figure 2. The Mescalero Apache Agency in
1880. Blazer's Mill was part of the small
non-Apache settlement that included the
agency building. Courtesy Center for Southwest Research, General Library, University
of New Mexico, neg. no. 000-064-0001.

Figure 3. The post trader's store at Fort
Stanton, with Sierra Blanca in the background. Probably taken in the 1870s. Courtesy National Archives, neg. no. 111-SC-
89514.

Figure 4. Lincoln, as seen from the south, in
a modern photograph. The House is hidden
behind the trees at the far left. Tunstall's
store (now a post office and museum) is just
to the right of the *torreón*, which is visible
near the center of the photo. The building
that housed the Ellis house and store, and
which marked the eastern edge of town, is at
the far right. Photo by Richard Federici;
courtesy New Mexico State Record Center
and Archives, State Planning Board Collection, neg. no. 11193.

Figure 5. The business premises of L. G.
Murphy & Co. and J. J. Dolan & Co. (the
House), later the Lincoln County courthouse. This photo dates from the mid-twen-
tieth century. The adobe bricks have been
stuccoed and the right balcony staircase has
been added, but otherwise the House has
changed little since 1878. Courtesy Center
for Southwest Research, General Library,
University of New Mexico, neg. no. 000-
434-0042.

Figure 6. Tunstall's store in 1926. The building originally had a flat roof. Courtesy Center for Southwest Research, General Library,
University of New Mexico, neg. no. 000-
118-0018.

Figure 7. The House brain trust in the post
trader days of the early 1870s. Left to right:
James J. Dolan, Emil Fritz, W. J. Martin
(whoever he was) and Lawrence Murphy.
Courtesy University of Arizona Library Special Collections Department.

Figure 8. Alexander McSween in the mid-1870s. There is only one authenticated photograph of McSween. During a 1926 tour of sites associated with the Lincoln County War, former Governor Miguel Antonio Otero and several friends visited Sue Mc-Sween at her White Oaks, New Mexico, home, and took a snapshot of her standing next to this portrait. Photo by Baltimore Studios, Baltimore; courtesy University of Arizona Library Special Collections Department.

Figures 9 and 10. Sue McSween. Photograph 9 was taken by Baltimore Studios, the studio that took the only known photograph of her husband, leading some to speculate the photographs were taken at the same time, perhaps on a honeymoon trip. But to my eye she looks several years older in this picture than he looks in his. According to Frederick Nolan, the studio proprietor was Sue's relative, which would explain why she returned to the same photographer on a subsequent trip back east. Photograph 10 was taken in 1926 at White Oaks by Governor Otero or one of his companions. Photo 9 courtesy University of Arizona Library Special Collections Department; Photo 10 courtesy Center for Southwest Research, General Library, University of New Mexico, neg. no. 000-118-0013.

Figure 11. John Tunstall. Courtesy University of Arizona Library Special Collections Department.

Figure 12. Chisum's South Spring River Ranch, outside Roswell, in the early 1880s. Courtesy New Mexico State Records Center and Archives, neg. no. SRC misc. 37983.

Figure 13. John Chisum. Courtesy University of Arizona Library Special Collections Department.

Figure 14. Rev. Taylor Ealy, M.D., and his wife Mary Ealy, in the mid-1870s. Courtesy Center for Southwest Research, General Library, University of New Mexico, neg. no. 000-443-0001.

Figure 15. Dick Brewer. Courtesy New Mexico State Records and Archives, neg. no. SRC misc. 11205.

Figure 16. Robert Widenmann in Haverstraw, New York. This undated snapshot was donated to the Museum of New Mexico by Widenmann's son. The caption on the back of the original states that the photo was taken "in later life," although it doesn't appear to have been all that much later. Courtesy Museum of New Mexico, neg. no. 36351.

Figures 17 and 18. Thomas B. Catron. Photograph 17 dates from around 1880. Photograph 18 was taken in Washington, D.C., while Catron was serving as one of New Mexico's first United States senators, 1912–16. Photo 17 by Edwin L. Brand, Chicago; photo 18 by Scherer Studio, Washington, D.C. Both photos courtesy Center for Southwest Research, General Library, University of New Mexico, neg. nos. 000-021-0054 and 992-008-0005.

Figure 19. Samuel B. Axtell around 1880. Courtesy New Mexico State Records Center and Archives, Shishkin Collection, neg. no. 22719.

Figure 20. The one, the only, the ubiquitous ferrotype of Henry McCarty. At Dudley's court of inquiry, he gave his name as William Bonney. Upon further questioning he admitted he was also known as "the Kid" and Antrim but, he added, "not 'Billy Kid,' that I know of." This image is authenticated in the sense that writers on the subject do not question its authenticity (how else would we illustrate our books?), but its provenance is established by tradition rather than research.

From time to time other purported photos of Billy the Kid surface. One likely candidate made national news in 1993. It showed a young man in suit and tie staring solemnly into the camera, arms folded in the universal school-picture pose – proof, if authentic, that the Kid could be as boring as the rest of us.

This ferrotype image was taken through the upper-left aperture of a four-lens camera and consequently differs slightly from the more familiar image, which was taken through the lower-right lens. The original of this image is the only one of the four whose whereabouts is known: it was donated to the Lincoln County Heritage Trust in 1985 by descendants of a Fort Sumner horse trader. Note the pinky ring and cardigan sweater. Courtesy Lincoln County Heritage Trust.

Figure 21. A postcard depicting Robert Brady, the oldest son of Sheriff William Brady, with an inset photo of his father. Contrary to the inscription, young Robert was not shot by the Kid or anyone else, although his mother once complained to Colonel Dudley that Doc Scurlock had fired in his direction to scare him, a charge Scurlock denied in writing. Postcard by Frashers Fotos, Pomona, Calif.; courtesy Center for Southwest Research, General Library, University of New Mexico, neg. no. 000-497-0289.

Major Wm Brady,
Sheriff, and
son Robert, of
Lincoln County,
New Mexico.

Sheriff Brady
was killed,
and son Robert
shot in the
mouth by
"Billy the Kid"
and
his gang.
April 1, 1878

SHERIFF BRADY

ROBERT BRADY   H!

Figure 22. Lew Wallace. Courtesy National
Archives, neg. no. 111-B-4922 (Brady Collection).

Figure 23. Edward Thornton, the British
minister to Washington who took an interest
in the Tunstall case. Thornton had previously
represented Her Majesty's government in
Brazil, where one of his consuls was the celebrated explorer Richard Burton. Courtesy
National Archives, neg. no. 111-B-3948
(Brady Collection).

Figure 24. George A. Purington, formerly a
captain in the Ninth Cavalry, was serving as
major in the Third Cavalry when this picture
was taken in 1885. Purington sits front left
with his white summer helmet in his hand.
Courtesy U.S. Army Military History Institute.

Figures 25 and 26. Nathan Augustus Monroe Dudley in the prime of life and a bit past it. Photo 25 courtesy U.S. Army Military History Institute (Roger D. Hunt Collection); photo 26 courtesy Massachusetts Commandery, Military Order of the Loyal Legion and the U.S. Army Military History Institute (27).

Figure 27. The Ninth and Tenth Cavalry were the
black regiments of the segregated cavalry. These
are members of the Tenth Cavalry camping near
Diamond Creek, 120 miles due west of Lincoln,
in 1891. This photo doesn't have anything to do
with the Lincoln County War, but it gives some
idea of what life away from the post was like for
the soldiers. Photo by Henry A. Schmidt; courtesy
Center for Southwest Research, General Library,
University of New Mexico, neg. no. 000-179-0728.

Figure 28. Roswell, New Mexico, 1887. Pat
Garrett is the tall man seated second from
right on the porch. Courtesy Center for
Southwest Research, General Library, University of New Mexico, neg. no. 990-026-0002.

The Cimarron News and Press gave Widenmann a forum to return *The Weekly New Mexican*'s favor. The Santa Fe paper's article, Widenmann wrote, was "full of Billingsgate and blatherskite." He suggested the editors "would have made excellent adobe layers for they could then have indulged in their favorite pastime to their heart's content."[16]

Widenmann told McClellan that he had laid the case before the British ambassador to Washington. His letter to the ambassador, Sir Edward Thornton, made the same points as the letter to McClellan, and was part of an extensive and remarkably successful letter-writing campaign. Thornton received communications from many quarters: McSween wrote the day after Widenmann did, and Tunstall's parents bombarded Thornton's superiors in Whitehall with letters and petitions, adding pressure from their end.[17] McClellan, the San Francisco lawyer, may well have done his share.

The Weekly New Mexican was moved to accuse Widenmann of treason for appealing to a foreign power. The more sympathetic *Mesilla Valley Independent* agreed that Tunstall's murder was "a disgrace to civilization" and that prompt measures should be taken to punish the guilty and prevent a recurrence. However, the paper added, "we have the utmost confidence that all this can be accomplished without having the British Government put to the inconvenience and expense of sending an Ironclad fleet up the Bonito or Ruidoso."[18]

Ambassador Thornton directed a cool diplomatic inquiry to President Hayes's secretary of state, William Evarts. Thornton first summarized the facts: Tunstall, a British subject, was murdered, and warrants were issued for the murderers' arrests and placed in the hands of a constable. The warrants were not given to the sheriff due to the belief "that that officer was indirectly connected with the murder." When the constable and posse attempted to serve the warrants, they were imprisoned by the sheriff. The sheriff "refused to allow them to make any arrests, though the alleged murderers of Mr. Tunstall were then and there with the Sheriff."[19]

Thornton concluded:

If the above mentioned statements be true, it would appear that a most inexcusable murder has been committed, and that the Sheriff of the County instead of assisting in the arrest of the murderers, as he is in duty bound, is impeding the course of justice. Under these circumstances I cannot doubt that the Government of the United States will promptly cause enquiries to be made into the matter, and will take such measures as it may deem expedient for investigating the conduct of the Sheriff of Lincoln County and for ensuring the arrest of the accused, and their being brought to trial.[20]

Matters in Lincoln County were outside the jurisdiction of the secretary of state, and so Evarts promptly (and probably gratefully) passed Thornton's note to Attorney General Charles Devens. Evarts requested Devens to "cause proper inquiry to be made."[21] Devens, in turn, forwarded a copy of the note to the United States attorney for the Territory of New Mexico with these instructions:

You will please make prompt inquiry into all the circumstances attending this murder and report fully to me with a statement of what measures have been or can be taken to bring to punishment the parties guilty of this crime.[22]

Tom Catron could not have been happy to receive these instructions. His plan was working beautifully. The only variable he had failed to take into account was Tunstall's nationality. But he can hardly be faulted for failing to understand how his handiwork would look to Her Majesty's minister in Washington.

Catron's response to his instructions was both uncharacteristic and understandable: he did nothing.

Meanwhile, McSween and Widenmann kept up the pressure, writing letter after letter, keeping Thornton apprised of all developments. And so, on March 27, 1878, eighteen days after his first note, Ambassador Thornton again dropped a line to Secretary of State Evarts. "I have the honour to inform you," the ambassador wrote with diplomatic asperity, "that I have received a letter from that place, of the 16th instant, in which it is charged that [Tunstall's murder] was incited by the District Attorney of the Third Judicial District and that the murderers are being screened or attempted to be screened by the Governor of the Territory and the Judge of the District."[23]

It was one thing to suggest some backwoods sheriff somewhere was corrupt. It was another thing altogether to suggest the district attorney committed murder and the governor covered it up. As the charges became progressively more sensational, they became that much less likely to be true – but that much worse if they were. Thornton's note acknowledged both points in a single deft sentence that started with an implied apology and ended by tightening the screws: "Without pretending that these charges are well founded until they shall be supported by further proof, it seems to me to be a case which demands prompt and searching investigation, and I am confident that the Government of the United States will not fail to give to the matter its early and serious attention."[24]

Secretary of State Evarts, who no doubt had enough to keep him occupied, again forwarded the ambassador's note to Attorney General Devens with a cover letter stating, "I have the honor . . . to invite your attention to his request that energetic measures may be taken to secure the arrest and conviction of the murderers."[25]

That was a blunt invitation. In reply, Devens informed Evarts that, upon receipt of the first note,

I addressed a letter to the District Attorney for New Mexico in which I directed him to institute a thorough inquiry into the circumstances of the murder. . . . I have not yet received a reply, but I have taken other measures to have the subject thoroughly investigated.[26]

In short, the Justice Department was forced to reach outside of its own ranks to find an investigator. Letters from Lincoln County and elsewhere continued to pour into Washington, many of them addressed to Secretary of the Interior Schurz concerning land fraud in northeastern New Mexico. Schurz had already resolved to send an investigator to New Mexico to ferret out that fraud, and also to examine the kleptocratic administration of New Mexico's Indian agencies. Under pressure from the British, the Justice Department signed on as cosponsor of the expedition, adding an inquiry into the murder of John Tunstall to the investigator's list of tasks.

The investigator chosen was Frank Warner Angel, a young lawyer from New York City about to take up duties as a federal prosecutor. Angel was appointed special agent in April, shortly after Ambassador Thornton's second diplomatic note and almost certainly in response to it; he arrived in Santa Fe a month later.[27] For Catron, Angel's investigation was a double torment. First, Angel was performing the task originally assigned to Catron himself, which meant Catron had lost the confidence of his superiors even before the investigation began. Second, and far worse, Catron knew the answers to the questions Angel was asking.

The Double Barrelled Bore

17

On March 10, well after dark, Dick Brewer rode into Lincoln, bringing news of the deaths of McCloskey, Morton, and Baker. The rest of the Regulators had scattered. Brewer arrived the day after the governor's flying visit and discovered that the governor had proclaimed him an outlaw for arresting Tunstall's murderers. He left town almost immediately.[1]

McSween and Deputy Barrier also ventured into town that night. Whatever hopes McSween had that the governor might declare a truce were quickly abandoned. He and Barrier also left town almost as soon as they arrived, taking refuge at John Chisum's ranch on the Pecos.[2]

All we know about Tom Hill (presumably an alias) is that he worked with Evans, helped to kill Tunstall, and made his living brutalizing other people. On March 13, Evans and Hill set out on a job together, as they had done so many times before. This time they descended on the camp of a sheepherder named John Wagner. Wagner was driving four thousand sheep from California all the way to Concho, Texas (near San Angelo), and had camped on the wide desert floor southwest of Tularosa. Wagner described what happened next: "Yesterday they stole a horse from me, broke open my trunks taking out all clothing and throwing it around, built a fire under my wagon, shot my driver in the leg, and took several articles from the wagon with them."[3]

The Mesilla Valley Independent identified the "they" of Wagner's letter as "some of our pet banditti who are now taking a little relaxation after their arduous labors as a sheriff's posse in Lincoln County."[4] The following week, *The Independent* explained what happened. Evans and Hill descended on the sheep camp while it was under the sole guard of

Wagner's Cherokee driver. It was a classic holdup. While one of the Boys kept the Cherokee covered, the other saddled a horse and mule belonging to Wagner (with Wagner's saddles) to assist their getaway. Then they entered the wagon and began forcing open trunks and boxes, looking for the money they knew Wagner must have with him to finance the long journey.

So intent were they that the Cherokee was able to reach a Winchester rifle. As if feeling sorry for Evans and Hill for having let down their guard, the Cherokee did something equally foolish: he told them to give up.

Evans and Hill did this sort of thing for a living: they drew their revolvers and fired. Realizing too late he was out of his league the Cherokee sprinted away, catching a bullet in his leg for his trouble. He dropped like a stone. *The Independent* reported, "The robbers, evidently believing they had finished him, proceeded with their work."[5]

But the Cherokee was not dead. He still had the Winchester. And he had learned from his experience. He crawled through the sagebrush until a clear shot presented itself, pulled the trigger, and Hill was dead.

Evans leapt on Wagner's horse and spurred it into a startled run even as the Cherokee shot again, shattering Evans's wrist but failing to knock him off the horse.

Evans rode the stolen horse sixty miles to his hideout at Shedd's Ranch, duplicating his ride of two months before when he rode all night with a bullet hole in his thigh.[6] Once more he was lucky to escape with his life, but only his powers of endurance made the luck work for him.

Evans was safe from the law at Shedd's Ranch, but anyone could see that he risked losing the arm to gangrene. And so, a day or two after arriving at Shedd's, Evans set out once more on horseback, riding this time all the way across the Journada del Muerte to Fort Stanton. Mesilla was closer, but Evans, whose name graced numerous Doña Ana County warrants, preferred to take his chances in Lincoln, where the governor had just annulled Justice Wilson's warrants. Evans was admitted to the post hospital. His wrist never healed properly but he lived.[7]

There was public jubilation at the news of Hill's demise. *The Independent,* which had erroneously reported Hill's death some months before, crowed, "Hill is dead and buried, there is no mistake about it this time."[8]

On March 13, 1878, Dr. Ealy wrote to his brother back home in Pennsylvania:

One of the worst men in this county on Sabbath broke his leg while trying to shoot an unarmed man in the street of Lincoln. Jumped from his horse before stopping him. I am careful. Keep in at night & am out very little in daylight. Many men in town will soon kill themselves drinking whiskey. . . .

We are well and happy.[9]

Special Agent Angel didn't have much use for Dr. Ealy, referring to him in his notes as "weak – not reliable – McSween man."[10] But since Ealy arrived in town the day after the shooting started, and everyone he met lived in fear of violent death, one can hardly fault him for acquiring a siege mentality.

Still, a certain prejudice can be detected in his reference to Jimmy Dolan as "one of the worst men in this county." And there is reason to doubt that Dolan broke his leg attempting to shoot an unarmed man, and not just because Dr. Ealy failed to identify the would-be victim.[11]

Opportunities for assassination presented themselves every day. Citizens of Lincoln spent a lot of time outdoors – drawing water from the well, going to the outhouse, feeding the chickens and horses, tending the garden, sitting on the porch. Dolan (or anybody else) could easily have rubbed out any unarmed man he chose without the inconvenience of jumping off a moving horse.

But Dolan didn't hire snipers to pick off his enemies, and neither did anybody else in Lincoln that spring. While each side accused the other of cold-blooded murder, both sides indignantly denied the charge. The House forces justified Tunstall's killing by claiming he was resisting lawful arrest. The Regulators justified the killings of Baker and Morton by claiming the prisoners first shot McCloskey and then tried to escape lawful custody. In short, even after the killings began, the rule of law remained in force: people still referred to legal norms as justification for their acts.

Governor Axtell began the process that changed all that when he proclaimed the Regulators outlaws. Axtell intended to strip the Regulators of their legal justification, perhaps believing they would give up the fight or at least lose popular support. Instead, he transformed a battle of jurisdictions between competing legal authorities into a small-scale partisan insurrection, with extralegal forces striking at the embattled established order.

The cloak of legality was a restraint on the Regulators; Axtell removed it. After the proclamation, the Regulators continued their campaign. Treated as outlaws, however, they increasingly came to act like outlaws. Moreover, the dishonesty of Axtell's attempt to remove Justice Wilson had its own corrosive effect, reducing still further the citizens' respect for their unelected government and its ability to maintain order.

The long-term effect was to encourage precisely the sort of half-random violence Ealy ascribed to Dolan. As the legal norms lost their meaning, the men of violence abandoned their pretense of legal justification. Men shot their enemies on sight. And when the enemies were gone, isolated farmers suffered.

But this dynamic had not yet spun out of control in early March. Dr. Ealy notwithstanding, it seems unlikely Dolan was trying to shoot an unarmed man when he broke his leg. But break it he did, and in the 1870s a broken leg meant more, or rather less, than an X-ray and a plaster cast. Dolan was laid up for weeks, recuperating in Santa Fe.[12] A note in the April 27 *Independent,* six weeks after the accident, said only that Dolan's leg was "improving." For the time being, Dolan was out of the picture.

The Regulators, helped along by the Cherokee sheepherder and a timely accident, had met with astonishing success in their campaign to avenge Tunstall's death. Of the six men named as Tunstall's killers in the inquest verdict, three were dead by the end of March: Hill, Morton, and Baker. Dolan and Evans were seriously injured, and Evans was held at the fort under arrest. Only one of the six was still at large: George Hindemann, the most obscure of the six, a House employee of no distinction or prominence, but a marked man nonetheless.

The reign of the Boys was over, with two dead, their leader under arrest, and the shadowy Rivers (according to Rob Widenmann) having abruptly decamped for Arizona.[13] The single blot on the tally sheet was the death under ambiguous circumstances of William McCloskey. Much remained to be done, but by the end of March the Regulators had good reason to be grimly pleased with their handiwork.

The turning point in the Lincoln County War occurred on March 8, 1878, but no one at the time recognized it as such. On that date, the commanding general of the U.S. Army, William Tecumseh Sherman, issued the following order:

The unexecuted portion of the sentence of a General Court Martial, promulgated in General Court Martial Orders No. 1, January 17, 1878, from Headquarters Department of the Missouri, in the case of Lieutenant Colonel N. A. M. Dudley, 9th Cavalry, is remitted.[14]

The Ninth Cavalry was the black regiment stationed at Fort Stanton.[15] On April 5, Dudley succeeded Captain Purington as commander of the fort.

Dudley had been court-martialed in January at Fort Union, New Mexico; he was suspended from rank and placed on half pay for three months. He had been found guilty of bringing his superior officer, Colonel Edward Hatch, into "contempt and disgrace in the estimation of the officers of the Army" by suggesting Hatch was skimming profits from the Fort Union depot. Not content with spreading rumors of corruption, Dudley told Hatch, his commanding officer, to his face: "'I will make your depot stink.'"[16]

Dudley was convicted despite a letter written on his behalf to the U.S. Army's judge advocate general. The letter writer, a citizen of San Antonio, Texas, claimed that Hatch had been gunning for Dudley since 1869, when the two served together on a military commission investigating a murder in Texas. According to the writer, Hatch accepted "courtesies" from the family of the accused, but Dudley refused to follow suit. "This made bad blood between Hatch and Dudley; in fact made them enemies."[17] When he faced charges for his conduct during the Lincoln County War, Dudley once more orchestrated a campaign to depict his accuser (Sue McSween, in that instance) as a moral monster. In both cases, the accusations appear to have been fabricated from whole cloth – a circumstance that did nothing to diminish the gale-force windiness of Dudley's self-righteousness.

The real issue is suggested by the charges of which Dudley was somehow acquitted at Fort Union: drunkenness on duty. Dudley had been convicted at another court-martial, in Arizona in 1871, for being drunk on duty. A later antagonist described him as "a whiskey barrel in the morning and a barrel of whiskey at night" – which helps to explain why Angel's notes on Dudley include the notation "talks too much."[18]

Dudley was tried at yet another court-martial, this one during the Civil War, after he falsely told a superior officer that their commander had ordered him to assist Dudley. Dudley's only defense was that he had no reason to lie, which overlooks the fact that his accusers had no reason to lie either. Dudley was acquitted, which may have layered a sense of invulnerability over his already-swollen ego.[19]

A formal photograph of Lieutenant Colonel Dudley shows him at attention, his left thumb hooked on his wide belt, a spiked helmet hanging by its strap from his elbow. An absurd monocle dangles from a cord around his neck. His chest is entwined in a yard or two of gold braid, and he wears a Bismarckian mustache. He looks like a vaudevillian playing a Prussian officer, down to the detail of a medal resembling the iron cross.

Dudley's stare of eagle-eyed alertness completes the parody. His white eyebrows are shaggy, his white hair close-cropped, his ears elephantine. The drawn-up seriousness of his face explains why so many of his fellow officers despised him.

Sue McSween returned from Kansas in March and joined her husband at his place of refuge, Chisum's South Spring River Ranch. The McSweens were joined there by an Englishman named Montague Leverson, a naturalized American citizen. Leverson suffered from delusions of grandeur: he bombarded President Hayes, Secretary Schurz, and various members of Congress with detailed letters describing events in Lincoln County in the belief that his voice crying in the wilderness would be heeded. Oddly enough, it was, after a fashion.

Leverson's long letters were full of grandiloquent flourishes. He told the president he was in Lincoln County to select "a suitable location for a colony to be chiefly composed of citizens from old and new England."[20] He envisioned thirty to forty thousand settlers farming peaceably in the lower Pecos valley,[21] but found a worm in Eden's apple: "On this mission I visited Mr Chisum's ranch on South Spring river and in that neighborhood I found all that could be desired except that security for life and property, to ensure which is the only excuse for the existence of government at all, instead of being afforded by the government is by the United States government in that region destroyed!"[22] Not to put too fine a point on it, he continued, "This County I am sorry to inform you is under the *rule of a gang of thieves and assassins at the head of whom are the United States officials.*"[23] Indeed, he asserted, "The state of affairs here is precisely that of the two Sicilies before they were freed by Garibaldi. The administrators of the law were the criminals and the honest men were driven to the mountains and pursued as bandits."[24]

No one else in Lincoln County wrote letters quite like these, and there was a steady stream of them, sometimes several a day, burdening the post office from Lincoln County to Washington. Special Agent Angel annotated Leverson's lengthy April 2 letter to the president, commenting in the margin: "Leverson is a man like Gov. Axtell, is liable to make himself a double barrelled bore." Leverson seems to have assumed that the President of the United States would pore over his letters, deeply concerned about such details of his "tour of inspection" as whether he started for Santa Fe on April 1 or a week later. (The White House passed the letters along, without comment, to the Departments of Justice and the Interior.)

McSween and Chisum appear to have humored Leverson. McSween was busy writing his own letters and encouraging others to do the same in an attempt to apply maximum pressure on Washington officials. Reverend Ealy wrote repeatedly to his uncle the congressman, who passed his letters along to the secretary of war. An attorney active in the Colfax County troubles weighed in with a letter bulked out with newspaper articles, which also found its way to the War Department:

> There is no doubt in my mind, from a mass of private information I have received, that the whole power of the territorial government, strengthened by the active aid of the U.S. military forces, has been either ignorantly or intentionally used to protect and assist a small combination of corrupt men – speculators in military and Indian contracts – against the best men in the county.[25]

Leverson's testaments could only aid this campaign, even if only as makeweight. Besides, maybe Leverson could deliver. If not thirty thousand settlers, perhaps three hundred – that would be a major influx.

And so Montague Leverson was entertained at Chisum's ranch for a week or two in late March. He happened to be present when Sheriff Brady rode up to the house at the head of a detachment of soldiers led by Fort Stanton's Lieutenant C. W. Smith to summon citizens for service on the Lincoln County grand jury that would meet in April.[26] That grand jury was to investigate Tunstall's murder and the embezzlement charges against McSween, among other less sensational crimes. The summons stated that court would convene on April 1.

Leverson assured President Hayes:

In conversation with Mr Brady he told me that he regretted having to come with troops, but that the citizens refused to accompany him, and I am assured on good authority that on his telling even native Mexicans who refused to accompany him that would be fined $30.00 for so refusing, they answered "Well then when we get the $30.00 we will pay it, but if you call on us to go in pursuit of the murderers of Mr Tunstall we will go at once."[27]

Sheriff Brady would hardly describe such bitter humiliations to the strange guest of his worst enemies, of course, and it is easy to guess who the "good authority" was. But beneath the surface implausibilities of Leverson's account lies a greater naïveté. The Lincoln County grand jury, when it finally met in April, issued a report spelling out the connection that Leverson, with his peculiar combination of ignorance and indignation, failed to make. The report described how Axtell's proclamation, by purporting to annul Wilson's appointment as J.P., "virtually outlawed Mr. Brewer and *posse*. In fact, they were hunted to the mountains by [Sheriff Brady] with U.S. soldiers."[28] That's what Brady and Lieutenant Smith were doing when they met Montague Leverson; the grand jury summons was little more than an excuse.

In the wake of Axtell's proclamation, Colonel Hatch had ordered Purington to consider Sheriff Brady "the proper person to render assistance to when required by him to preserve the peace and sustain the laws."[29] It is hard to fault a military man for obeying an order to respect civilian authority, but to many in Lincoln County Purington's decision to help Brady meant the army was taking sides. Purington became a hated man; Colonel Dudley, when he assumed command in April, was celebrated as a savior.

All of this was lost on Leverson. But he set the sheriff straight on a few matters:

I stated to Mr Brady "A complaint has been lodged with the County Commissioners to the effect that you and your bondsmen are insolvent and to require you to furnish good bonds. If this be so I advise you to seize the opportunity this affords you to resign. You have done many illegal perhaps criminal acts for which you are likely to be held to strict accountability and from what I have seen of the temper of good and quiet citizens I believe your life is in danger. You have a wife and children and your resignation, by throwing everything into the hands of the U.S. Marshal at Santa Fe will save your skin and get the county out of its present troubles."[30]

Leverson's account brings to mind the image of an overdressed Englishman in rotund middle age dressing down the frontier sheriff, who bashfully traces lines in the dust with the tip of his boot, nodding in rueful agreement as his transgressions are examined. Did Leverson himself believe it happened?

McSween did not show his face during Brady's visit. He later told Special Agent Angel, "John S. Chisum informed me that Brady then and there assured him that he did not want to arrest me and would not as he knew I would be at court."[31] McSween added that he had no faith in Brady's assurances, but it is interesting to note that Brady knew perfectly well McSween was there. According to Leverson, Sue McSween negotiated with the sheriff on behalf of her husband, abandoning all pretense that his whereabouts were unknown. But even with the cavalry backing him up, Brady made no effort to arrest the fugitive.

Leverson told the president that Lieutenant Smith "pledged his word as *an officer and a gentleman*" that if McSween sought shelter in Fort Stanton until court convened, "he should not be placed in jail or in the guard house." To seal his promise, Leverson claimed, Lieutenant Smith volunteered this preposterous oath: "'You may make a football of my head if a hair of his head be injured or if the least insult be given him by word or sign from the highest to the lowest.'"[32]

April Fools' Day

18

On March 29, Deputy Barrier left for home, his strange odyssey almost over. He told Special Agent Angel that "hearing of the losses in my business, in consequence of my absence from home, I felt it my duty to return."[1] While no doubt his business did suffer, there was another reason for his decision to return home just three days before the April term of court: if he had escorted McSween to the courthouse, he would have been arrested.

Two days after Barrier's departure, McSween set out for Lincoln accompanied by his wife, Chisum, and Leverson. Heavy rains blew in that afternoon and the mud slowed their progress to a crawl. Consequently, as Leverson confided to President Hayes, "we were obliged to put up on Sunday the 31st March at a ranch about 10 miles below Lincoln having made about 20-miles that day."[2]

Everyone who planned to testify before the grand jury arrived in Lincoln that rainy night. Bonney, Middleton, and Waite, who were prepared to describe how the posse attacked Tunstall, arrived in the company of three other Regulators, Frank MacNab, Henry Brown, and Jim French.

MacNab worked as a cattle detective for Chisum, an odd-sounding job title that meant he was a private undercover cop, dressing and working as a cowboy but paid to investigate rustling.[3]

As for Henry Brown, it would be fun to believe, as several writers have contended, that he was the same Henry Brown who gained a lasting place in the hearts of Western history buffs as town marshal of Caldwell, Kansas in the early 1880s. That Henry Brown supplemented his income by knocking over banks in neighboring towns. His double life wasn't suspected until he and three companions first bungled a job by killing a cashier, then bungled their escape. Brown was lynched. Sadly, while Marshal Brown wrote a moving letter to his wife from jail, Lincoln County's Brown couldn't even spell his own name.[4] Besides, many people on the frontier called themselves "Henry Brown," usually with good reason. One of them – possibly the Kid's companion – was shot and killed in Albuquerque in 1881.[5]

Little is known of Jim French except that he had a reputation as a hard case. A couple of months later, he was indicted for livestock theft.[6]

Rob Widenmann hooked up with the Regulators at some point on the evening of March 31. Widenmann was never accepted by the others – he was a clerk, not a cowboy – but he, too, planned to testify before the grand jury. Besides, he had the key to the Tunstall store. So when it began raining, the Regulators holed up inside. Gathered together, with the rain beating on the roof, undoubtedly apprehensive about showing their faces in the morning, most likely passing around a bottle, the Regulators had plenty of time to rehearse their testimony, and their grievances.

Early the following morning, jurors began gathering on the steps of the Lincoln County courthouse, an unimpressive small building at the east end of town. But an unintentional April Fools' joke had been played on everyone. Because of a stupid clerical error, the jury duty notices contained the wrong date. Court would not convene until the following week.[7]

It fell to Sheriff Brady to break the news to the jurors. Around nine o'clock he stepped out of the House and ambled the half-mile or so down the street to the courthouse. Four men walked with Brady: George Hindemann, Billy Mathews, George Peppin, and Jack Long.[8]

Justice Wilson (or was it ex-Justice Wilson?) was hoeing the onion patch next to his house, which was across the street from Tunstall's store. It was a peaceful weekday morning in a town where little distinction was made between weekdays and weekends. Brady and his deputies commiserated with the unwanted jurors, chatting amiably for a few minutes on the courthouse steps, then began strolling back to the House. They were even with Justice Wilson when the shooting began.

Brady dropped to the ground with a half-dozen bullets in his body. Hindemann was also hit. He fell, then tried to drag himself clear. The other three men, uninjured, sprang for cover. Wilson pitched into his onion patch, his buttocks creased by a stray bullet.[9]

Brady groaned audibly and died. When Hindemann cried out for water, Ike Stockton, a small-time saloon keeper, ventured out with a cup.[10]

The shooting had come from the adobe-walled corral behind Tunstall's store. The gate to the corral swung open and Bill Bonney scurried to Brady's side. He knelt, picked up something, and started back for cover when the street once more echoed with gunfire. A bullet caught Bonney in the thigh, yet somehow he threw himself through the gate, which swung shut behind him. Both Billy Mathews and Jack Long later took credit for that shot.

What did Bonney pick up? Robert Utley asserts that Bonney rifled Brady's clothes, searching for the arrest warrant with McSween's name on it. But Bonney had no reason to risk his life for McSween. His loyalty was to the memory of Tunstall, not to McSween. There is no evidence Bonney and McSween were even acquainted with each other at this time. And, according to *The Mesilla Valley Independent*, "the so-called 'regulators' . . . indignantly disclaim all connection or sympathy with McSween or his affairs. They say that the only object they have in view is to destroy the original band of thieves and murderers and kill them."[11]

Bonney had no reason to think Brady had the warrant in his possession when he died. Besides, the current warrant for McSween's arrest was the second one issued. There was nothing to prevent Judge Bristol from issuing a third, and then a fourth, so there was no point in risking one's neck for that particular scrap of paper.

The Weekly New Mexican reported that Bonney grabbed the rifle Brady had dropped.[12] Gregorio Wilson, son of the justice, was just a boy when his father was grazed by that stray bullet. Many decades later he fleshed out the newspaper report, telling two different interviewers that Bonney ran into the street to retrieve the rifle Brady had confiscated weeks earlier, when he, Waite, and Constable Martínez were thrown in jail. Brady had since adopted the rifle as his own. This story has indirect corroboration: Constable Martínez testified that after he was released by Brady his arms were not returned to him.[13] Brady was even less likely to return a rifle to the much more dangerous Kid.

It has become common to attribute Brady's murder to Bonney, and indeed Bonney was eventually sentenced to hang for it. But everybody who shot at the sheriff shared the intent to kill. Probably all six Regulators shot at the sheriff; we know that multiple bullets hit him. (Perhaps seven men shot — Widenmann admitted being in the corral when the shooting started, though he said he was just there to feed Tunstall's bulldog.)

George Hindemann died shortly after Stockton gave him water.

The sensational April Fools' Day killings played in contemporary newspaper accounts and in countless subsequent books as the assassination of Sheriff Brady, but Brady's killing is actually harder to explain than Hindemann's. Before April 1, Hindemann was the only one of the six killers of Tunstall identified in the inquest verdict to remain alive and uninjured. *The Mesilla Valley Independent* reported:

> One of the murderers subsequently stated that Brady was killed by accident; that it was their intention only to kill Hindemann, as one of the murderers of Tunstall, and that one of the shots intended for Hindemann took effect on Brady. This statement, however, is negatived by the fact that Brady's body was literally riddled with bullets after he fell, while Hindemann, who lay near him, still alive but mortally wounded, was not again fired upon.[14]

More gunfire was heard when Middleton, Waite, French, Brown, and MacNab rode out of town; according to some accounts, Jim French was winged. Dr. Ealy wrote in his memoirs that "John Middleton, while riding away, deliberately got off his horse & took rest upon his knees, & fired back at a crowd which was firing at him and his companions." This was correct technique (cavalrymen dismounted before firing) but it was also style, a cool display, and no doubt the House men dived for cover.[15]

But they could count. Only five Regulators left town; Bonney was left behind. He was in no condition to ride. Dr. Ealy said he "came walking into our back door. The ball passed through his left thigh. I drew a silk handkerchief through the wound, bound it up and he was taken charge of by Sam Corbet."[16]

That casually described silk handkerchief is painful even to contemplate, but Bonney kept moving. He knew what would happen if he stopped. Brady's deputies eventually followed the trail of blood to Ealy's back door, but at the point where Bonney's wound was dressed the trail went cold. Bonney had disappeared.

Sam Corbet, the man who took charge of him, was a young, scrawny clerk in Tunstall's store who hid his youth and scrawniness behind a fan-shaped black beard. Dr. Ealy said that Corbet "sawed a hole through the floor under a bed and as there was not any cellar under the house laid him on a blanket on his back with 2 revolvers in his hands." Another, more romantic version says that Bonney hid in a flour barrel while a local housewife rolled tortillas on the lid.[17]

The House men gave Bonney a head start: they didn't have the nerve to search for him without assistance. One of their number rode to Fort Stanton to summon the military. Captain Purington must have been stunned: just three days earlier he had reported to his superiors in Santa Fe that "affairs are running smoothly" in Lincoln County, adding, "I apprehend no further trouble in civil matters."[18]

Thanks to Catron's intervention, orders had gone out from the Secretary of War to General Sherman to General Sheridan to Colonel Hatch to Captain Purington that the Ninth Cavalry should assist Sheriff Brady.[19] But no one told Purington what to do if Brady died. He was on his own. It couldn't have made him comfortable to realize from what lofty vantage points his conduct would be judged.

To make a trying situation worse, it was Purington's last week as commanding officer of Fort Stanton. Colonel Dudley had arrived at the fort, prepared to take over on April 5. Consequently, when Purington learned the sheriff had been assassinated, he was placed in the awkward position of being in charge and at the same time performing under the eye of his commander.

Rob Widenmann described what happened when Purington and his twenty-five soldiers reached town:

On the first day of April, 1878, Capt. Geo. Purington, Co. H, 9th Cavalry, rode into the town of Lincoln with a company of soldiers and surrounded the house of Mr. A. A. McSween. I stepped out of the house, it being at the time my place of residence and greeted Capt. Purington. He asked me whether I had had anything to do with the killing of Brady, to which I answered that I had not and that I had very nearly been killed myself. He then began cursing and using abusive language. I told him that I had thought he was impartial to which he answered that he was. I said his present actions did not seem to show it when he turned to Lieut. Smith and ordered him to arrest me which he did, though no warrant was shown or legal process taken.

Soon after one Geo. W. Peppin, claiming to be deputy sheriff, stepped up to me and said, "Widenmann I want you." I asked him whether he had a warrant and he said he had. I then demanded to have the warrant read to me when Capt. Purington said: "Don't put on any frills now Widenmann, come along," and through the orders of Capt. Purington I was by force of arms arrested and held prisoner.[20]

The McSweens hit town shortly after the soldiers did. Too late they learned of the killings. Having once made their appearance on Lincoln's streets, there was no returning to the safety of Chisum's ranch.[21]

Montague Leverson, with characteristic blithe disregard for reality, strolled down Lincoln's only street to the post office, concerned to pick up his mail. It is safe to assume he was the only person in Lincoln who expected the post office to be operating normally that day. "On my way," he wrote to President Hayes, "I saw a company of Cavalry under the command of Brevet Col. Purington . . . and was informed by Mr Shield that he and Mr Widenmann, deputy U.S. Marshal, and two colored boys had been arrested *by Colonel Purington* without warrant, color or authority of any kind."[22] The "colored boys" were George Robinson and George Washington, ex-troopers employed by McSween, who could not have been happy to be arrested by their former officer. There seems to have been no reason to arrest Shield, Robinson, and Washington except that they were in the general vicinity of Tunstall's store — eating breakfast at home, according to one account — when the shooting occurred.

Special Agent Angel's note in the margin of Leverson's letter to the president reads: "Col. P. is understood to have acted under Peppin Dep Shff." It's true that George Peppin presented himself to Captain Purington as a deputy sheriff and the sole surviving civil authority in town. But who was acting under whom? This was how McSween remembered it:

> G. W. Peppin went to Col. Purington and asked him if he would allow him (Peppin) to search my house for arms, Purington replied in the affirmative. Peppin and posse then went to the house to search, I forbade them to enter unless they had a warrant for that purpose. I said these words on that occasion: "Peppin, you know that you are not an officer, but were you [one], you can't search without a warrant for that purpose." Whereupon Mathews replied, "We can't, aye, we'll show you what we can do." Then Peppin replied that Col. Purington gave him permission to search the house.[23]

Purington, however, denied he gave anyone permission to do anything. He wrote to Special Agent Angel:

None of the acts of G. W. Peppin, Deputy Sheriff, were endorsed by me, neither did I disapprove of them. I informed every one that whatever the Deputy did was on his own responsibility. The soldiers were there only for the preservation of life, and property, and were not directed to assist the Deputy Sheriff or Posse in searching houses.[24]

Peppin referred to Purington, who deferred to Peppin. Widenmann, Shield, and the rest believed they were arrested by Purington, while Purington denied he arrested anyone, and of course he had no authority to round up civilians on his own. But Peppin was just being a realist when he claimed to be searching houses at Purington's sufferance, since no one was going to resist him as long as the soldiers stood behind him – a neat reversal of Widenmann's predawn raid on the House.

McSween added to the confusion by arguing that Peppin wasn't a deputy sheriff at all. How could he be the deputy of a dead man? According to McSween, Peppin's commission died with Brady.

Confusion compounded confusion. And so Captain Purington spent a frantic afternoon trying simultaneously to impose order on the explosive situation and to distance himself from his ally in that task. Confronted with McSween's legalisms and Widenmann's smart-alecky remarks as well as the sheer bloody brutality of the killings, the captain began to lose control. It was at this point that he once more ran into Montague Leverson, this time at the home of Isaac Ellis. Leverson, in his inimitable way, described what happened when Peppin and the soldiers arrived:

Up till that day I had had some belief in the sacredness and efficacy of the laws and constitution of the United States. I urged on Mr Ellis to refuse admission *alike to officers and the alleged deputy,* until they procured a search warrant, but to offer *the moment they procured one,* to throw open his doors; and that then, if in the face of his refusal they attempted to force an entrance *to shoot them down,* pledging myself, although not a citizen of the Territory, to stand by unto death, as the rights not only of the people of the Territory but of every inhabitant of the United States were imperilled by the ruffianly defiance of the rights secured by the constitution of which the military [were] even now the accomplices. I also warned some of the troops, that the conduct of their officers was *illegal* and *criminal,* that they (the soldiers) would be criminally as well civilly liable if they obeyed illegal orders, and that the orders of their officers would *not* excuse them in the committal of illegal acts.[25]

According to Widenmann, Leverson "called Purington's attention to the provisions of the Constitution of the United States" that forbid houses to be searched without a warrant. Pushed past the breaking point, Purington responded, "Damn the Constitution of the United States and you for a fool!"[26]

Purington, no doubt, had awakened that morning with no greater wish than to get through his last days of command with his dignity intact, his authority unimpaired. His worst nightmare could not have equalled the strain of that brutal, confusing, dangerous day. Not only did he wind up damning the Constitution, but McSween recalled that he "cursed fearfully and insultingly abused Rev. T. F. Ealy, a Presbyterian minister." Widenmann remembered that Purington "cursed Leverson and other citizens present in the presence of ladies and his subordinate troops, using language unbecoming to a gentleman and an officer."[27]

Dr. Ealy was a target for Purington's wrath because he had given Bonney the sort of medical treatment Dr. Mudd gave John Wilkes Booth. It was bad enough that a man of the cloth had facilitated the killer's escape. Still worse was the realization, as afternoon faded into evening, that nothing had been accomplished. Houses were ransacked and enemies made, but the United States Army couldn't find Bonney even when it knew within a few hundred yards where to find him.

Purington's frustration must have been brought into painfully sharp focus by the only possible explanation for the army's failure: Lincoln's citizens were sheltering their sheriff's murderer.

McSween and the arrested men applied to Purington for protection, sure that incarceration in the Lincoln County jail would be fatal. Still bitter two months later, McSween told Special Agent Angel that Purington

> acknowledged that if he left me in custody of Peppin, Mathews, et al., he believed that I would be killed by them, but he claimed that he had no place for me in the fort. My friends insisted that W. Dowling, Post Trader at Fort Stanton, had a room that I could secure.

Purington contended that he had not. After much entreaty he consented to take me up to the fort. . . .

He appeared to be anxious to leave me in the custody of Peppin though he heard one of Peppin's posse say that I was the man they wanted, that they wanted him (Purington) to turn me over to them, that they would care for me.[28]

Purington's indecision circled back to the original question: who arrested these men, the captain or the deputy? Purington said Peppin did. If so, the military had no business taking them to the fort. But Purington eventually gave in, implicitly conceding that he was in charge after all.

At the end of that long day, Alexander and Sue McSween, Rob Widenmann, David Shield, George Robinson, and George Washington traveled to Fort Stanton in McSween's wagon. But even in the sanctuary of the fort, controversy erupted when Robinson and Washington were thrown into the guardhouse. To the ex-troopers, it must have seemed the military was reaching into their civilian lives to drag them back into its clutches. McSween testified that they were "obliged to work during their stay there."[29]

Purington told Special Agent Angel that Robinson and Washington were confined in the guardhouse because the racist post trader had refused to let them stay in his building. Purington also claimed, inconsistently, that he would have locked up the whites, too, had the guardhouse been large enough.[30] Although the whites stayed with the post trader, Purington posted guards outside the door "with orders to shoot any and all of us who left the rooms without permission," according to McSween, who complained he was not allowed visitors even though he was required to pay room and board.[31]

Four days later, Colonel Dudley assumed command and he permitted Widenmann, Shield, and McSween to apply formally for military protection. Once they did so, they were permitted the freedom of the fort. They remained at Fort Stanton, safe from their enemies, until Judge Bristol gaveled Lincoln County's grand jury to order the following week.

Blazer's Mill

19

Dr. Joseph Blazer earned his title pulling soldiers' teeth in the Civil War. After the war he moved to New Mexico, where he bought a sawmill and became one of Lincoln County's most prominent citizens. He was one of the original commissioners named to the Lincoln County Commission.[1] Blazer's Mill was located on the crest of the pass across the mountains, an island of private land surrounded by the Mescalero Reservation. The tiny settlement commanded a gorgeous view of the volcanic slopes and magnificent evergreen forest – which Blazer's men decimated to feed the sawmill.

A short distance from the mill stood an imposing two-story building, which Dr. Blazer leased to the government to house the Mescalero Apache Agency. Blazer maintained a small office in the agency building. The Indian agent in the spring of 1878 was the corrupt Major Frederick Godfroy, who was just months away from his forced resignation.

While Major Godfroy supplemented the family income by selling the Apaches' food and blankets to the House, Mrs. Godfroy served meals and put up travelers in the agency building, thereby extracting a subsidy from the government, which paid the rent but shared none of the profits. The isolation of Blazer's Mill, and its location along the Lincoln-Mesilla trail, ensured Mrs. Godfroy a steady stream of customers. There was nowhere else to go to get a proper meal for many miles in any direction. When the Regulators piled into Mrs. Godfroy's restaurant three days after the Brady shooting, they were motivated by nothing so much as the promise of a good lunch.

It was a large crowd. Brewer, who was conspicuously absent at the time of Brady's assassination and who, according to *The Mesilla Valley Independent,* "declared that he neither advised nor consented to the commission of the dastardly act," was once more at the head of a formidable force of fourteen.[2] The wounded Bonney had slipped out of Lincoln to rejoin his comrades. Middleton and Waite were there, along with Frank MacNab, Jim French, and Henry Brown, all of whom had been behind the adobe wall when Brady was shot. Those seven were joined by Doc Scurlock, Charles Bowdre, and the cousins Frank and George Coe, who lived long enough to see their memories and tall tales polished by ghostwriters and published in New York. Rounding out the crew were the relatively obscure Stephen Stevens, John Scroggins, and Ignacio González.

Lincoln County had always been a dangerous place for the Regulators; now it was even more dangerous. Brady's friends would want revenge. There was a rumor the House had offered a bounty.[3] Stopping for lunch at Mrs. Godfroy's wasn't a discreet thing to do, but there was safety in numbers.

While the Regulators were tucking into lunch, Andrew Roberts rode up to Blazer's Mill on a mule, leading a packhorse. Roberts worked for the House and had accompanied Deputy Mathews on both of his trips to Tunstall's ranch. After the first trip, Mathews promised Brewer he would return with just one other man to round up the cattle. A few days later, he and Andrew Roberts rode up to the front door of Tunstall's house while the rest of the posse, including the four Boys, hid in ambush. That incident tells us everything we need to know about Roberts: he tried to lure Tunstall and his men to their deaths.[4]

Both John Middleton and Henry Brown signed affidavits that referred to "Bill Williams *alias* A. L. Roberts," but neither explained how he knew that "Andrew Roberts" was an alias.[5] Jimmy Dolan never explained how he knew that Bill Bonney's real name was Antrim either, but he did. It seems that Bonney's past simply followed him, a faint doppelgänger, and it is likely that Andrew Roberts's past followed him the same way.

All sorts of legends have attached to the fellow. Maybe he was a Texas Ranger, or maybe he killed a Texas Ranger in a gunfight. It is sometimes said that Roberts spoke with a Deep South accent. It is also said that he was a small man, that he rode a mule rather than a horse on all occasions, and that he had restricted use of his right arm ever since he caught a load of shotgun pellets in the shoulder, an incident that gave rise to his supposed nickname "Buckshot Roberts," a nickname with the tin ring of a buff's fabrication.[6]

Two competing stories explain his presence at Blazer's Mill that April noontime. Paul Blazer, who was born twelve years after the events he described, wrote that Roberts had decided to leave Lincoln County and had sold his farm. He was at Blazer's Mill waiting for the mail wagon to bring a check from the buyer in Santa Fe. But who sells land through the mail? Not even Andrew Roberts was dim enough to send a deed to a distant city and then wait for a check to arrive in the mail. Moreover, it was unlikely he had worked the land long enough to claim title under the Desert Lands Act.

The alternative story has this virtue: the Regulators believed it. This story says that Roberts was out to collect the reward offered for Brady's killers. Anyone could guess that the Regulators were hiding in the mountains. It is certainly possible that Roberts thought he could track the Regulators and ambush them on the high slopes (which would explain why he rode a sure-footed mule rather than a horse), then return to Lincoln to collect his reward.

The third possibility is the most plausible, however: Roberts wasn't working alone. He might well have arranged with other House adherents to rendezvous at the mill; he just happened to be a couple hours early.

After riding all morning, Roberts was naturally feeling a bit peckish when he reached Blazer's Mill at lunchtime. There was no sense eating the food he had packed when he could pick up a better meal at Mrs. Godfroy's.

Roberts and his mule ambled right past the corral where the Regulators had left their horses. But either Roberts failed to notice the fourteen or more animals milling about or, more likely, he never paused to wonder about their owners. John Middleton, who had been left outside to keep a lookout, stepped into the restaurant to announce Roberts's arrival.

According to Walter Noble Burns's 1925 best-seller, *The Saga of Billy the Kid*, Frank Coe is alleged to have said in later life that he went outside to talk to Roberts for no other reason than that he finished lunch first.[7] It is certainly plausible that Coe went outside to talk to Roberts. Coe hadn't participated in Brady's murder, so it wasn't likely that Roberts would shoot him on sight. Besides, both Coes were gregarious sorts who got along with everybody.

As it happened, the Regulators had a warrant for Roberts's arrest. Roberts wasn't one of the six killers fingered at the inquest, but his role in Tunstall's murder was known. Justice Wilson had issued the warrant for his arrest as accessory. A number of other men were wanted as accessories, none of whom ever became targets of the Regulators' wrath: Pantelón Gallegos, and Robert Beckwith, Thomas Green, Ham Mills, and other small-fry members of the posse who neither made any decisions nor pulled any triggers. Because Roberts fit into this category, it seems unlikely that anyone would have bothered to arrest him if he hadn't ridden right up to the Regulators, armed to the teeth.

When Coe and Roberts sat down on the porch of the agency building, on the opposite side from the restaurant, Coe's line of argument probably went like this: There are fourteen of us and only one of you. There's no sense in fighting. Give us your guns and Justice Wilson will bind you over to trial. You'll be free on bail and no one will get hurt.

Roberts's problem, once he finally realized his blunder, was that he didn't trust the Regulators. He was right not to trust them, of course. Hadn't they killed Morton and Baker after they surrendered? Didn't they shoot Sheriff Brady and Hindemann from ambush? If he gave up his guns, what was to stop any one of the fourteen from doing to him what he'd planned to do to them?

It may have been a question of pride, too. How could he explain that the Regulators captured him the first time he climbed off his mule? Or perhaps he was just delaying, hoping his friends would show up soon.

Burns describes Roberts patting the Winchester he held across his lap and telling Coe, "As long as I've got a load in old Betsy here, there ain't nobody going to arrest me, least of all this gang."[8] Burns invented this sort of dialogue, inspiring the decades of Hollywood hacks who wrote the westerns. Now it sounds like parody, and it gets worse. When certain of the Regulators demand Roberts's surrender, Burns has Roberts exclaiming, "Not much, Mary Ann!" as he brings his rifle to his hip.[9]

Maybe Roberts really did talk that way. If so, who can blame the Regulators for gunning him down?

What appears to have happened is this: Coe and Roberts talked for a long time. Coe gave Roberts an opportunity to surrender, but he refused to do so. Burns romanticizes Roberts's defiance as the courage of one man against the odds; Robert Utley describes Roberts as "a tough scrapper, not easily intimidated."[10] But only a moron could have failed to be intimidated by the odds Roberts faced. Indeed, the sheer uselessness of resistance allowed Roberts to get the drop on the Regulators, who assumed he would act rationally. The gunfight at Blazer's Mill remains unique for that reason: the person who blundered into the trap used the element of surprise to his advantage.

While Coe and Roberts jawed, the other Regulators became antsy. It wasn't safe for them to hang around Blazer's Mill, but as long as that nut with the gun was sitting on the porch they were pinned down. If they tried to ride away, Roberts might shoot them. So, after a while, Bowdre, Middleton, George Coe, and perhaps one or two others came around the corner of the building with their guns drawn and told Roberts to surrender. At this point it was a question of arithmetic rather than trust.

Roberts still didn't get it. He raised his rifle from his lap and squeezed off a shot. The bullet, according to legend, creased Bowdre's side in such a way that it neatly severed his gun belt, which fell around his ankles. The same bullet, slightly deflected – and this part is documented in photographs – crashed into George Coe's right hand, ripping away his forefinger.

Bowdre shot Roberts in the middle of his chest, knocking him to the floor of the porch. Roberts dropped his carbine. People didn't recover from chest wounds in the days before sterile surgery and antibiotics. Roberts was dying. None of the Regulators tried to stop him from crawling into Dr. Blazer's modest office.

And then the incredible happened: a shot rang out and John Middleton fell down, nicked on the shoulder. Roberts had reached Dr. Blazer's buffalo hunting rifle, which had been hanging on the office wall as a souvenir. He had even managed to find bullets, sixty-caliber monsters. And, since Roberts was now lying on the floor of the office behind a half-closed door, there was no way to get a clean shot at him except to stand in front of the door, right in the line of fire of Dr. Blazer's cannon.

Bill Bonney risked it. Despite the wound in his leg, he was the only Regulator reckless enough to try. He ran along the side of the building and, without slowing down, thrust his pistol through the door, firing wildly. But he missed.

If the Regulators got on their horses and rode away from the agency, one of them might find a shell the size of Texas imbedded in his spine. But if they stayed put, Roberts's friends might reinforce him: the Regulators had no assurance he was working alone.

Dick Brewer realized it could take Roberts all day to die, and he wasn't prepared to wait that long. He took his rifle and circled down from the restaurant, behind the corral, and worked his way across the sawmill yard, finding cover behind the logs, until he had reached a position directly in front of the door behind which Roberts lay dying. He popped up once and squeezed off a shot. But Roberts was lying on the floor and the shot went high.

There was a pause and no answering shot. Brewer popped up a second time; Roberts destroyed the top half of his head.

The End of the
Original Struggle

20

McSween wrote Brewer's obituary in a letter to the editor of *The Cimarron News and Press* dated the day after Brewer's death:

> Outside "the House" no one knew Mr. Brewer but to respect him. He was a young man without vices of any kind. Had he been content to enslave himself, he would, no doubt, be living now, but to a man of kingly nature, existence would be intolerable under the conditions sought to be imposed.
>
> Murderers and horse thieves hated him; their friends hated him. But the people, Mexican and American, held him in the highest possible esteem. He had a fine ranch on the Rio Ruidoso, which he had been cultivating for the past four years. It was his intention to make Lincoln County his permanent home.
>
> Peace to your ashes, Dick! as you were familiarly called. Sweet and pleasant be your slumbers! Ever green and fresh be your memory. Some will malign you, but that will not disturb you, for when the mist has cleared away and the horizon of truth is clearly seen, even they will be shamed to silence. Death has deprived your father and mother of an obedient and loving son; your sister and brother of the prince of brothers; the county of Lincoln of one of her best, most industrious, sober, upright, and honest citizens. He died young – 27 years of age.[1]

As if to prove McSween right, Dolan did his churlish best to malign Brewer's memory in a subsequent letter to *The Weekly New Mexican:* "R. M. Brewer I always considered an honest man and treated him as such until he became contaminated with Mr. McSween, his 'legal advisor.'" Dolan then told a hilariously unconvincing tale about the time Brewer tried to sell John Riley stolen cattle. Naturally, Riley was shocked – *shocked* – that anyone would offer him stolen cattle "and advised him to return them to the owner."[2]

The dueling letters continued all spring. McSween (signing his letters "Stanton") and Dolan ("Cow-Boy") each gave as good as he got in long letters of painstakingly thorough invective. The newspapers themselves joined in the fray. *The Weekly New Mexican* did not scruple to print Dolan's description of "that filthy sheet called the 'Cimarron News and Press.'" A week later, Dolan, who was good at this sort of thing, described an article in *The Mesilla Valley Independent* as "a sickly effort to wiggle out of a most malicious attempt through the instrumentality of a barefaced lie to . . . injure by all means, fair or foul, the characters of Major Murphy, Mr. Riley and myself." *The Mesilla News* piled on, denouncing its crosstown rival for its "unmanly assault upon gentlemen" in Lincoln. Marion Turner of Roswell published a letter in *The Las Vegas Gazette* that captured the views of the Seven Rivers ranchers: suspicious but tolerant of the House (which bought their cattle), suspicious but intolerant of McSween, and full of loathing for the dread figure they saw behind it all – John Chisum. Even a Colorado newspaper got into the act: John Riley ridiculed its "lame statement" about the troubles.[3]

In this way the troubles in Lincoln County kept the entire territory entertained.

On April 4, 1878, Reverend Brooke Herford, pastor of the Church of the Messiah in Chicago, wrote a letter to General Sheridan about the Lincoln County troubles, stating that troops were being used to shield Tunstall's murderers. Herford's interest in Lincoln County is not clear, but he probably was related to a citizen of Lincoln County with the same last name. Sheridan, who was stationed in Chicago, immediately forwarded Herford's letter to General Sherman, averring that Herford "is of the highest character and responsibility in this city." He even sent a telegram telling Sherman, "I think this matter worthy of investigation."[4]

Sheridan's message went up the ladder, and the secretary of war's response came down: Sherman told Sheridan that the secretary wished him to inquire of General John Pope whether Herford's allegations were true.[5] The directive appears to have lost its force by the time it trickled down to Colonel Hatch, assuming it did. But Sheridan was disturbed enough by Herford's letter that he followed up, pressing for an investigation and making his case with humor:

> The population of that section [i.e., Lincoln County] is divided into two parties, who have an intense desire to exterminate each other, and are only prevented from accomplishing their purpose by the presence of a small military force. It is said that one of these parties is made up of cattle and horse thieves, and the other party of persons who have retired from that business.[6]

On May 14, the secretary of war authorized Sheridan to send an officer to Lincoln County to investigate.[7]

Preparing for the April 8 term of court, Judge Bristol was confronted with the peculiar problem of the prisoners incarcerated at Fort Stanton. McSween had pointed out the dubious legality of the arrests made by George Peppin, the deputy of a dead sheriff. When Brady died, the office of sheriff became vacant. How could Peppin be the deputy of a vacancy? New Mexico law did not address the situation except to provide that when the office of sheriff was vacant, a judge issuing warrants could appoint "some proper person, who is hereby fully authorized to serve such process." In other words, the judge could appoint someone to serve warrants as a kind of temporary sheriff.[8]

So Bristol issued arrest warrants for Shield, Widenmann, Robinson, and Washington and put them in the hands of John Copeland, who had once had been involved in the cattle business with John Riley. Bristol probably expected Copeland to be a House man. It helped that he was not beholden to the House in the obvious way of an employee.[9]

Copeland dutifully arrested Shield, Widenmann, Robinson, and Washington at Fort Stanton. The formal arrests were in a sense absurd, since the arrested men were already in custody and evinced no desire to leave what was for them more a safe haven than a prison. But the arrests tidied up a loose end for the judge and deprived the prisoners of a possible defense at trial.

The arrests also magically transformed Copeland into a figure of authority. By performing the sheriff's task, he became the acting sheriff in many citizens' eyes. When the Lincoln County commissioners met to appoint a new sheriff, they chose John Copeland.[10]

On April 5, 1878, Lieutenant Colonel Dudley's first day of command, he was informed by Lawrence Murphy that, according to rumor, the Regulators (or, rather, "fourteen outlaws") intended to ambush and kill Judge Bristol on his journey to Lincoln. Having "every reason to believe" the rumor was true, Dudley immediately ordered a military escort to protect the judge, no doubt an alarming novelty for Bristol.[11] By playing concerned citizen, clever Murphy influenced Dudley and simultaneously gave the judge a personal stake in the Lincoln County troubles.

Nonetheless, Bristol failed to show for the first several days of court. Court records show that each morning the clerk called court to order, noted the judge's absence, and then adjourned for the day. When Bristol did appear, the New Mexico Organic Act obliged him to attend to federal cases first.[12] He finally convened the Lincoln County grand jury on April 13, 1878. The grand jury consisted of fifteen men, among them Dr. Blazer (who became foreman) and Juan Patrón.

Judge Bristol delivered a lengthy charge, laying out the various allegations of criminal conduct the grand jury was to investigate. *The Las Vegas Gazette* devoted half of its front page to Bristol's stem-winding oration, then jumped to an interior page, sixty column inches in all. Fifty-five of those inches were devoted to the embezzlement charge against Alexander McSween. Only in his closing sentences did the judge add that the grand jury should also consider the possibility that other criminal acts may have been committed by other people in Lincoln County. He devoted sixty words to the death of Tunstall.[13]

The words of the charge confirm the impression left by its proportions. Bristol began by discussing a matter close to his own heart: he complained that McSween "and his partisans have been busy in their endeavors to manufacture public opinion favorable to McSween and prejudicial to your Judge and the court." The judge explained, "Among the falsehoods put in circulation for this purpose, one is, that the Courts of New Mexico are controlled by a corrupt ring. Another is that the Court with the officers is arraigned on the side of Murphy, Dolan and Riley for the purpose of crushing McSween." Now why, asked the judge, would McSween say such things? He answered himself: "The circumstances of the case point to one conclusion as to the motive, and that was to induce desperate men to come to the aid of McSween, armed with deadly weapons, for the purpose, among other things, of offering open and violent intimidation or resistance to the Court."

After Brady's death and Murphy's warning, Bristol's fear of assassination was hardly irrational. But by delivering himself of such strong feelings he only confirmed the very rumor he was at such pains to suppress. And one reason *The Gazette* devoted so much space to the charge was that it allowed the paper to print, without fear of prosecution for criminal libel, the accusation that Catron's ring controlled the territory's courts.

Having thus expressed his personal hostility to McSween, and his fear of the Regulators, Bristol turned to the embezzlement charge. He discussed the circumstances of McSween's planned trip to St. Louis and summed up, "If these facts are true it is pretty strong evidence tending to prove embezzlement."

Bristol next discussed the attachment of John Tunstall's property. Bristol told the jury that at the preliminary hearing held at Bristol's house in Mesilla, John Tunstall testified "that he and McSween were partners in trade, that they owned as partners the stock of goods in the store on Mr. McSween's premises here, that the stock of goods was worth a considerable amount, I forget how much; and, that McSween had a half interest, or thereabouts."[14] This amounted to the judge testifying in his own courtroom, an unusual practice.

William Keleher points out that Bristol addressed only the incriminating evidence and ignored evidence that might exonerate McSween, exactly as a prosecutor argues his case to the jury.[15] That point is obvious enough. A more subtle tension can be found just below the surface of the judge's words.

"The administrators," Bristol told the jury, "were perfectly justified in believing that McSween had an interest in that store that could be reached by process of attachment." Although he spoke of the administrators who asked for the writ of attachment, he was referring above all to himself, the man who issued it. Bristol was a hack, but that doesn't mean he felt no horror when he learned that his signature on an illegal writ of attachment killed a man. There is an unintended pathos in the judge's words: he wanted the jury to believe him, that it wasn't his fault, that he was "perfectly justified."

It didn't work. After hearing witnesses called from across the county (not an easy task: the first of two reports to the judge spoke of "the great difficulty that has been experienced in obtaining the attendance of witnesses" and the "fact that a great portion of the testimony taken before us was palpably prejudiced, and of a contradictory character"), the jury reported:

> Your Honor charged us to investigate the case of Alex. A. McSween, Esq., charged with the embezzlement of $10,000 belonging to the estate of Emil Fritz, deceased; this we did but were unable to find any evidence that would justify that accusation. We fully exonerate him of the charge, and regret that a spirit of persecution has been shown in the matter.[16]

A pithier repudiation of the judge could hardly be imagined. But the jury was referring to more than the criminal charge of embezzlement. Since no evidence at all justified the criminal charge, it followed that no evidence supported Bristol's writ of attachment in the parallel civil suit.

The grand jury report continued:

> The murder of John H. Tunstall, for brutality and malice, is without a parallel and without a shadow of justification. By this inhuman act our county has lost one of our best and most useful men; one who brought intelligence, industry, and capital to the development of Lincoln County.

In the same paragraph the grand jury added, "We equally condemn the most brutal murder of our late sheriff, William Brady, and George Hindemann."

Jesse Evans, Miguel Segovia (also known as "The Indian"), and Frank Rivers were indicted for Tunstall's murder. James J. Dolan and Billy Mathews were indicted as accessories.[17]

For Brady's murder, Bonney, Middleton, Waite, and Brown got the hook. Shield, Widenmann, Washington, and Robinson were not indicted, and so were freed from their not-entirely-involuntary confinement in Fort Stanton.

The grand jury also passed out indictments for the death of Roberts. Bowdre was indicted for murder, and most of the other Regulators (but not the Coe cousins) for aiding and abetting. John Riley was indicted for receiving stolen cattle.

The grand jury did not hesitate to lay blame for the state of affairs in Lincoln:

Had his excellency, S. B. Axtell, when here, ascertained from the people the cause of our troubles, as he was requested, valuable lives would have been spared our community; especially do we condemn that portion of his proclamation relating to J. B. Wilson as J.P. Mr. Wilson acted in good faith as such J.P. over a year. Mr. Brewer, deceased, arrested, as we are informed, some of the alleged murderers of Mr. Tunstall by virtue of warrants issued by Mr. Wilson. The part of the proclamation referred to virtually outlawed Mr. Brewer and *posse*. In fact, they were hunted to the mountains by our late sheriff with U.S. soldiers. We believe that had the governor done his duty whilst here, these unfortunate occurrences would have been spared us.

The Las Vegas Gazette summed up the proceedings: "The McSween party have evidently come out ahead, both in the courts and out of them. They have routed the opposition horse, foot and dragoon, though the latter seem to have had the moral support of Judge Bristol, District Attorney Rynerson and Governor Axtell's proclamation." The editor added that McSween's exoneration "must be taken at least as an authoritative rebuke to the extraordinary measures of arrest and attachment to which the administrators had been instigated [a cunning use of the passive voice] and which led to such disastrous results."[18]

The Mesilla Valley Independent printed the grand jury's reports in the same issue that carried a small advertisement placed by McSween, announcing that Tunstall's father would pay a $5,000 reward for the "apprehension and conviction" of Tunstall's murderers. The advertisement continued, "The actual murderers were about twenty in number, and I will pay a proportionate sum for the apprehension and conviction of any one of them."

Printed immediately below McSween's notice was another small advertisement, this one of much different character:

A CARD TO THE PUBLIC

The condition of affairs now existing in this county is such as to make it unsafe for the undersigned to further continue business as they have heretofore done. They take this occasion to assure their friends and the public that the suspension will only be temporary, and that they will resume when peace and quiet shall take the place of lawlessness and order be restored in the county. Asking for continued confidence, and hoping for a renewal of business relations, we remain,

Lincoln, N.M. April 23, 1878   Very Respectfully,
                                            JAS. J. DOLAN & CO.

The suspension was anything but temporary. The House was dead and gone. Shortly afterward, the partnership was formally dissolved. Tom Catron sent his twenty-one-year-old brother-in-law Edgar Walz, fresh from Minneapolis, to manage his newly acquired Lincoln County real estate, including, in addition to the House, Dolan's cow camp in Seven Rivers.[19]

The Lincoln County War was fought because Tunstall and McSween tried to break the House's monopoly. They succeeded, but at a terrible price. The House, aided by Catron, fought back with the embezzlement charge, but it didn't stick. Those things for which a short and bloody war had been fought were now settled with the finality of death and bankruptcy. McSween had won.

A town meeting was called on an hour's notice on April 24, 1878, immediately following the adjournment of the grand jury. *The Independent* reported that "citizens of Lincoln County from every section thereof, assembled at the Court House to express their sentiments relative to the present troubles. The room was crowded." Juan Patrón called the meeting to order, and nominated Judge Florencio Gonzáles for president of the meeting, with Captain Saturnino Baca and José Montaño for vice-presidents. McSween and Isaac Ellis were nominated as secretaries. The five men nominated were, with Patrón himself, the town's most substantial citizens.[20]

Gonzáles made an impromptu speech, which "was vociferously cheered, and interrupted by frequent applause." Patrón, Montaño, and a man identified as "Mr. Hereford" – possibly a relative of Chicago's Reverend Herford – also made speeches. The latter said, in words that express the sense of an era passing, "I trust that the pledges of friendship and good feeling made this evening in so solemn and appropriate a manner may never be marred or broken." A committee consisting of Patrón, John Chisum, and Avery M. Clenny (who, like Patrón, had served on the grand jury) was named to draft appropriate resolutions. This is what it came up with:

Be it Resolved,
That it is the sense of this meeting that our present troubles are only a continuance of old feuds, dating back five or six years, that they will now cease, as the cause has been removed.

This was Patrón's theory expressed: the troubles were an expression of long-simmering hostilities. Everyone in Lincoln County caught the reference to the "cause" that had been "removed." The House had shut its doors the previous day.

The resolution thanked Colonel Dudley "for his conduct as an officer and a gentleman. . . . We do and will consider the day he took command at Fort Stanton an important era in the history of our county." More was said in the same vein, and a delegation was nominated to present a copy of the resolution to Dudley personally. Even drunken Colonel Dudley must have caught the drift: thank God Purington was reduced to second in command.[21]

The resolution continued:

Be it Resolved,
That we condemn without qualification the conduct of the Governor S. B. Axtell while here in March last. That his refusal to investigate our troubles, stamps him as a little one sided partisan. That his conduct and proclamation of March 9th, 1878 are unworthy of an officer filling his exalted station. That as a result of that proclamation, he is responsible for the loss of life that has occurred in this county since his visit.

There was much more to the resolution, including the expression of gratitude from town to army and of friendship between Anglos and Hispanics. The resolution was intended to express both an end and a new beginning. As far as the citizens of Lincoln County were concerned, their war was over.

At least 150 citizens attended the meeting. That's how many signed a memorial for Dick Brewer published in *The Cimarron News and Press*. The memorial began:

> We the undersigned residents of Lincoln County, in the Territory of New Mexico, deeply deplore the loss our county sustains by the death of Richard M. Brewer, a young man of irreproachable character, who commanded the respect and admiration of all who knew him. Some of us have been acquainted with him over eight years and none ever knew his name to be associated with anything of a questionable character. He was a hard working, generous, sober, upright and noble minded young man.[22]

After briefly summarizing Brewer's pursuit of Tunstall's murderers, and Axtell's proclamation, the memorial concluded:

> Brewer and *posse* knew well that if the late sheriff arrested them they would be murdered, so they took to the mountains.
> We tender our heartfelt sympathy to the aged parents of the late Richard M. Brewer, and other relatives in Wisconsin, and we beg to assure them that while they have lost a good son and relative, we feel that our county has lost one of her best citizens.

Many other men died in the Lincoln County War; none was so mourned.

Dudley Takes Over
(and Everything Changes) **21**

The collapse of the House was an economic catastrophe for the small ranchers of Seven Rivers. For years they had sold their cattle to the House. Jimmy Dolan had maintained a cow camp on the Pecos where he fattened up the cattle he purchased from them. Suddenly, that cow camp was being run by a twenty-one-year-old Minnesotan who had never previously set foot in Lincoln County. The big Santa Fe and Las Vegas firms could no longer count on the House to supply the beef and grain to fulfill their contracts with the government. When those contracts were next put out for bid, who would acquire the stranglehold?

John Chisum.

Some of the Seven Rivers ranches were small only by comparison with Chisum's spread. An 1886 map designates "Beckwith's Rancho" as one of the landmarks of southeastern New Mexico. But the comparison with Chisum was the essence of Seven Rivers, an irreducible fact of economic life. To the injury of Chisum's massive economies of scale had been added the rankling insult of the "War on the Pecos," when the Beckwith family, pinned down in their own home, watched helplessly as the Chisum men appropriated cattle from their corrals.

Then, following Brewer's death, Frank MacNab succeeded to the leadership of the Regulators. From the point of view of the Seven Rivers ranchers, this meant that Chisum's cattle detective was riding at the head of any army of vigilantes ruthless enough to kill the sheriff — a terrifying prospect. They were determined not to suffer a second "War on the Pecos." So, late in April, they mobilized. Seventeen of them (romantically termed the Seven Rivers Warriors by some writers) armed themselves and rode from their ranches toward Lincoln and a showdown with MacNab.[1] They were not motivated by a desire to help the House, which was beyond help. Rather, they were banded together against a common enemy who happened to be the House's enemy also.

The "Warriors" were accompanied by eight House men, including Dolan, Mathews, and Peppin, who probably were the chief organizers and were, of course, pursuing their own agenda. They camped for the night of April 29 on the banks of the Bonito, some eight miles downstream from Lincoln.[2]

The same evening, by evil coincidence, Frank MacNab, Frank Coe, and a Coe in-law named Ab Saunders set out from Lincoln on their way to Saunders's home on the Rio Hondo. Eight miles from town they rounded a bend and found themselves without warning in the midst of twenty-four armed men who wished them harm.

Everyone was surprised. But surprise for MacNab, Coe, and Saunders meant irretrievable seconds of confused hesitation. For the Seven Rivers men, it meant only that their plan was put into action sooner than anticipated. Someone shot, then everyone was shooting. MacNab, Coe, and Saunders wheeled around; then MacNab pitched from his horse, dying or already dead.

Coe and Saunders spurred forward, but then Saunders, too, was hit. Coe, riding alone, knew he couldn't make it back to Lincoln. When his horse was shot he flung himself into a dry arroyo, a crumbling dirt breastwork.

His pursuers, once they realized where Coe was hidden, understood the stalemate. When the excitement of the chase had passed and everyone had caught his breath, it turned out that they really had nothing against Coe, who was a small-time farmer rather like themselves. For that matter, they had nothing against Ab Saunders either, who now lay groaning in the grass, a fact that may have pricked the consciences of men who, for all their toughness, were landowners and family men.

Coe gave up and was held prisoner. Some of the very men who had shot at Saunders helped transport him to Fort Stanton, where Dr. Appel did his bit. Saunders was not expected to live. A couple of days later, Frank Coe, having obtained freedom for himself, came to the fort to care for his relative. His solicitude outraged Lieutenant Colonel Dudley. In Dudley's mind, Coe stood convicted of Roberts's murder, despite the grand jury's refusal to indict him. In his weekly report, he described how he chased Coe from the fort "and told him if I caught him on the [military] reservation again I would place him in irons and put him in the Guard House."[3]

The Seven Rivers men hadn't even reached Lincoln, but they had already decapitated the Regulators. Still, they couldn't just turn around and go home. The remaining Regulators were still at large, and the authorities (whoever they happened to be at the moment) would have some questions about the killing. At some point the music would have to be faced, better together than separately. So the whole crew continued into Lincoln late that night or early the following morning, holding Frank Coe prisoner.

But by transporting Saunders to the fort's hospital, the Seven Rivers men helped to spread the news of the gun battle. Their decency cost them. By the morning of April 30 the Regulators were ready for them, holed up in the McSween house and the Ellis store. The situation quickly evolved into a replay of the "War on the Pecos," this time with the roles reversed: the Seven Rivers men were the prudent besiegers, scattered over the hills across the river, trading potshots from impossible distances with the Regulators.[4]

George Coe, knowing his in-law was wounded and his cousin was held prisoner, positioned himself on the roof of the Ellis store. Beside him was Henry Brown. The two were boasting about their marksmanship. Coe saw a man sitting on a cow skull on the hillside, too far away to be identified. (He was Dutch Charley Kruling, a member of the sub-posse that chased after Tunstall.) Coe said he could nail Kruling. Brown scoffed. Coe squeezed off a shot and, sure enough, Kruling crumpled to the ground, his ankle shattered.

Brand-new sheriff John Copeland dealt with the situation sensibly, riding to Fort Stanton and returning shortly with Lieutenant Smith and enough troopers to cool everyone's ardor. The Seven Rivers men rode with the soldiers back to Fort Stanton, where they were given the freedom of the fort. Frank Coe took advantage of the confusion to walk away from his captors.[5]

The justice of the peace for San Patricio, in whose precinct MacNab had been killed, duly issued warrants for the arrest of the killers. These were given to Copeland, who arrested the men at the fort the following day. Copeland asked Colonel Dudley for a military escort to transport the prisoners to San Patricio for their preliminary hearing. Surprisingly, Dudley refused to provide an escort — unless Copeland first agreed to arrest the Regulators.

It was a crime to refuse to assist the sheriff.[6] But Dudley didn't exactly refuse; he set conditions for his aid. When Copeland, who had little choice, acceded to Dudley's demand, it meant that Dudley had effectively taken over the role of Lincoln County sheriff. The nominal sheriff was following his orders.

Copeland pointed out that he had no warrants to arrest any of the Regulators. Dudley took care of this technicality, arranging for Peppin, Long, and Mathews (but not any of the Seven Rivers men, quickly reduced to bit players in their own drama) to swear out affidavits describing how the Regulators attacked their besiegers without provocation. The affidavits were then rushed by a soldier to David Easton, the justice of the peace for Blazer's Mill. (Since Wilson had purportedly been removed from office by Governor Axtell, there was no longer a justice in Lincoln; Blazer's Mill was the precinct closest to the fort.)[7]

But there was a catch. Under New Mexico law, a justice of the peace could issue warrants only after a criminal complaint was filed, which hadn't happened. Moreover, a justice was required "to examine the complainant and any witnesses who may be introduced by him, under oath."[8] Easton could hardly examine witnesses who had remained behind at the fort.

Nevertheless, Easton issued the arrest warrants. But he sent them to Dudley with a cover letter in which he stated his belief that Lincoln County's troubles were largely caused by officials "taking partisan sides." He added, "I do not wish to commit the same." Then he resigned his position as J.P.[9]

Copeland and his posse of troopers transported the Seven Rivers men to their preliminary hearing in San Patricio and, after they were bound over, back to the fort. On the return trip, he and the soldiers arrested various Regulators on the authority of Easton's illegal warrants, adding another dozen or more riders to the caravan.

On May 4, Dudley submitted an official report of his first month in command. That report, with its news about military escorts for the judge and soldiers arresting civilians by the dozen, created a small sensation in Washington. Secretary of War George W. McCrary directed Judge Advocate General W. McKee Dunn to determine "whether there is any violation of law in the use of troops in [New Mexico] Territory in the facts as reported by Colonel Dudley."[10]

Dunn did not find the question difficult. Five days later he responded that Dudley's actions were "without authority of law." Colonel Hatch was ordered by telegraph to suspend operations in Lincoln County immediately.[11]

Back at Fort Stanton, Dudley recognized the necessity of separating his two groups of prisoners. So he put the McSween men in the guardhouse while the Seven Rivers men continued to enjoy the freedom of the fort, an arrangement that makes one wonder whether Dudley was taking advice (or cash, which in New Mexican public life virtually amounted to the same thing) from someone with a motive to dispense it. For reasons of his own, Dudley specified that Doc Scurlock be shackled.[12]

Maybe Dudley just welcomed the opportunity to demonstrate his toughness to his new subordinates after the disgrace of his recent court-martial. Lincoln County, with its factions clashing and quarreling like the mini-states of Germany, needed its Iron Chancellor.

But by handling the first crisis of his new command with Prussian firmness, Dudley kicked the props from beneath Lincoln County's last credible institutions of civil authority. He showed that the sheriff could be made to follow orders. He demonstrated that a judge could be persuaded to break the law. Any force that commanded sufficient firepower could take people prisoner without any legal authority and the civil authorities were powerless to resist.

In short, Dudley confirmed beyond the last hope of redemption the most sourly cynical suspicions of Lincoln County's citizens. Seeking order, he created the conditions for blood-spattered anarchy.

Exasperated and humiliated, Sheriff Copeland released all the prisoners, telling everyone to go home and quit fighting.[13] That ended all efforts to prosecute those who shot MacNab and Saunders, a point that could not have been missed by the surviving Regulators.

A week later, the Regulators staged a raid on Dolan's Seven Rivers cattle camp. A group of twenty or so swooped down on the camp and drove off twenty-seven horses. They also killed Miguel Segovia, "the Indian."[14]

As always, the Regulators had their legal excuse, but this time it wasn't a very good one. Scurlock, purportedly now one of Copeland's deputy sheriffs (an appointment as provocative as Brady's appointment of Mathews and Morton), claimed to be attempting to rearrest MacNab's killers. The sympathetic *Cimarron News and Press* reported that Segovia had been involved in the MacNab killing, which was probably true. The reason Segovia was executed while Dolan's other hands were permitted to flee, however, was that the grand jury had indicted him for the murder of Tunstall. The Regulators clung to the idea of retributive justice based on law: Bonney and the others saw themselves as executioners pursuing the condemned. The indictment, like the verdict of the coroner's jury, became a death warrant.

The first posse Dick Brewer organized captured the Boys and brought them back to Lincoln, even though Brewer correctly predicted the Boys would be freed from jail. And on their first ride, the Regulators had permitted Morton to post a letter and made some effort to transport him and Baker to jail – they weren't killed until their fourth day of captivity, and then supposedly while trying to escape. But now, in raiding Dolan's cattle camp, the Regulators made no serious pretense that Segovia's killing was anything but revenge. And there was no reason to steal or scatter the horses except to deprive their enemies of transportation. Sheriff Copeland immediately disclaimed any responsibility for Scurlock's actions.[15]

The Regulators had ceased to justify their actions with reference to legal norms except in the most perfunctory and unconvincing way. To some extent this reflects a loss of leadership – there was no Dick Brewer, not even a Frank MacNab. But it was also necessity: what else could the Regulators do with Segovia? Despite the indictment, they could hardly imprison him at Fort Stanton. Dudley would arrest them and turn Segovia loose. The Lincoln County jail had demonstrated its porousness. And even if he could be held in prison, Segovia would be tried before Judge Bristol – a joke. A quick bullet solved the problem.

Dudley, Bristol, Catron, Dolan, and Murphy had all, in their different ways and with their different motives, pursued policies of expediency. But by ignoring the law's restraints they corrupted their enemies. The causes of the fighting had been removed; that made the fighting much more dangerous.

However, Dolan's cattle camp didn't belong to Dolan any longer. The leaderless Regulators may not have known of the foreclosure, or maybe they didn't grasp its significance. In late May 1878, Tom Catron wrote a letter to Governor Axtell that read in part:

A party of men under the charge of a man claiming to be deputy sheriff, went to the ranch where my cattle were, and killed the herder and wounded two other men, and then drove off all the horses and mules, leaving my herd entirely unprotected and uncared for. . . .

There seems to be no authority in the county of Lincoln to compel people to keep the peace or obey the law, and there seems to be an utter disregard of the law in the county, as well as of life and private rights.

I would most respectfully request that some steps be taken to disarm all parties there carrying arms, and that the military may be instructed to see that they keep the peace.

I am informed that the sheriff keeps with his deputies large armed posses, who are of one faction only and who take occasion at all times to kill persons and take property of the other faction whenever they get an opportunity.

There is no power, from what I can learn, that can keep the peace in the county except the military, of whom both parties have a healthy dread.

Hoping your Excellency will take such steps as will insure peace and preserve the lives and property of citizens and persons in that county, I am,

Very respectfully,
T. B. Catron[16]

On May 28, Axtell issued a proclamation giving Catron everything he wanted. The second paragraph of the proclamation read:

I command all men and bodies of men now under arms and traveling about the country to disarm and return to their homes and their usual pursuits, and so long as the present sheriff has authority to call upon U.S. troops for assistance, not to act as a sheriff's posse.[17]

Like its predecessor, Axtell's May 28 proclamation suffered from the vice of illegality. It was a crime in New Mexico to refuse to assist a sheriff. Yet here was the governor of the territory commanding the citizens of Lincoln County to break the law.

The first paragraph of Axtell's proclamation also reveals Catron's hand:

John H. Copeland, Esq., appointed sheriff by the county commissioners, having failed for more than thirty days to file his bond as collector of taxes, is hereby removed from the office of sheriff, and I have appointed George W. Peppin, Esq., sheriff of Lincoln County.

This part of the governor's proclamation may have been technically legal, if only because the law on the subject was unclear. The legislature had not anticipated this particular situation. New Mexico sheriffs doubled as tax collectors and were required to post a bond within twenty days of assuming office, which usually happened January 1, almost two months after the election. The statute did not specify what should happen when a sheriff was appointed to fill a vacancy rather than elected. The bond was to be posted "in a sum to be determined by the judge of the District Court." Since Judge Bristol had not determined the sum, Copeland could not post a bond in that amount. But that circumstance arguably gave the governor authority to remove him from office and name his replacement.[18]

Sheriffs were also required to post a second bond, to indemnify victims of wrongdoing.[19] Copeland's failure to post this bond, rather than his failure to post the tax collector's bond, was the real issue: Catron couldn't have been happy to discover he had no recourse for the value of the twenty-seven horses driven off by a purported sheriff's deputy.

Catron wanted Copeland removed from office; Axtell removed him. Catron wanted the military to safeguard his property; Colonel Hatch ordered Lieutenant Smith to Roswell with Company H, Ninth Cavalry.[20]

So George Peppin, who had acted as sheriff after Brady's death and conducted the futile house-by-house search for the wounded Bonney, became sheriff. His choice was vintage Axtell: heavy-handed, politically obtuse. Special Agent Angel, who arrived in Lincoln County at the end of May, commented on the transfer of power: "The Governor immediately seized the opportunity to aid Murphy, Dolan & Riley. He this time acts strictly within the law, and would that I could say the intent of the law and non-partisan."[21]

Peppin's assignment was simple: rid the county of everyone who opposed Catron's interests. Within three months, Sheriff Peppin sought protection at the beef contractor's slaughterhouse two miles below Fort Stanton, afraid to walk abroad in the county where he was the chief law enforcement officer.[22] But by that time he had largely completed his assignment.

The Rio Grande Posse

22

Special Agent Angel assembled an enormously detailed record. He was a skillful attorney – thorough, painstaking, and sheathed in steel-plated self-confidence – the first federal official involved in the Lincoln County War to perform his duties honestly and competently.

Lincoln County's troubles were just one of the many matters he was sent to investigate. The Departments of Interior and Justice were also curious about affairs in Colfax County. Gold had been discovered near Elizabethtown on the east side of the Rockies in northeastern New Mexico, near the present-day resort of Red River. Soon afterward, Tom Catron acquired a controlling interest in the Maxwell Land Grant, a small patch of land near Las Vegas. The Maxwell Land Grant had never been properly surveyed, so Catron hired a surveyor. The surveyor, who happened to be Stephen Elkins's nephew, completed his survey in a miraculous two weeks. Lo and behold, it turned out that the Maxwell Land Grant encompassed Elizabethtown and all of the gold fields. Catron and his partners tried to complete their land grab by evicting all of the prospectors, but the prospectors put up a stiff resistance.[1]

As he did in Lincoln County, Axtell did everything within a governor's power, and more, to help his "good friend" Tom Catron.[2] He joined a plot to invite several leaders of the protestors to a supposed secret meeting with the governor. At the signal, the sheriff was to arrest one of the men. Axtell wrote to the district attorney for northern New Mexico, "Have your men placed to arrest him and to kill all men who resist you or stand with those who do resist you. . . . Do not hesitate at extreme measures." Fortunately, the protest leaders smelled the rat.[3]

There were sufficient allegations of corruption – against Axtell, Catron, and the Mescalero Apaches' agent, Frederick Godfroy – to keep Angel busy all summer. *The Mesilla Valley Independent* noted with satisfaction that Angel was "stirring things up in different parts of the Territory."[4] He covered a lot of ground, both figuratively and literally. He traveled hundreds of miles, interviewing dozens of people in a sustained explosion of investigative energy that horrified everyone in New Mexico who enjoyed the way things were. *The Weekly New Mexican,* friendly to the Santa Fe Ring, was moved to new heights of venomous rhetoric: Angel, having been "spewed out of the White House, evolved from the inner consciousness of the administration," had earned "the confidence of at least one of the editors of the *Independent,* of a sleeve button lawyer in Santa Fe, of two butchers, and of four pimps at large. Can a mere man hold any more and not burst?"[5]

The problem with Angel was that he was the product of someone else's patronage system. The ring couldn't touch him.

Angel was in Lincoln County in late May and early June. His visit coincided with the arrival of John Kinney. Kinney was the sophisticated Mesilla Valley outlaw who built a crime syndicate from his butcher shop, controlling every aspect of the business from the initial rustling to the retail sale of the choicest cuts. Kinney could be a demanding boss: in 1883, according to *The Rio Grande Republican,* Kinney pistol-whipped one of his men so savagely that the street rang with "a sound like the strokes of an axe on an oak log." All told, Kinney kept some thirty men under arms, and he had the sheriff of Doña Ana County thoroughly intimidated.[6]

Colonel Albert Fountain thundered against Kinney and the Boys from his bully pulpit as editor of *The Mesilla Valley Independent.* For his pains, the paper's offices were shot up at least once. (Some years later, Fountain and his son were murdered.)

But Kinney was more than New Mexico's most notorious, most feared, and most outrageously swaggering outlaw; he was also a Texas Ranger. He was an outlaw and a lawman at the same time.

Kinney and his men served as Texas Rangers in El Paso, forty-five miles downriver from Mesilla, and were extraordinarily successful in pacifying that city after the disturbances of the El Paso Salt War. They turned it into a ghost town and its five thousand Hispanic residents into refugees.

There was nothing complicated about the El Paso Salt War.[7] It began as a feud between two politicians and escalated into one of the ugliest race riots in American history – and the most inglorious chapter in the history of the Texas Rangers.

El Paso in the 1870s was a pleasant town, famed for its wines, the historic port of entry connecting Mexico with the United States. A large Hispanic population was dominated, both politically and commercially, by a minuscule group of Anglos.[8]

El Paso had been the salt capital of northern Mexico for generations, and in the 1870s salt remained a principal item of trade. The salt was gathered from a shallow saline lake some one hundred miles east of El Paso in the terrible Big Bend Desert. Under Mexican law, salt lakes were common property owned collectively by the entire community. And in New Mexico, it was a crime to claim private ownership of a salt lake. But the Texas Constitution of 1876 effectively stripped land titles from everyone who had acquired title during the days of Mexican governance. The Texas Supreme Court subsequently voided that section of the Constitution, finding at least three violations of the federal Constitution. For good measure, a federal appeals court also found a violation of the Treaty of Guadalupe-Hidalgo, by which the United States pledged to honor Mexican land titles.[9] But in 1877 it was the supreme law of Texas, and it allowed one of the feuding politicians, an Anglo named Charles Howard, to lay claim to the entire salt lake despite the community's prior claim of common ownership. Howard posted notices threatening to prosecute anyone who stole "his" salt.

When two men whose families had gathered salt for generations defied the notices, Howard had them thrown in jail. A mob, composed entirely of Hispanics, freed the prisoners and took Howard hostage.

At that point, the other feuding politician intervened – on behalf of his rival. Louis Cardis was an Italian whose business and political success (he owned a stagecoach line and served as a state representative) had made him a leading citizen in his adopted homeland. Cardis arranged for Howard's release in exchange for a promise that he would never return to El Paso.

Howard retreated to Las Cruces and bombarded the governor of Texas with telegrams warning of imminent armed invasion from Mexico. The governor took the telegrams seriously enough to ask President Hayes to send troops to investigate. Hayes complied. Howard rode into town with the troops, strode into Cardis's office with a shotgun, emptied both barrels into Cardis's body, then rode with the soldiers back to Mesilla.

The Texas governor resolved to send his Rangers to El Paso to keep things from getting out of hand. But the westernmost battalion of Rangers was garrisoned in San Antonio, 550 miles to the east. Transporting them to El Paso would be slow and expensive, so the governor did the next best thing: he sent the battalion's commander, Major John Jones, to El Paso to organize a new battalion. But few Hispanics would serve, and there weren't many Anglos. So Jones was forced to swear in a pack of semiliterate layabouts.

His job completed, Jones returned to San Antonio, leaving his ragtag Rangers to their own devices. Then several Hispanic men organized a wagon train to go to the salt lake. Hearing this, Howard once more rushed to El Paso, this time in the company of ten men, employees of John Kinney. He was met at the edge of town by the twenty Rangers, who acted as his bodyguards, escorting him about town as he threatened salt gatherers. In the evening, Howard and his bodyguards retired to the Rangers' headquarters in the nearby hamlet of San Elizario.

Predictably, the mob reformed. The former sheriff of El Paso, a man named Ellis, slipped from the headquarters and mingled with the crowd. According to a letter published in *The Mesilla Valley Independent*, he maddened the crowd with his patronizing advice, saying:

> "What does this mean, boys? Don't act foolishly; let me advise you for your own good," and other remarks to the same effect, when León Granillo cried out, "*Ahora es el tiempo*" (now is the time). Then Eutemio Chávez rode up on horseback and threw a lasso over Ellis and started on the run, dragging the unfortunate man. After he had dragged him some distance he got down and cut his throat and his body was thrown to the coyotes.[10]

There was no going back after that. Rangers' headquarters was besieged, with constant sniping and several deaths. Finally, after five days, Howard gave himself up. He was summarily shot. Two other Anglos were also executed "on general principles," in memoirist W. W. Mills's phrase. The Rangers and Kinney's men were allowed to go. The town quieted down.

The local sheriff, who referred to his constituents as "greasers," had quailed in his house during the riot. When calm returned, so did his courage. He received telegraphed permission from the governor to raise a second battalion of Rangers and found the men he wanted in Las Cruces and Mesilla. John Kinney and his entire band of professional thieves and killers were all sworn in as Texas Rangers.[11]

They cleaned out El Paso. The first two Hispanics they found were hog-tied before they were shot. Another man was killed and his wife seriously wounded inside their own house. They hadn't even opened the door. Army officers later counted fifteen bullet holes piercing the door from the outside, none emerging from within. A half-dozen other murders followed; all of the victims were Hispanic. Army officers were unable to determine exactly how many women were raped by the Rangers, but the number is probably roughly equivalent to the number of women the Rangers found in town.

The rest fled with their families into the Mexican interior. At Christmastime (about the time McSween and Chisum were arrested in Las Vegas), Captain Thomas Blair of the U.S. Army wrote that most of El Paso's citizens were "perishing for want of food and from exposure to the cold in and around Saragossa, Mexico."[12] Finally, on New Year's Eve, frustrated by the lack of any other targets, one Ranger killed another. That was the signal that El Paso was well and truly pacified, and the Rangers' mission was declared a success.

When George Peppin took over as sheriff of Lincoln County, the first thing he did was swear in John Kinney and his entire band as deputy sheriffs. Kinney and his men had developed a taste for law enforcement; it gave them immunity from prosecution for doing the things they normally did anyway.

Kinney, of course, didn't work for free.

Tom Catron knew all about the Salt War and so did the residents of Lincoln. It was much on everyone's mind at the town meeting held after the grand jury's adjournment. Among many other resolutions adopted at the meeting was the following:

Be it Revolved, . . .
That we recognize with expressible pleasure the good and united feeling that binds all our people, Mexican and Americans, together. We recognize our mutual dependence upon each other, and we pledge our lives and our property to the protection of each other and the maintenance of the laws.[13]

The resolution was prompted by the widespread concern that Lincoln County's troubles were rapidly developing into a replay of the Salt War.

In El Paso, Kinney and his men had to kill a few people and rape a few women before they succeeded in depopulating the town. It was easier at Lincoln, where the depopulation began almost as soon as his presence became the subject of rumor. On June 14 Rob Widenmann left Lincoln, never to return. Juan Patrón and Judge Florencio Gonzáles sought refuge at Fort Stanton; Patrón later retreated all the way to Las Vegas. Chisum took a trip to St. Louis. McSween, Bonney, the rest of the Regulators, and anybody who was afraid he might be mistaken for a Regulator fled to the hills.

Neutrals fled in unrecorded numbers. A nascent settlement on Chisum's land along the Pecos was abandoned. Farmers and ranchers quietly moved on to more peaceful pastures. An anonymous correspondent told *The Mesilla News:* "Col. John Kinney holds Lincoln. And Lincoln I regret to say presents an appearance as melancholy as an old toper when about to join the Sons of Temperance."[14]

Colonel Hatch was happy to order troops to Roswell to protect Catron's livestock. Earlier, he had instructed Captain Purington to assist Sheriff Brady. Such employment of the military in nonmilitary matters was common in the 1870s. In 1878, one Democratic congressman put it this way: "During the last ten years not one-half of our Army has been employed for legitimate purposes. Its use has consisted mainly of running elections and keeping the dominant party in power." A southern Democratic senator said: "The Army has not only been used in the collection of the internal revenue in a way not authorized by law, but it has been used and prostituted to control elections repeatedly. Statehouses have been seized over and over again, and not a great while in the past." An Illinois Democrat, illustrating how the nascent labor movement found common cause with southern conservatives, declared: "The people of this country . . . are not willing to have an army either for the purpose of falsifying ballot boxes or for shooting down American laboringmen."[15]

With left and right united, Congress passed the Posse Comitatus Act as an amendment to the U.S. Army's appropriation bill. Effective June 18, 1878, it forbade the use of the military as a posse, except in specified circumstances amounting to armed insurrection.[16] General Sherman's staff wasted no time in preparing and distributing a memorandum explaining the act, and by June 25 Colonel Hatch had received explicit orders, originating with Secretary of War McCrary, that "the use of Troops in Lincoln County, under the call of the Governor, must be discontinued."[17]

However, there was no telegraph line to Fort Stanton.

Meanwhile, in Lincoln County, June passed in a series of inconsequential skirmishes as the three forces in the field maneuvered for position. The Regulators feared the army and were reluctant to engage Kinney's "Rio Grande Posse" (an innocuous name that, like "the House" and "the Boys," and perhaps also the more literal "Kid," concealed the speaker's antipathy with intentional transparency). On June 26 Kinney's force, with Sheriff Peppin tagging along, made an assault on San Patricio, the Regulators' safe haven. McSween and the Regulators, outnumbered, retreated into the hills. Nothing happened except that a horse belonging to Jack Long (now a deputy sheriff) was shot and killed.[18]

Dudley again was outraged that the Regulators should resist their attackers and sent thirty-five troopers under the command of Captain Henry Carroll to restore order. But by the time the soldiers arrived in San Patricio, they were the only thing disturbing the cicada-buzzing peace of the hot summer's afternoon. Nonetheless, Carroll led his men into the mountains in pursuit of the Regulators, trailing them for forty-five miles – the first chase since Brady's death.[19]

Carroll and his men were in the field when Lieutenant Colonel Dudley received the secretary of war's order, delivered by courier from Fort Craig on the Rio Grande. According to the War Department's legal officer, Dudley's actions were illegal even before the Posse Comitatus Act was passed. Dudley had shrugged off that opinion, ignoring the order to "discontinue operations." After all, one man's opinion is not the law. But now Congress had acted. He sent a soldier after Captain Carroll to recall him to the fort.[20]

In early July, the Seven Rivers men again mobilized, this time attacking Chisum's South Spring River Ranch. It must have been exhilarating for the Beckwiths and their friends to pockmark Chisum's adobe ranch house with bullets. That was all they accomplished, but they rode home satisfied.[21] The Seven Rivers men didn't do foolish things that might lead to loss of life, particularly their own lives. They proved a major disappointment to Dolan and Catron, who had hoped to rely on their (unpaid) assistance. Their independence, and the reasonable curbs they placed on their appetite for revenge, had forced Catron to hire John Kinney.

A more serious incident occurred on July 10 with a second assault on San Patricio. McSween described the scene for *The Cimarron News and Press:*

> Headed by Axtell's sheriff and J. J. Dolan the Rio Grande posse killed and stole horses in San Patricio last week, and at the same time and place, they broke windows and doors, smashed boxes and robbed them of their contents; from an old woman who was living alone they stole $438. They tore the roof off of Dow Bros. store; threw the goods out on the street and took what they wanted. Towards women they used the vilest language. Citizens working in the fields were fired upon but made good their escape up the river. . . . Kinney said in town that he was employed by the Governor and that he and his men would have to be paid $3.50 a day by the county, and that the sooner the people helped him arrest the Regulators, the sooner their county would be relieved of this expense; Dolan endorsed this speech.[22]

Kinney's speech is humorous enough to sound authentic, though perhaps McSween shouldn't be faulted for failing to see the humor. But how did Kinney's men get the roof off the store?

The San Patricio incident involved a lot of bluster and threats, and maybe even robbery. But its psychological effect went much deeper. It was a reminder of what Kinney had done in El Paso, and that if the fancy took him he would do the same to little San Patricio.

Colonel Dudley received a report on the incident from the same Captain Blair who investigated atrocities in El Paso. Blair's account was much less colorful than McSween's but largely corroborated it. Blair agreed that the posse acted "to some extent (exactly how far does not appear) under Mr. Dolan's instructions," and that it

> tore down a portion of a house, forced and tore open a number of doors, and searched houses without showing or claiming to have any legal warrants for so doing, [and that it appears] that the searches were conducted in a discourteous, uncivil, and even rude manner.[23]

The San Patricio raid convinced McSween and the Regulators that they couldn't hide forever. The citizens of San Patricio had, in effect, become hostages. The assaults on the citizens would continue – and would get worse with each visitation – until the Regulators rode down from the hills for a final showdown.[24]

The Regulators also faced a more mundane type of pressure. In his letter, McSween bragged that "the Regulators now number over 200 able-bodied men, well equipped," at least a fourfold exaggeration. He added, "They have now detailed 50 of their number to harvest each other's wheat." But of course it was a difficult thing to harvest one's wheat under these conditions, even assuming the Regulators had found time to plant and care for it. A farmer standing in his field is peculiarly vulnerable. McSween's letter was probably mostly wishful thinking. But with the wheat ripening in the fields, the Regulators knew they faced destitution if they stayed in the hills.

McSween's letter also referred in passing to "the petition sent by the people to Governor Axtell asking the removal of Peppin." Since McSween's letter was dated July 11, and Peppin had only become sheriff on June 28, it had taken remarkably little time to gather signatures for the petition.

The position of sheriff was normally filled by election in New Mexico. Peppin wasn't elected; he wasn't even chosen by elected officials, as John Copeland had been. Rather, he was appointed by a governor who was himself unelected, and he understood very quickly how profoundly he was despised by the citizens who were his charge. It made him abjectly dependent on John Kinney. Peppin had no political legitimacy but he had the Rio Grande Posse (or it had him), and in the short term that was more important.

The Five Days' Battle

23

On the night of July 14, 1878, McSween and the Regulators occupied Lincoln. The Regulators had picked up reinforcements from San Patricio and neighboring Hispanic villages; their ranks were swollen to a fighting force of fifty to sixty men, by far the most formidable army yet to take the field in the Lincoln County War, save only the U.S. Army itself. The men were deployed in three strategic locations: at Ellis's store on the east, commanding the road into town; at McSween's house; and, between those two locations, at José Montaño's home on the south side of the road.[1]

The augmented Regulators timed their nighttime descent on Lincoln well. Kinney, Peppin, and most of the Rio Grande Posse were on the road, hunting for Regulators. Kinney had left behind a skeleton force to guard the town, under the uncertain command of Deputy Jack Long. Long and his four or five men were holed up in the stone tower or *torreón* across the street from Montaño's house. Either they failed to notice the arrival of fifty or sixty armed men (not impossible, if a couple bottles of whiskey had found their way into the *torreón*) or they disliked the odds – there was no shooting.[2]

The *torreón* was built when Lincoln, or rather La Placita del Rio Bonito, was little more than an outpost, its handful of residents dreading the Apaches. They built the *torreón* to the specifications of a castle keep, suitably scaled down: it was cylindrical, twenty feet in diameter, and twenty feet tall, built of stones mortared with adobe. It was intended to be large enough to house the entire community and strong enough to withstand the most persistent siege.

McSween owned the *torreón,* which stood a short distance from his home, as well as the house next door to the *torreón*. He rented both to Captain Saturnino Baca, a black-bearded grizzly of a man and Lincoln County's former sheriff. Baca's wife had recently given birth. Since the refugee life is hard on newborns and recovering mothers alike, the Baca family stayed behind in Lincoln when most of their neighbors fled. Desiring to remain on good terms with everyone, they did not resist when Deputy Long commandeered the stone watchtower in their backyard. They even fixed meals for him.[3]

This irritated McSween. From McSween's point of view, his tenant was sheltering gunmen intent on bumping him off, not the sort of thing to warm a landlord's heart. But it wasn't mere spite that made McSween serve a notice to quit on Captain Baca. What he wanted wasn't Baca's house but the *torreón,* which was located on the same plot of land. If its occupiers failed to heed the notice to quit, wouldn't the landlord be justified in evicting them? The purpose of the notice to quit was to justify, in any subsequent criminal prosecution, the Regulators' planned assault on the *torreón.*

From Baca's point of view, however, he and his family were being evicted as punishment for having previously been victimized by Jack Long. After all, it wasn't Baca's idea to cook dinner for the deputy. Being forced to move his wife and their newborn deeply offended Baca's notions of decent behavior and challenged his honor. At the same time, he didn't particularly care to defy fifty or sixty armed men. A former Union officer who had served with the New Mexico Volunteers during the entire course of the Civil War, he knew where to turn for help. He wrote to Lieutenant Colonel Dudley, requesting the assistance of soldiers to move his household to the Wortley Hotel.[4]

Colonel Dudley immediately sent Post Surgeon Appel to look into the matter. The idea of the United States Army intervening in a landlord-tenant dispute is peculiar, to say the least, but it is all too easily explained: Dudley wanted to help Baca, his fellow officer, and he wanted to hurt McSween.

Appel shuttled back and forth between McSween, Baca, Long, and the Regulators holed up in the Ellis store. McSween made it clear that he was only interested in clearing the House men out the tower, agreeing to allow soldiers to take up residence. On behalf of the Regulators, Doc Scurlock promised in writing that the House men could leave the tower unmolested. But Long, who recognized the *torreón*'s strategic importance, and who may not have trusted Scurlock anyway, refused to budge.[5]

At each of their three strongholds, the Regulators dug gun ports in the adobe walls and reinforced doors and windows with sandbags, the same preparations some of them had made at Tunstall's home five months before. Each of the flat-roofed houses had an adobe parapet; portholes and notches were dug in the parapets, transforming them into breastworks.

As Appel left Lincoln at dusk, he ran into John Kinney and the Rio Grande Posse hurrying back to town. Appel was still within earshot when Charles Crawford, nicknamed the Lallycooler, fired the first shots in the air. Former Justice of the Peace David Easton saw puffs of powdered adobe where bullets hit McSween's house.[6]

That evening and the three following days were taken up with inconclusive shooting reminiscent of the attack of the Seven Rivers "Warriors" weeks before. The only locations Kinney's men could command were Dolan's store on the extreme western edge of town and the Wortley Hotel across the street.[7] It was impossible to communicate with Long and his little band holed up in the *torreón*. They, meanwhile, faced all of the predictable miseries of prolonged confinement: dwindling food and water supplies, overflowing chamber pots.

Moreover, as quickly became clear, the Rio Grande Posse was badly outnumbered. Kinney's twenty or so men were tough as nails, with less conscience, but the odds were three to one against them. Dolan sent out a frantic appeal to the Seven Rivers men, who responded, but that only improved the odds to three to two, and the Seven Rivers men had already demonstrated their unreliability. There was no hope of retaking the town without reinforcement, but John Kinney was so feared in Lincoln County, and George Peppin so despised, that help could not be found in the civilian population.

Kinney's two raids on San Patricio had driven many peaceful men into the ranks of the Regulators and alienated everyone else from the sheriff's cause. This is perhaps the most striking feature of the posse commanded by Sheriff Peppin: there were no members from Lincoln or the surrounding mountain villages other than House employees. Peppin was isolated in his own county seat, able to draw support only from the Seven Rivers region 150 miles away, and then only because the Seven

Rivers men had their own quarrel with Chisum. Otherwise the sheriff was entirely dependent on the mercenary outlaws of the Rio Grande valley.[8]

There was only one place in all of Lincoln County where he could turn for help. "If it is in your power to loan me one of your Howitzers," read a penciled note sent to Colonel Dudley over Peppin's signature, "you would confer a great favor on the majority of the people of this County, who are being persecuted by a lawless mob." Peppin admitted he didn't write this note, and he claimed not to remember who did.[9]

Dudley was receptive to the appeal. He knew a showdown was looming. He wrote in his official reports, "I fear [the House forces] will get the worst of it." He warned his superiors of the necessity for "some very decisive action" by the governor or the military.[10] Nonetheless, he had to contend with a nagging problem: the Posse Comitatus Act made it illegal for him to give the requested assistance. He responded with a note of his own, delivered by Private Berry Robinson:

> My sympathies and those of all my officers are most earnestly and sincerely with you on the side of law and order. . . . Up to the present time I have endeavored in all my official acts to avoid in any possible way, by act or expression, to act otherwise than in strictly an impartial manner towards both factions in Lincoln County, but I do not hesitate to state now, that in my opinion you are acting strictly within the provisions of the duties incumbent upon you as Deputy U.S. Marshal and Sheriff, and were I not so circumscribed by law and orders, I would most gladly give you every man and material at my Post to sustain you in your present position, believing it to be strictly legal.[11]

Dudley knew what he wanted to do; his "sympathies," as he put it, were fully engaged. The only thing holding him back was his duty to obey the law. This conflict was familiar to Colonel Dudley. His desire and his duty were frequently at odds: he was controlled by his emotions, and his emotions were controlled by drink. It was only a matter of time before he allowed himself to do what Congress forbade.

The sheriff's brain trust, Dolan and Kinney, could easily read the message between the lines of Dudley's note: give me a good enough excuse and I will help you. So they manufactured one. Someone in the Wortley Hotel wrote a response to Dudley's note for Peppin's signature:

Am very sorry I can't get the assistance I asked for but I will do the best I can. The McSween party fired on your Soldier when coming into town. My men on seeing him tried their best to cover him, but of no use. The soldier will explain the circumstances to you.[12]

Dudley seized the opportunity. While the Regulators and the Rio Grande Posse sniped at each other across long distances, a panel of officers descended on the town to conduct an investigation into the shooting incident. The panel reported:

After considering all the evidence before it, the board finds that Private Berry Robinson, . . . who was ordered to Lincoln to carry a dispatch to Special Deputy U.S. Marshal and County Sheriff Peppin, as he approached the town and when within five hundred yards of it several shots were fired at him by parties concealed within Mr. McSween's house. Said Robinson was in uniform and it was broad daylight.[13]

Five hundred yards from town was more than five hundred yards from McSween's house. At that distance, how could Robinson know the bullets came from McSween's house? Robinson's own statement, or at least the statement attributed to him, explains: Jimmy Dolan told him so. The board of officers then confirmed the story by talking to Dolan.[14]

There is reason to doubt whether the statement was actually made by Private Robinson, since it describes in some detail how Peppin called for a candle to write his response.

Robinson approached town from the west, and the House and Wortley's hotel were west of McSween's house. If bullets "whistled" past Robinson's horse's head, as Robinson stated, they were almost certainly intended for those inside the House and hotel and had overshot their mark.

The story accepted by the board – that McSween's men deliberately shot at a soldier in "broad daylight" – was the least likely explanation for the incident. Among other things, Robinson's statement said he left the fort at 6:30 P.M. and "rode pretty fast to get [to town] before dark."[15] But with his experience on the receiving end of military law (two military courts convicted him and two others assembled damning evidence against him), Lieutenant Colonel Dudley knew the importance of supporting evidence. The phony assault was a manufactured bit of evidence justifying the course of action Dudley had already determined to take, one dictated by his "sympathies."

Dr. Appel, Dudley's confidant and most trusted associate, was a member of the board of officers. While in Lincoln he tended to the first casualty of the Five Days' Battle, which came on its third day, July 17. The Lallycooler, a House employee of long standing who had previously threatened to kill "all the old damn son of a bitches" living in the lower part of town, had been stationed on the hills overlooking town. After a day and a half of inconclusive sporadic firing, he grew careless about staying behind cover. Fernando Herrera, one of the newly recruited Regulators, plugged him from the roof of the Montano store. Crawford fell unconscious. No one in Peppin's command had the courage to come to his rescue. He was left to bake in the July sunshine for hours before Dr. Appel finally administered first aid and arranged to have him moved to the Fort Stanton hospital, where he died a week later.[16]

The following evening, July 18, the Regulators suffered their first casualty. At twilight Ben Ellis ventured out from his store to tend to his horses. Some sheriff's sharpshooter saw him. The shot grazed his neck, dangerously close to the spot where pigs are stuck.

Dr. Ealy and his family were living inside the Tunstall store. They barricaded the windows with their trunks, laid their mattresses on the floor, and tried to conduct life below the level of the windows. After nightfall they heard an unexpected knock on the door. Two muddy men from the Ellis store had come to summon the doctor. Unable to take the direct route up the street, which led past the *torreón*, they waded waist deep up the Bonito in the darkness until they were opposite the store. Then they did the combat crawl across the corral to the door.

Dr. Ealy agreed to see Ellis, which meant he agreed to repeat in reverse order the route the messengers had taken. Portly Dr. Ealy did his best. He did the combat crawl across the dust and dried manure; he blundered in the darkness through the undergrowth of the Bonito's bank; he slithered into the rushing waters of the mountain stream; he tried gamely to keep his footing in the darkness on the moss-covered, water-rounded rocks of the streambed even as Jack Long's men fired round after round over his head – but he couldn't do it. Dr. Ealy's daughter Ruth wrote in her memoir, "It was a long time before he came back," but he did so without seeing the patient.

The next morning Dr. Ealy hit upon a simpler stratagem for covering the few hundred yards to the Ellis house. He walked up the street. But he took a few precautions: he carried his baby and walked with his daughter. Ruth Ealy doesn't record what her mother thought of this arrangement, but it worked: Long's men held their fire. By that time Ellis had lost a great deal of blood, but Ealy was able to clean and dress the wound and Ellis lived.

A few hours later, shortly after noon on July 19, Lieutenant Colonel Dudley rode into town at the head of a column of some forty soldiers. He brought along every officer in the post but Lieutenant Samuel Pague, who was left in charge. He also brought a Gatling gun, an early machine gun, with three thousand rounds of ammunition as well as the requested nine-pound howitzer "with ample ammunition," along with rations for three days.[18]

Why did Dudley come? A military court of inquiry convened the following year to consider that very question. Dudley testified that "my object in going to Lincoln was to give protection to women and children."[19] He did so by offering to escort the very few women and children remaining in Lincoln to the fort, an exercise that could have been accomplished by one soldier and a few teamsters driving wagons, without all the bother of transporting the howitzer and Gatling gun.

So why was everyone else there? The prosecution presented testimony that on July 18, Jimmy Dolan rode to the fort and entered into a deal with Dudley. The defense countered with Jimmy Dolan himself, who testified that while he did indeed ride to the fort and talk with Dudley, they didn't discuss the nonstop shooting that had turned Lincoln into a war zone. Somehow the subject never came up.

Dolan's testimony continued:

> Q. [by Colonel Dudley's lawyer]: Did you have any conversation with Col. Dudley about 30 feet west and in front of the porch of his quarters, or anywhere in front of or about his quarters in the evening preceding or at any time during the day before the 19th day of July last in reference to his moving troops to the town of Lincoln in the month of July last in which conversation Col. Dudley said to you "to go down and stand them off and he would be there by 12 o'clock," or anything to that effect?
>
> Dolan: No sir. Never had any such conversation with Col. Dudley at that time and place.[20]

On cross-examination the prosecution naturally asked whether Dolan and Dudley had such a conversation at any other time or place. Dudley's lawyer objected and the court sustained the objection, for no good reason except, perhaps, that the fix was in.[21]

Dolan was, at the time of his conversation with Dudley, under indictment for accessory to murder. His partner, John Riley, was under indictment for cattle theft. They were bankrupt, merchants without a store. It is difficult to imagine any nonconspiratorial reason why Dudley was chatting with Dolan at all.

Dudley's actions upon reaching town were efficient, methodical, and effective. First he trained his mountain howitzer on the Montaño house. He delivered the message that if the men stayed inside the Montaño store, "the women and children had better leave." So Mrs. Montaño and her five children left, only to hear from Colonel Dudley that he didn't have enough soldiers to protect them.[22]

The howitzer was a great persuader, exactly as predicted. The Regulators fled out the back door, hustling down the street to join their companions in the Ellis store.

Then Dudley marched over to the Ellis store and again aimed the cannon. This time, all the Regulators mounted up and rode into the hills north of town. No one gave chase. When some of the Regulators tried to return to town later, Dudley trained the Gatling gun on them and they faded away. Among the Regulators to flee Lincoln that afternoon were John Middleton, Doc Scurlock, and Charles Bowdre.[23]

Dudley marched back down the street and aimed the howitzer at McSween's front door. This time no one fled.

In just a few minutes Dudley had broken the standoff of the previous four days, but now he faced a different kind of standoff. If McSween had been of a mind to flee he would have had all of John Kinney's butcher boys and a good portion of the United States Army on his tail. McSween knew that, of course, and after a while Dudley grasped that military bluster alone wouldn't do the trick.

So, leaving a few men to guard McSween's house, he ordered his troops to set up camp. Three times that day Dudley summoned Peppin into camp, each time providing him with two soldiers to walk at his shoulders. According to Peppin's later testimony, Dudley kept recalling him into camp for no other purpose than to repeat the same warning.[24] The story reveals a great deal about the sheriff: he was prepared to lie under oath, but he wasn't clever enough to come up with a plausible story.

Shortly after settling into camp, Dudley staged a curious replay of the incident of the previous month in which the J.P. for Blazer's Mill was bullied into issuing illegal arrest warrants. Dudley demanded that the justice of the peace for Lincoln be brought into camp. The J.P. was once more John B. Wilson, who had been reelected to his old post at a special election. Dudley demanded that Wilson issue warrants for the arrest of everyone inside the McSween house. Their crime was the assault on Private Robinson.

Wilson demurred, pointing out that the Constitution did not permit him to issue warrants on demand, but only "upon probable cause, supported by Oath or Affirmation." So the three officers who served on the investigative board signed affidavits, although none of them had first-hand knowledge of the incident (assuming that it even happened). Wilson then suggested that shooting at a soldier was a federal crime over which he had no jurisdiction.

Issue the damned warrant, Dudley roared, or I'll have you thrown in irons.[25]

It was a persuasive legal argument. Wilson issued the warrant. Joseph Nash and Bob Olinger, two of the Seven Rivers men, tried to serve it, shouting through McSween's window that they had a warrant for everyone's arrest. According to Nash, McSween's men responded that they "had warrants in their guns for all of us."[26]

Of course, Dudley didn't expect McSween to open his door when the deputy knocked. The sole purpose of the warrants was to provide some legal camouflage for the colonel's next move.

The colonel's foresight paid off. Justice Wilson's warrants were repeatedly brought up at the court of inquiry, as Dudley took every opportunity to remind the judges that the men inside the McSween house were resisting lawful arrest.

Inside the house were Alexander and Sue McSween, Sue's sister Elizabeth Shield and the Shield children, and Susan Gates, the schoolteacher, along with Bill Bonney and Jim French, two of the original Regulators.

Also inside the house was Harvey Morris, a young man from Kansas who had come to New Mexico seeking relief from tuberculosis and who was reading law in McSween's office. All Morris wanted to do was become a lawyer. He was inside the house only because that was where he lived, and it suddenly had become dangerous to leave.

Also inside were Francisco Zamora, Vicente Romero, Eugenio Salazar, Ignacio González, José Chávez y Chávez, and Tom O'Folliard, even younger than the Kid, who was to prove the Kid's most loyal companion.[27]

They knew how desperate their situation had become. If they surrendered to Peppin and Kinney they (or at least some of them) would be put to death: Bonney and French would get it as revenge for Brady, McSween because he was McSween, some of the others for "trying to escape." And as long as the Gatling gun commanded the hills, no one was going to ride to their rescue. They were opposed not just by the sheriff's posse and the most notorious gang of cutthroats in southern New Mexico (one and the same, actually) but by the United States Army itself. The cops, the crooks, and the military were joined in alliance for the sole purpose of annihilating them.

So McSween resolved to negotiate. He tried to open communications with Dudley, his agitation evident in the note he sent to the lieutenant colonel:

Would you have the kindness to let me know why soldiers surround my house. Before blowing up my property I would like to know the reason. The constable is here and has warrants for the arrest of Sheriff Peppin and posse for murder and larceny.
Respectfully,
A. A. McSween[28]

Dudley dictated a response that captures the very essence of his personality:

I am directed by the commanding officer to inform you that no soldiers have surrounded your house and that he desires to hold no correspondence with you; if you desire to blow up your house, the commanding officer does not object, provided it does not injure any United States soldiers.[29]

McSween wrote in terror for his life; Dudley tweaked him on his choice of words. Since Dudley had ordered that the howitzer be trained on McSween's front door, he understood perfectly well the implied subject of the first clause of McSween's second sentence: "Before *you* blow up my property." Moreover, McSween's house *was* surrounded by a mixed group of soldiers and civilians. But the majority were Kinney's men, who took up position after the soldiers passed through town, and so Dudley was being accurate, in his perversely pedantic way, when he said the house was not surrounded by soldiers.[30]

The significance of the colonel's note lies not in his spite but in his refusal to conduct any correspondence. Dudley would not consider a negotiated settlement. He wanted a fight to the finish.

Dr. Ealy had demonstrated that the Rio Grande Posse was reluctant to shoot little children. Would they also hesitate to shoot women? Sue McSween, determined to talk to Dudley, put it to the test. She left the house mid-afternoon and walked down the street in the direction of the cavalry camp. No one fired.[31]

The first thing Sue saw were two men, Sebrian Bates and Joe Dixon, picking up logs from a large pile of lumber. In her testimony at Dudley's court of inquiry, Sue described the men as "colored servants of mine." Three well-armed posse members, whom Sue described only as "Murphy men," were overseeing the labor. When Sue asked Bates and Dixon what they were doing, they told her that Peppin and Colonel Dudley had ordered them to stack lumber against the wall of the McSween house to facilitate its burning.[32] Sue "begged" Bates and Dixon not to do it, but the Murphy men said, "If they don't want to get into trouble they had better not refuse."

Like a pilgrim in a morality play, Sue continued down the road when whom should she meet but Sheriff Peppin. (Peppin testified that he was ensconced in the safety of the *torreón* when Sue "hollered" up to him.)[33] Sue said that she asked Peppin "why he was trying to force my servants to help burn down the building."

> He then said that if I did not want my house burned down I must make those men who were in the house get out of it, that he was bound to have those men who were inside today dead or alive. [He said] that he was tired of this and would give them enough of it today.

Sue then continued down the road to the army camp. She found Dudley and told him what she had seen: men held at gunpoint, the sheriff plotting arson. She asked for protection. According to Sue, Dudley responded "that he had nothing to do with these troubles, that he had only come there to camp and did not intend to have anything to do with either party – that he knew nothing about the matter."

Sue told Dudley that "it looked strange to see his men . . . guarding Peppin back and forth through the town and sending soldiers around our house and sending us such word as he had sent us if he had nothing to do with it." She testified that she also asked him "why he camped there in the middle of the town and just on that day when these men were trying to do their dirty work." She added, "The soldiers in camp laughed out loud at that expression, which appeared to aggravate Col. Dudley." Dudley replied, "Madam, the ladies I am accustomed to keep company with never make use of such a vulgar phrase."[34]

Sue then tried to explain what her husband had meant when he wrote the note about "blowing up my house," but Dudley insisted that McSween meant he would blow up his own house, reading from the letter to prove his point. Sergeant Baker said that when Sue took a couple of steps as if to snatch the letter, "Colonel Dudley gave me orders that if she attempted to take the letter, to snatch the letter out of his hand, to shoot her." However, Dudley was smiling as he spoke, and the men laughed at the sport.[35]

Sue refused to be cowed by ridicule and continued to press her point. Dudley was an old bachelor who had spent his adult life in the army. He was not used to the company of strong-willed women and eventually lost patience, telling Sue that it was none of her business what he did with his soldiers, that he would send his soldiers wherever he pleased, and that she had no business complaining about it "when such men as Billy Kid, Jim French and other of like character [were] in her house."[36]

Dudley said he was in town to protect women and children. Sue pointed out that Miss Gates and Mrs. Shield and her children were in the McSween house. Dudley said, well, they shouldn't be in that house and so he wouldn't protect them. If they didn't want to get hurt, they must leave the house.

The discussion went downhill from there. Sue asked why the military was trying to kill McSween when they didn't even have a warrant for his arrest. Dudley (not denying that they were trying to kill McSween) responded that they did indeed have a warrant, and then accused Sue of being inconsiderate to Saturnino Baca's wife. Completing the descent to the schoolyard, Dudley, Sue testified, "made sport of me being Mrs. McSween, as though it was degrading to be called Mrs. McSween."[37]

Deputy Jack Long, newly liberated from the *torreón*, tried his hand as arsonist. He and Buck Powell, one of the Seven Rivers "Warriors," sneaked up to the northeast corner of the house, the enclosed winter kitchen, and splashed coal oil everywhere. But the fire they started was extinguished immediately.[38]

Worse, they were almost killed. The Regulators caught them in the act and opened fire. Long and Powell fled across the McSween yard and leapt into the first shelter they could find, which unfortunately turned out to be the McSween outhouse. Since the outhouse walls were thin, Long and Powell had no choice but to descend to the pit. So the deputy who spent the first four days of the Five Days' Battle cooped up in the *torreón* spent the final day standing knee deep in excrement.[39]

But the posse didn't give up easily. Andy Boyle, a former Brady deputy from Seven Rivers, successfully started a fire at the opposite corner of the house, in the half-open summer kitchen, once again using coal oil as an accelerant.[40]

Peppin did not oversee the fire-bugging. The sheriff had given all his warrants for the arrest of McSween and the Regulators to his deputy, Bob Beckwith, and retreated into the *torreón*. He hid until the following day, no longer even pretending to be in charge of the operation.[41]

The fire spread from room to room around the U-shaped structure. Toward evening, the Shield family, Miss Gates, and Sue McSween were persuaded to seek shelter with the Ealys in the Tunstall store next door. As night fell, Reverend Ealy decided it was time to evacuate the store, too. Since Lieutenant Colonel Dudley claimed to be in Lincoln for the purpose of protecting women and children, and most of the women and children in Lincoln were now huddled together inside the Tunstall store, Ealy went to the army to seek help.

Ealy's concern for his family, and for Miss Gates, Mrs. McSween, Mrs. Shield, and the Shield children gave Dudley the perfect opportunity to settle scores. Ealy was the doctor who treated Billy the Kid following the assassination of Brady, allowing him to escape – a painful humiliation for the soldiers sent to capture him. Dudley could not pass up a chance to get even. He told Ealy to leave the army camp immediately or he would be thrown out. It was the third time that day Dudley refused to aid women and children.

Ealy was escorted out of camp. Having achieved his revenge, Dudley sent an aide after him with the message that the colonel would be willing to consider a written plea for help from Ealy's wife. With her children's lives possibly hanging on her choice of words, Mrs. Ealy wrote the begging letter.[43]

Dudley was magnanimous in victory and sent a volunteer crew to move the Ealys to safety.

The fire by now had consumed most of the house and the inhabitants were crowded into the winter kitchen and an adjoining room. About this time, according to Bates, Dudley "went to drinking his lager beer or some kind of drink. Then he said, have you not got those fellows burnt out yet, Peppin? He says, you were a hell of a while getting those fellows burnt out there. Peppin said, they ain't got but one more room to stand in and then we will have them burnt out."[44]

After dark, a group of McSween men made a break for it: José Chávez y Chávez, law student Harvey Morris, and Bill Bonney were in the first wave. Others followed, including Jim French. They ran first for the Tunstall building, hoping the roar of the fire and the dense smoke would conceal their movements. But as they sprinted across the open ground toward the store they were backlit by the flames and the posse opened fire. Not only that. According to Bonney and Chávez y Chávez, three uniformed soldiers joined the fusillade.

Morris was hit. The others gave up all hope of reaching the store and veered for the river, plunging into the underbrush. There was no pursuit.

Concentrated fire from the posse and soldiers pinned down the remaining McSween men. The house was almost completely consumed. McSween and the rest hid behind the last remaining wall, flames at their back, John Kinney's posse and U.S. soldiers in front. Escape was impossible. Fifteen minutes after the first group made its break, McSween called out that he surrendered.

McSween, Zamora, and Romero were the first three to emerge from the burning building into the yard. Deputy Beckwith, armed with the warrants, stepped forward to arrest the men.

Beckwith, trying to do his duty, thought the plan was to arrest McSween. He was mistaken. It was a firing squad. McSween was hit five times. Zamora and Romero were also killed. One of the McSween men got off a shot that hit Beckwith in the eye, killing him instantly. The surviving McSween men fled to the riverbed and escaped.[45]

John Kinney's men broke into the Tunstall store. In the morning, Tunstall's loyal clerk Sam Corbet arrived at the store in time to see Jesse Evans, newly released from the custody of the fort, in his underclothes, trying on a new suit.[46] Ex-Justice of the Peace Easton called Sheriff Peppin, who declared himself powerless to prevent the looting. Easton boarded up the windows and the door, but shortly afterward the store was broken into again. Lieutenant Colonel Dudley was present at least part of the time.[47]

Sometime during that summer's morning, Dudley strolled from the store to the spot where McSween's house had stood. The fire had died out; the house was ashes. Dudley told the court of inquiry:

> I saw the body of McSween lying in the yard of the McSween house. Two or three chickens were around the body pecking at it. I drove them away myself and ordered a bed quilt that was lying in the yard spread over the body.[48]

McSween's body was covered with a quilt looted from Tunstall's store. The Lincoln County War was over.

Part Three

THE KID

*Anything that the
imagination can
concoct in the way of
murders and desperate
deeds may be heard
upon the streets now in
regard to Billy the Kid,
but getting at the truth
of the many rumors is
another thing altogether.*
The Daily New Mexican
May 5, 1881

The End of the Regulators

24

Members of John Kinney's Rio Grande Posse had a different explanation for McSween's death. Andy Boyle claimed that a few minutes after McSween called out that he surrendered, he suddenly yelled, "I shall never surrender!" and his men opened fire. Of course, the posse had no choice but to fire back.[1]

Boyle had good reason to lie: by torching the McSween house and then joining in the shooting, he made himself eligible for the death penalty unless the killings were done in self-defense.

In any case, if McSween decided at the last second not to give up, it was because he feared being killed immediately upon surrendering.

On one side, McSween, Zamora, Morris, and Romero were killed, and Salazar and González were wounded (Salazar lay in the yard feigning death even as John Kinney kicked him). On the other side, only Bob Beckwith was shot. *The Albuquerque Review* commented, "The death of so many men where only one of their assailants, Beckwith, is reported killed, indicates that foul play had in all probability been resorted to."[2] It seems clear who used the element of surprise.

Dudley's military success created a black hole where Lincoln County's civil authorities used to be. Peppin, who hid in the *torreón* while his posse killed four men, had no stomach for law enforcement. Once John Kinney returned to take care of business in Doña Ana County and the Seven Rivers men went back to their homes on the Pecos, Peppin found himself uncomfortably alone. He hied himself to the post contractor's slaughterhouse, lying low and learning the butcher's trade, sheriff in name only until his defeat in the November elections.

Like any vacuum, this absence of any effective law enforcement sucked in stray particles from all around. John Selman, who later had himself elected marshal of El Paso and killed John Wesley Hardin, was, in 1878, making a career on the other side of the law. Hearing there was fun to be had in Lincoln County, he drifted in from Texas and hooked up with a number of like-minded fellows, who formed themselves into an organization peculiarly dubbed "the Wrestlers."[3]

Robert Utley speculates that many of the Wrestlers were veterans of the Rio Grande Posse who had been promised the Tunstall herd as compensation for services rendered.[4] Whether or not there was an explicit quid pro quo, they helped themselves.

The Wrestlers didn't stop there. For two months they rode around Lincoln County doing whatever they liked. It was a period of random violence, related to the highly purposeful fighting of the Lincoln County War only by proximity in time, closely analogous to the period of looting that follows the passage of an invading army in more conventional wars. Farmers were shot in their fields for target practice. Women were raped. Judge Bristol couldn't hold the October term of court because he couldn't find sufficient men to serve as jurors.[5]

The New York Times ran its first news story on the violence in Lincoln County in late summer, a description of the outrages of the Wrestlers.[6] The barbarity of the Wrestlers fit comfortably with New Yorkers' dime-novel image of the western frontier. All that had gone before, which didn't fit that image quite so neatly, had been ignored. *The Times* added a word of thanksgiving that New Mexico, home to "a handful of uneasy, wandering and lawless people . . . mostly Mexicans and other mixed races," had not been admitted into the union.

On the night of McSween's death, Bill Bonney and his surviving comrades made their way on foot across the river and into the hills, where they met up with the remaining Regulators. Their first task was to find horses for Bonney and Tom O'Folliard. This is the first of only two times we know for certain that Billy the Kid stole livestock after his arrival in Lincoln County.[7]

The newest Regulators – those Hispanic farmers from San Patricio and surrounding villages who had become involved only in reaction to the excesses of John Kinney's men – faded away. Continued association with such men as Bonney was only likely to attract the wrong sort of attention.

Besides, there was no purpose to continued association. A dwindling band called the Regulators continued to exist only because it was too dangerous for the best known of the men to go home. Some, such as Bonney, had no home. Reduced to a core of Bonney, Bowdre, Scurlock, Frank and George Coe, Henry Brown, John Middleton, Fred Waite, Tom O'Folliard, and sometimes joined by a few others, the Regulators became a mutual aid society dedicated to keeping each other alive.

By the end of August they were in Fort Sumner on the northern stretches of the Pecos in San Miguel County. There they discovered they were celebrities. The Las Vegas newspapers had covered every move in the Lincoln County War, and the citizens of Fort Sumner knew all their names. Attention focused on the teenaged Kid, who stepped off the front pages into the dusty streets speaking fluent Spanish. The fighting had already passed into folklore; the Regulators' defeat made them more romantic, for their struggle had been doomed from the start. The days and nights in Fort Sumner became one long farewell party.

But the dolce vita could not last forever. The romantic mood had its source in the shared knowledge that the Regulators had reached the end of the road. Frank and George Coe were the first to go, heading for the San Juan River valley in northwestern New Mexico. Bowdre and Scurlock took jobs as cowboys for Pete Maxwell, whose family had sold Catron the fabulous Maxwell Land Grant. Bonney, O'Folliard, Brown, Waite, and Middleton crossed the border into the Texas Panhandle, safely beyond the reach of New Mexican law.

Lieutenant Colonel Dudley had legal problems of his own. He cleverly fired a preemptive strike, informing his superiors in Santa Fe on August 10 that he had not received an official interpretation of the Posse Comitatus Act.[8] No doubt it is possible to parse this statement in a way that makes it truthful. If pressed on the point, Dudley might have claimed he only meant that he hadn't received a detailed legal memorandum. But of course he knew about the Posse Comitatus Act: he sent a soldier to recall Captain Carroll to the fort in response to passage of the act. Even before, he knew that the War Department's lawyer had ruled that his use of troops in Lincoln County was illegal.

Colonel Hatch's staff knew that Dudley knew. An August 15 letter reminded him of the earlier orders to suspend operations, informed him that he was not authorized to act as he had, and concluded, "This use of Troops is entirely illegal and must be stopped immediately." Dudley replied, "I regret my wrong interpretation of [the Act] but am glad to receive so positive an order as the one contained in yours of the 15th."[9]

His free-lancing was just a technical dispute about an abstract question of law; his sarcasm dared Colonel Hatch to do something about it.

Morris J. Bernstein was the clerk of the Mescalero Apache Agency, working for the corrupt Major Godfroy. On the side, he kept the House's books.[10] Like another clerk, Rob Widenmann, he seems not to have known when to keep his mouth shut. When Dr. Blazer, owner of Blazer's Mill, gave a sworn statement alleging corruption at the agency, Bernstein called him a liar. Dr. Blazer declared, in front of witnesses, that nobody could call him a liar and live. Bernstein refused to back down and threats were made back and forth. The two men agreed to fight to settle their differences.[11]

During the next day or two, Dr. Blazer made dark remarks to Major Godfroy, suggesting the wisdom of firing Bernstein without delay. And then, two or three days after Dr. Blazer threatened to kill him, Bernstein was killed. When asked about his whereabouts at the time of the killing, Dr. Blazer said he had heard gunshots and so climbed, by himself, to a secure room at the top of one of the buildings, where no one could see him.

Since troops were at the agency at the time Bernstein was shot, Dudley assigned Captain Blair to investigate the matter. Blair reported that Dr. Blazer "neither expressed surprise nor regret at the murder of Mr. Bernstein, nor sympathy for his friends. He also insinuated to me that Mr. Bernstein had frequently tampered with his letters. I consider the life of Major Godfroy in very great danger." Therefore, Blair concluded, he could only agree with Major Godfroy that the culprit was the Spanish Inquisition.

Actually, they both blamed the murder on the surviving Regulators, but the evidence implicating the Spanish Inquisition was at least as strong. There were no witnesses placing any of the Regulators within twenty miles of the agency, there was no physical evidence linking them to the crime, and they had no motive to kill Bernstein.

It isn't hard to understand why Major Godfroy, anxious to regain his position on Dr. Blazer's good side, chose to blame his subordinate's death on phantom villains. Captain Blair's report is more puzzling. After assembling a remorseless sequence of circumstantial evidence allowing of just one conclusion, Blair reaches a different one, as if the end of a different report had been pasted to his pages.

The New Mexican published a joint statement by Dudley and Peppin, squarely placing blame for Bernstein's death on the Regulators.[12] But Peppin, working in the slaughterhouse, was hardly in a position to know about the matter. And Dudley's public statement was contradicted by his private report that "in my judgment, the whole trouble at the Agency on the 5th was brought about by the continual personal misunderstandings between Dr. Blazer, Bernstein and Godfroy." Dudley added, without elaboration, "The conduct of Major Godfroy has been so singularly strange since the 5th."[13]

It would appear, then, that both Dudley and Peppin concluded it was useful to depict the Regulators as cold-blooded killers for reasons unrelated to their knowledge of the circumstances of Bernstein's death. One such reason might have been the circumstances of McSween's death. Seen in this light, Captain Blair's non sequitur conclusion makes perfect sense: that's the way his commanding officer wanted it.

One imagines no one called Dr. Blazer a liar again.[14]

The ongoing carnage in Lincoln added urgency to Special Agent Angel's investigation. In early August, Angel submitted to the United States attorney, Thomas B. Catron, a packet of affidavits and deposition testimony concerning his conduct in office, particularly his involvement in Lincoln and Colfax counties. Angel asked Catron to respond to the evidence.

Catron, a good lawyer, immediately went into a stall. He asked Angel to distill specific written questions from the mass of evidence. Angel complied (Catron later acknowledged Angel's "gentlemanly and courteous manner"), drafting detailed interrogatories and giving Catron thirty days to respond. Catron then asked for sixty days.[15]

When Angel balked, Catron went over his head, writing a four-page letter to Attorney General Devens, delivered by his old partner Elkins. Catron's letter argued that thirty days was an unreasonably short time to answer the interrogatories. Catron would have to drop everything to defend himself, resulting in "very great pecuniary loss to myself and clients."[16]

Devens found it difficult to sympathize with a rich man who was reluctant to spend money in his own defense, and it probably didn't help that Catron spelled his name "Devins." His chief clerk wrote a single-sentence response: "Attorney General replies to your letter 19th ultimo, presented yesterday by Elkins, that you have had ample opportunity to answer charges and no extension of time can be granted."[17]

Catron, as always, was persistent. On September 13 and again on September 17, he wrote to Devens, informing him he had mailed his interrogatory answers and supporting affidavits to Angel. Catron asked again for an extension of the deadline to allow him to gather additional evidence. This time he appealed to Devens's political instincts, arguing that Angel's investigation was threatening the Republican stranglehold on New Mexico politics in an election year.

Unfortunately for Catron, his only bargaining chip was the promise of continued political control of a remote and unimportant territory, a matter of far greater interest to him than to Devens. Moreover, Devens had little room to maneuver. His Justice Department was being pressured by the State Department, which in turn was being pressured by the British ambassador, who refused to allow the question of Tunstall's murder to fade without an answer.

Also, the very reason Angel was sent to New Mexico was to make good Catron's dereliction of duty. Devens explained this point in a letter to Secretary of State Evarts enclosing Angel's final report:

Upon being advised by you that your attention had been called by the British Minister to the killing of Tunstall, I immediately directed the United States Attorney for New Mexico to institute thorough inquiry and report to me.

It not appearing that that officer had at once undertaken such investigation, an agent of this Department was sent to the Territory, charged among other duties, with that of specially learning all the particulars of the murder as well as the causes which led to the same.[18]

Only after the Justice Department engaged a special agent to do Catron's job did the reason for Catron's inaction become clear: he was involved up to his ears. Given a chance to defend himself against charges of corruption, Catron asked for a delay so that exposure of his misdeeds would not cost him either financially or politically.

The denouement was inevitable. On October 10, Catron wrote Devens, "In accordance with a purpose long entertained, I hereby tender my resignation as United States Attorney for New Mexico, to take effect November 10th 1878."

The story of Angel's investigation of Catron does not end there. Angel filed a report concluding that Catron, profiting from his reputation as the foremost American authority on Spanish and Mexican land grants, had fraudulently assured a purchaser that a transparently fake Mexican deed was genuine. In return he received a share of the purchase price. Angel's report on the oddly named *Uña de Gato* (Cat's Claw) grant was submitted to the attorney general, who passed it on to the Department of the Interior, which loaned it out to the Division of Lands and Railroads, where the paper trail ends.[19]

To understand the disappearance of the report, we have to fast forward to 1893, when Catron was in the midst of his carefully planned political comeback. His mentor and former partner Stephen Elkins was secretary of war for lame duck President Benjamin Harrison. Catron was concerned that the new Democratic administration might make Angel's report public, discrediting him anew.

Catron's biographer, Victor Westphall, writes, "Catron requested that Elkins secure the report and destroy it. Elkins replied that he had caused diligent search to be made in the attorney general's department for Angel's report but that it could not be found."[20]

Maybe Elkins just looked in the wrong place. Or perhaps the report was innocently lost. But a politician of Elkins's silkiness would never admit in writing that he had destroyed government records. Whatever the full explanation for the missing report, we can be sure Catron breathed easier knowing it could not be found, like a man whose wish had been granted.

Ben-Hur

25

Special Agent Angel also presented the governor with a list of thirty-one questions. Emulating his "good friend," Axtell asked for an extension of time. Angel gave him the thirty days he requested, but in the end Axtell never exactly answered. He gave a copy of Angel's questions to *The (Santa Fe) Rocky Mountain Sentinel* with his response, and then sent a copy of the newspaper article to Angel in New York. His response was a mixture of bluster and lies. Angel asked, "Have you acted under and by the advice of Hon. T. B. Catron, U.S. District Attorney, in the issuing of your proclamations as to the Lincoln County troubles, knowing that said Catron has large interests at stake in said County?" One thinks immediately of Catron's letter asking the governor to protect his stake in Dolan's cow camp, and Brady's telegram to Catron asking him to see the governor, which the governor forwarded to President Hayes. But Axtell replied with haughty insouciance, "The questions relating to Hon. T. B. Catron are also easily disposed of. I have received no letters from him."[1]

Axtell also claimed he did not remove Justice Wilson from office ("he was not in office"), defended his appointment of Peppin, explained away the involvement of Jesse Evans and the Boys, explained some more about John Kinney, admitted borrowing $1,800 from Riley, and all but conceded his involvement in the Colfax County murder plot. In short, he confirmed most of the charges against him.[2]

Axtell was a patronage pol to the tips of his well-greased fingers and assumed everyone else was, too. He could think of only one reason why Interior Secretary Schurz might want to get rid of him: he "evidently wants the place for some friend of his."[3]

Axtell wrote Collis Huntington, from whom he had accepted bribes for years, that there wasn't a single blot against his integrity. Wishing to err on the side of caution, however, he also asked Huntington to intercede with Secretary of State Evarts to "modify" Angel's report before it was filed. "This Evarts can have done, as those men are his men."[4] All to no avail.

Axtell's replacement, Lew Wallace, was to the political manner born. His father was successively Indiana's governor and congressman while his uncle was governor of Idaho and Washington and congressional delegate from both territories. His brother-in-law became Indiana's governor and later United States senator.[5]

At the outbreak of the Civil War, Wallace raised his own regiment and became its colonel. He dressed his soldiers in Zouave uniforms, whose flowing vivid colors reflected his romantic yearning for glory. His rank was a more cynical emblem: it revealed his political connections.

Nonetheless Wallace succeeded in covering himself with glory at Fort Donelson, rallying his troops by riding along the line shouting, "You have been wanting a fight; you have got it. Hell's before you!"[6] A 1863 narrative of the war thus far contains this index entry: "Wallace, Gen., heroic struggles of."[7] For his efforts Wallace was promoted, becoming the Union's youngest major general.

Then came Shiloh. In his late novel *The Prince of India,* Wallace wrote, "How many there are who spend their youth yearning and fighting to write their names in history, then spend their old age shuddering to read them there!"[8] He was writing about himself. He never lived down the fame he won at Shiloh, when he took all day to move his regiment five miles from camp to the battlefield. Grant and Sherman made him the scapegoat for the battle's carnage, and Wallace never again held an important field command.[9]

After a lengthy leave, he was placed in charge of the defenses at Cincinnati, where he took the unusual but effective step of declaring martial law and suspending commercial activity in order to throw all available resources into defense of the city. The power to rule by fiat appealed to Wallace; he later sought to declare martial law in New Mexico.

Wallace made a career of serving on commissions – he could be counted on to convict. He was part of the tribunal that found Major General D. C. Buell incompetent in command at the Battle of Perryville. He convicted John Wilkes Booth's conspirators, four of whom were executed two days after the verdict came down, limiting their right of appeal. He presided over the commission investigating atrocities at the Andersonville prisoner-of-war camp in Georgia, whose Swiss commandant was speedily sent to the gallows.

In the 1876 presidential election, Rutherford B. Hayes lost the popular vote to Samuel Tilden. The Republican party needed help, so it named Lew Wallace to the commission supervising recounts in Louisiana and Florida. The commission converted thin Tilden victories to solid Hayes majorities by disqualifying a disproportionate share of Democratic ballots.

The scandal of the stolen election stank up Washington for the four years of the Hayes administration. Wallace was dragged into the mire when Samuel McLin, a member of Florida's canvassing board, claimed that Wallace had promised him political favors in return for adjusting vote totals.[10] Wallace denied it. He had made no promises. He'd simply pointed out that the party looked after its loyal soldiers – and then recommended McLin for a federal judgeship in New Mexico. Hayes forwarded the nomination to the Senate.

But the Senate, showing its contempt for a weak president, defeated the nomination. Meanwhile, Wallace expected his labors to be rewarded, too, and at Hayes's request modestly expressed interest in serving as minister at a "second-class" station such as Italy, Brazil, Spain, or Mexico.[11] But Hayes was spooked by the McLin debacle. He gave Wallace nothing.

Months later, the president offered Wallace the ambassadorship to Bolivia. Nettled by the long delay, Wallace said no. The salary was too low, he explained, to justify moving his family. The real reason was pride.

A couple of weeks later, he became governor of New Mexico. *The Grant County Herald* commented, "General Lew Wallace must have a position for services rendered."[12]

The Wallaces lived in Santa Fe's Palace of the Governors, a crumbling adobe rabbit warren of interconnected rooms that offered plenty of quiet for undisturbed composition. Wallace's wife, Susan, wrote an engaging memoir of New Mexico that compared its landscape to the Holy Land: "It is all like the old Bible pictures."[13] The comparison could hardly have been lost upon her husband, whose landscape descriptions – composed without benefit of travel to Palestine – comprise some of the most vivid passages of *Ben-Hur*.

Even before assuming office, Wallace solicited reports from Colonel

Hatch, Judge Bristol, and Marshal Sherman concerning the troubles in Lincoln County. On October 5, 1878, just three days after taking office, he was able to tell Secretary Schurz exactly what needed to be done:

> In my judgement nothing remains for me to do except call upon the President to exercise his constitutional authority and declare the existence of insurrection in the County of Lincoln, place the county without loss of time under martial law, suspend the writ of habeas corpus therein and appoint a military commission to come and hold sessions there for the trial and punishment of offenders.[14]

In other words, Wallace wanted to recreate the conditions of his wartime service. Two days after receiving this telegram, President Hayes issued a proclamation that began with a dramatic drumroll:

> WHEREAS, it has been made to appear to me that by reason of unlawful combinations and assemblages of persons in arms, it has become impracticable to enforce, by the ordinary course of judicial proceedings, the laws of the United States within the Territory of New Mexico, and especially within Lincoln County therein; and that the laws of the United States have been therein forcibly opposed and the execution thereof forcibly resisted.[15]

But this elaborate windup exhausted the president, and perhaps it was just as well that he contented himself with officially "admonishing" the citizens of Lincoln County to cut it out: "I do hereby warn all persons engaged in or connected with said obstruction of the laws to disperse and return peaceably to their respective abodes on or before noon of the thirteenth day of October, instant."

Wallace didn't get what he wanted, but he made the best of what he got. After thirty days he assured Secretary of the Interior Schurz that "there has been no instance of violence" in Lincoln County since the proclamation was issued. He concluded that

> the people might be in a state of mind to avail themselves of amnesty for the past, and begin anew. It is easy to see now, without something of the kind, the vendetta spirit which has marked the outbreak might go on indefinitely. Accordingly I have this day issued a proclamation announcing the end of the disturbances, invit-

ing peaceably disposed citizens who have been driven away to return to their homes, and offering a general pardon, the latter carefully worded in expression and limitation.[16]

Wallace's November 13, 1878, amnesty proclamation optimistically declared that "the disorders . . . have been happily brought to an end" and pardoned all crimes committed between February 1 and November 13, 1878. The pardon was limited to two classes of citizens:

> It shall not apply except to officers of the United States Army stationed in [Lincoln] County during the said disorders, and to persons who, at the time of the commission of the offense or misdemeanor of which they may be accused were with good intent, resident citizens of the said Territory, and who shall have hereafter kept the peace, and conducted themselves in all respects as becomes good citizens.[17]

The pardon did not apply to pending prosecutions. Those already under indictment, such as Bill Bonney, were not off the hook.

The Mesilla Valley Independent, which in other circumstances might have warmly supported a reformist governor, observed that peace had not, in fact, descended on Lincoln and suggested that Wallace pretended otherwise merely to speed his Senate confirmation and avoid another McLin debacle.[18]

In the same issue in which it printed the amnesty proclamation, *The Mesilla News* labeled it "a libel on the gallant officers" of Fort Stanton, since it implied that they needed to be pardoned. Wallace wrote to Dudley, asking him if he had read the article in *The News*: The editor "goes for me in grand style because I presumed to include officers of the Army in the terms of my amnesty. I had a good reason for that, by the way, which I will explain when I see you." It was months before he got the chance to explain his good reason: he had learned that Sue McSween intended to press murder and arson charges against Colonel Dudley. Wallace, believing he had done Dudley a favor, signed his letter "Your friend."[19]

Encouraged by *The News,* however, Dudley had already acquired a smoldering sense of grievance that he nursed into a firestorm. On the very day that Wallace wrote his friendly letter, Dudley composed a letter of his own, an open letter to Wallace that he published in the Santa Fe

Ring—controlled *Weekly New Mexican.* "I am aware that it is not within the province of an officer of the Army, to make suggestions to a civil functionary, occupying the high position held by yourself, much less criticize his official course," Dudley wrote, then proceeded to do so at great length. Dudley criticized the governor for making "false and unjust accusations" against him personally and against "the gallant officers of my command" by implying, however indirectly, that they might have done something for which they needed to be pardoned. On behalf of himself and his officers, Dudley defiantly refused to accept the offer of amnesty.[20]

The colonel was reduced to misty-eyed incoherence as he described his role in Lincoln County: "Wherever the colored cavalry have made their appearance, doors that have for weeks and months been barred and barricaded, windows have been opened for a few hours, husbands and sons have enjoyed the luxury of a night's rest at their homes, whenever troops have camped a single night near their ranches."

Wallace hadn't intended to insult Dudley, but Dudley certainly intended to insult him. The two men, who had never met, became mortal enemies.[21]

Chapman in Battle

26

In biographical briefing papers he prepared for Lew Wallace, Special Agent Angel had this to say about Sue McSween: "Sharp woman – now that her husband is dead a tiger."[1] Wallace's amnesty proclamation was intended to usher in a new era of good feeling, but Sue was in no mood to forgive and forget. She knew, better than most, that her husband had been murdered, and she knew which lieutenant colonel was responsible.

Sue McSween took temporary refuge in Las Vegas with her sister and her sister's family. Once in Las Vegas, however, she sought out a lawyer to keep the fight going (her brother-in-law, David Shield, an ordained Presbyterian minister, had too much sense). She found Huston Chapman.

Never did a lawyer more clearly perform the role of hired gun. Chapman's job was to make Colonel Dudley's life miserable. He threw himself into the job with a pugnacious enthusiasm that suggests he failed to grasp how easily he could share McSween's fate.

On October 24, Chapman wrote a letter to Governor Wallace claiming that he was "in possession of facts which make Col. Dudley criminally responsible for the killing of McSween, and he has threatened that in case martial law was proclaimed that he would arrest Mrs. McSween and her friends immediately. Through fear of his threat Mrs. McSween left Lincoln."[2]

There was more in this vein, all of it essentially true but conveyed in a highly colored style that invited incredulity. Wallace (not yet the target of Dudley's broadside in *The Weekly New Mexican,* and counting on Dudley to enact his plan to impose martial law) sent a copy of Chapman's letter to Colonel Hatch with a note saying the accusations "strike me as incredible." At Wallace's request, Hatch sent a copy to Dudley, which Dudley inevitably saw as an act of aggression. Dudley warned Wallace: "I am prepared to defend myself from any and all attacks, coming from whatever source they may," a not-very-veiled reference to Wallace himself. Wallace's reply was studiedly calm, assuring Dudley that "the indignation you showed was not displeasing to me, but rather the reverse. I think the same charges against me, if untrue, would have moved me in the same way."[3]

Nonetheless, Wallace must have been startled by the manner in which Dudley chose to defend himself. The governor couldn't have known how characteristic it was. At his Fort Union court-martial, Dudley obtained a third party's statement that Colonel Hatch hated him because Hatch was corrupt and Dudley wasn't. Faced with accusations made by Sue McSween's attorney, Dudley once again adopted the "best defense" strategy, submitting third-party statements attacking Sue exactly the way one would expect an unmarried middle-aged Victorian military man to attack a woman he didn't like: he claimed she was a "lewd bad woman." Sheriff Peppin swore that he "witnessed her in actual criminal contact with a well known citizen of Lincoln County, this in the spring of 1877." A twenty-year-old named Francisco Gómez, who was probably illiterate in English, swore that "Mrs. McSween persisted in advances" of a "palpably lewd and libidinous manner" until he succumbed "in the brush near the river." Peppin, a busy voyeur, added that he had been "forced to witness" Sue and Gómez romping on the riverbank, and that "Mrs. McSween's lascivious conduct towards Francisco Gómez . . . was too disgusting to relate." Saturnino Baca, who later testified that he could speak "only few words" of English, signed an affidavit that repeated, word for word, passages from Peppin's statement. Baca's affidavit said that he had "heard Mrs. McSween charged to her face, and in the public street, and in the presence of her husband, A. A. McSween, with having come from a house of ill-repute to Lincoln." Jack Long, the would-be arsonist who was standing knee deep in human excrement when McSween was murdered, and who had solemnly promised not to help hang Reverend Ealy, complained that Sue was "both profane and vulgar." And so on.[4]

Chapman, whose fatal flaw was an unreasoning refusal to give in to fear, was not cowed. His father provided one explanation for his son's blind tenacity: "On account of an accident in his early youth our son lost one arm. . . . He spurned the idea that he could not accomplish with one hand anything that others could do with two."[5]

Long accustomed to bucking the odds, Chapman pressed his fight against Sue's enemies. In November, he and Sue traveled to Lincoln, where he managed to antagonize almost everyone. He bombarded Wallace with complaints about the army, and about Wallace himself. Much as Colonel Dudley had done in his open letter, Chapman wrote, "You will pardon me for presuming to advise you," and then did so vehemently, castigating the governor for not traveling to Lincoln to see for himself the deplorable state of affairs brought about by the lawless actions of the military, who rousted citizens from bed in the middle of the night and left them deep in the woods dressed only in their nightshirts, prevented other citizens from voting, and caroused drunkenly through town with sheriff's deputies, firing their guns in the air. Chapman added, "I have advised the citizens here to shoot any officer who shall in any manner attempt their arrest, or interfere with their rights."[6]

In mid-December, events in Lincoln took a decidedly surrealistic turn. On December 13, Lieutenant French was ordered into town to search for Dudley's bugbear, Doc Scurlock. Late that evening he knocked at the door of a Hispanic couple named de Guebare. When they asked who was there, French unconvincingly replied in pidgin Spanish, "Una amigo." The de Guebares understandably declined to open the door, prompting French to begin kicking it in. One of the soldiers with him was able to speak Spanish and tell the de Guebares they were military men, and the door was opened. Lieutenant French then sat before the fire, playing with his revolver, asking about Scurlock in a rambling, confusing way. He removed a cartridge from his gun, pried it apart, and held it up to Mr. de Guebare's nose, asking, "See how nice the powder smells?"[7]

At one point when Mrs. de Guebare spoke, Lieutenant French told her to shut up. He pointed the gun at Mr. de Guebare and seemed to be drunk. But after a while he left with his company of soldiers. They headed down the street to the former home of Saturnino Baca, where Sue McSween and her attorney were staying. Once inside the house, French waved his pistol around and declared he was a better lawyer than Chapman. When Chapman refused to be intimidated, giving back as good as he got, French abruptly tore off his tunic and blouse, shouting, "God damn you, Sir, you have got to fight me!" He called for his men to tie one of his arms behind him to make it a fair fight.

In December, Will Dowlin, harvesting the field planted by Tunstall and McSween, bought the House. Tom Catron had loaned the House at least $23,000, but Dowlin took the premises off his hands for just $3,000. Two years later, Dowlin sold the building to the county for use as a courthouse for $15,000.[8] So Catron's name must be added to the long list of those who lost the Lincoln County War.

Also in December, the bodies of two members of John Kinney's Rio Grande Posse were found along the trail from Lincoln to Las Cruces. The men had been shot. Their killer was never located.[9]

That same month, coincidentally or not, Bill Bonney returned to Lincoln County, but we have no record of his movements until February 18, the anniversary of John Tunstall's death. On that day he met with Jimmy Dolan and Jesse Evans to negotiate a treaty. The Kid wanted peace.[10]

According to Lieutenant Colonel Dudley, who claimed to have seen the letter, Bonney sent written word to Evans proposing a truce. Evans agreed to talk. The two men, each accompanied by several companions, arrived after dark at the prearranged place, hiding behind adobe walls on opposite sides of the street. Bonney and Evans shouted back and forth until finally, prepared to trust each other at least that much, they stepped into the street and met face to face.

Evans couldn't resist saying something to the effect that he ought to shoot Bonney right then and there. It wasn't a matter of temper or even hostility exactly: it was just Evans's style to push, to see how far he could go. Bonney, like Dick Brewer before him, wasn't easily scared – which was probably all Evans wanted to know.

Bonney was accompanied by Tom O'Folliard, and Eugenio Salazar, the man who feigned death in McSween's yard even as John Kinney kicked him, and by a character named Joe Bowers, who may also have been inside the burning McSween house.

On his side, Evans had Jimmy Dolan, Billy Mathews, and a man known as Billy Campbell. Campbell, a newcomer to Lincoln County (perhaps one of the Wrestlers), was a large man and a mean drunk, violent and impulsive. *The Daily New Mexican* reported, ridiculously, that he "was probably the notorious Jesse James," thereby giving birth to the weirdly persistent legend of a summit meeting between America's two most celebrated outlaws.[11]

The agreement reached was straight to the point: the fighting would end and none of the parties would testify against any of the others, on pain of death. It was mutual obstruction of justice.

The Lincoln County War would never have been fought if Evans, Dolan, Bonney, and the rest were able to focus on their long-term self-interest. If Bonney's only motivation was the avoidance of trouble, he would have stayed in Texas. The truly self-interested citizens of Lincoln County were the wagonloads who bolted for the horizon.

Something beyond pure practicality was behind the antagonists' decision to make peace. And that something else is as obvious as the dangers they had faced for the previous 365 days: they were tired of fighting.

Except for the newcomer Campbell. Campbell hadn't been around for most of the bloodshed and apparently regretted his tardiness.

After the ceremonial signing of the treaty, Evans and Dolan broke out the whiskey. Bonney, who (it's true) never drank, was the only sober one in the group. Many others joined in the celebration, so that perhaps twenty armed cowboys (plus Bonney) were sloshing drunkenly up and down Lincoln's single street that anniversary night.

In the course of the celebrations they met Juan Patrón. Campbell pulled out his gun and pointed it at Patrón. Patrón, however, had not survived this long without acquiring a certain nimbleness. He dove for cover. Campbell was quickly calmed down by his buddies, but the peace treaty was already violated.

About ten o'clock, Huston Chapman ventured into the street. According to a letter signed "Max," which appeared in *The Las Cruces Thirty-Four,* Chapman "went to a neighbor's to get some bread to make a poultice for his face. He was suffering from a severe case of neuralgia."

Returning home, Chapman bumped into the carousers. Someone, probably Campbell, demanded to know who Chapman was. Chapman told them. Campbell pulled out his pistol and pressed it to Chapman's chest. According to later courtroom testimony, Campbell actually delivered that two-reeler villain's line: "Then you dance."

Surrounded by drunken cowboys, a pistol to his chest, suffering from facial pain severe enough to warrant a bandage of wet bread, Chapman irrationally refused to give in to fear. "Max" quotes Chapman as saying, "You cannot scare me, boys. I know you and it's no use. You have tried that before."

The version given in the later courtroom testimony is different. In that version, Chapman asks, "Am I talking to Mr. Dolan?"

Jesse Evans answers, "No, but you're talking to a damned good friend of his."

Dolan stood behind Chapman, holding his Winchester rifle. He fired. Campbell shot, too – at such close range that the flaming powder ignited Chapman's clothes. Either that or, as "Max" had it, Campbell poured whiskey on the body and set it afire. Lincoln's inhabitants were too frightened to extinguish the blaze; *The Mesilla Valley Independent* reported that Chapman was burnt "to a crisp."

Dolan's role in the murder remains uncertain, perhaps because Dolan himself couldn't remember. At first he denied any knowledge of Chapman's death, then he admitted being with the killers but denied firing any shots, then he admitted firing into the ground to distract the group.[12] But others said he shot Chapman.

According to some witnesses, Campbell boasted, "I promised God and Colonel Dudley that I would kill Chapman, and I have done it."

Chapman's murder finally convinced the governor that his presence was needed in Lincoln. He arrived in town two weeks after the killing. Colonel Hatch happened to be at Fort Stanton on a tour of inspection of the forts in his realm at the same time. Wallace persuaded him to transfer Dudley to Fort Union, near Las Vegas. Wallace next met with Lincoln's citizens to hear their grievances. He then organized a voluntary militia called the Lincoln County Mounted Rifles and placed it under the command of Juan Patrón. He compiled a list of thirty-five desperadoes – including Evans, Dolan, Campbell, Bonney, and O'Folliard – and instructed Fort Stanton's new commander, Captain Henry Carroll, to work with Patrón to round them up.

Bonney and O'Folliard gave the captain the slip, but Evans, Campbell, and Dolan were quickly incarcerated at the fort. The governor turned his energies to convincing the citizens that they ought to testify to what they knew. The citizens were, not unreasonably, reluctant to do so. Wallace had reached the familiar impasse: he had his criminals in custody, but no one to testify against them.[13]

And then he received this letter:

To his Excellency the Governor,
Gen. Lew Wallace,

March 13, 1879

Dear Sir

I have heard that you will give one thousand dollars for my body which as I can understand it means alive as a witness. I know it is as a witness against those that murdered Mr. Chapman. If it was so as that I could appear at Court I could give the desired information, but I have indictments against me for things that happened in the late Lincoln County War and am afraid to give up because my enemies would kill me. The day Mr. Chapman was murdered I was in Lincoln at the request of good citizens to meet Mr. J. J. Dolan to meet as friends, so as to be able to lay aside our arms and go to work. I was present when Mr. Chapman was murdered and know who did it, and if it were not for those indictments I would have made it clear before now. If it is in your power to annul those indictments I hope you will do so as to give me a chance to explain. Please send me an answer telling me what you can do. You can send answer by bearer. I have no wish to fight any more, indeed I have not raised an arm since your proclamation. As to my character, I refer to any of the citizens, for the majority of them are my friends and have been helping me all they could. I am called Kid Antrim but Antrim is my stepfather's name.

Waiting an answer, I remain,
Your obedient servant,
W. H. Bonney[14]

Wallace responded with his own note, dated March 15, which reveals his fondness for the mechanics of conspiracy, so similar in their intricacy to nineteenth-century potboilers:

Come to the house of old Squire Wilson (not the lawyer) at nine (9) o'clock next Monday night alone. I don't mean his office, but his residence. Follow along the foot of the mountain south of the town, come in on that side and knock at the east door. I have authority to exempt you from prosecution if you will testify to what you say you know.

The object of the meeting at Squire Wilson's is to arrange the

matter in a way to make your life safe. To do that the utmost se-
crecy is to be used. *So come alone.* Don't tell anybody – not a living
soul – where you are coming or the object. If you could trust Jesse
Evans, you can trust me.

At the time of the meeting Bonney meant nothing to Wallace except as
a witness to Chapman's murder. Years later, however, when Wallace recalled the meeting in a newspaper interview, the Kid's nickname was as
well known as it remains today. The dreary task of lining up testimony
for a criminal prosecution had been magically transformed into a story
to dine out on.

Wallace provided the interviewer with a polished anecdote:

Billy the Kid kept the appointment punctually. At the time designated, I heard a knock at the door, and I called out, "Come in." The
door opened somewhat slowly and carefully, and there stood the
young fellow generally known as the Kid, his Winchester in his
right hand, his revolver in his left.

"I was sent for to meet the governor here at 9 o'clock," said the
Kid. "Is he here?" I rose to my feet, saying, "I am Governor Wallace," and held out my hand. When we had shaken hands, I invited
the young fellow to be seated so that we might talk together. "Your
note gave promise of absolute protection," said the young outlaw
warily. "Yes," I replied, "and I have been true to my promise," and
then pointing to Squire Wilson, who was the only person in the
room with me, I added, "This man, whom of course you know, and
I are the only persons in the house."

This seemed to satisfy the Kid, for he lowered his rifle and returned his revolver to its holster. When he had taken his seat, I proceeded to unfold the plan I had in mind to enable him to testify to
what he knew about the killing of Chapman at the forthcoming
session of court two or three weeks later without endangering his
life. I closed with the promise, "In return for your doing this, I will
let you go scot free with a pardon in your pocket for all your misdeeds."[15]

The only authenticated photograph of Bonney is a ferrotype, which
produces a mirror image of its subject. In the ferrotype, Bonney appears
to wear his pistol on his left hip and hold his carbine in his right hand.

Wallace relied on this mirror image rather than his memory for the details of the Kid's dramatic entrance.

Wallace's anecdote reads like a passage from Sir Walter Scott; the plan he unfolded was like a plot device. The Kid would submit to a fake arrest. This would provide him with a cover for his testimony while allowing him to be placed in protective custody.

Wallace and the Kid seem to have had a grand time working out the details of the sham arrest. "The Kid talked over the details of this plan for his fake arrest with a good deal of zest," recalled Wallace, even volunteering that he should be handcuffed. Wallace, the author of the plan, was no less enthusiastic. Still, the Kid wanted time to think it over.

Just hours after this meeting, however, all bets were off. Jimmy Dolan, Jesse Evans, and Billy Campbell "escaped" from the Fort Stanton guardhouse.

Sheriff-Elect Garrett

27

Governor Wallace immediately sent word to Juan Patrón, leader of the Lincoln County Mounted Rifles, of a generous $1,000 reward for the capture of Evans and Campbell. Two days after the escape Justice Wilson received this note:

> Please tell you-know-who that I do not know what to do, now as those prisoners have escaped, to send word by bearer, a note through you it may be, that he has made different arrangements. If not, and he still wants the same, to send: William Hudgens as Deputy to the Junction tomorrow at three o'clock with some men you know to be all right. Send a note telling me what to do.
>
> W. H. Bonney
>
> P.S. Do not send soldiers.

Bonney wanted to go forward with the plan because he wanted the promised pardon. From the governor's point of view, however, what was the point? Bonney's testimony against Campbell meant little while Campbell was in Texas. Still, this is how Wallace responded:

The escape makes no difference in arrangements.

To remove all suspicion of understanding, I think it better to put the arresting party in charge of Sheriff Kimball, who shall be instructed to see that no violence is used.

This will go to you tonight. If I don't receive other word from you, the party (all citizens) will be at the junction by 3 o'clock tomorrow.

Bonney wrote back (the "bearer" must have worn out his horse riding between them):

Sir: I will keep the appointment I made but be sure and have men come that you can depend on. I am not afraid to die like a man fighting but I would not like to be killed like a dog unarmed. Tell Kimball to let his men be placed around the house and for him to come in alone; and he can arrest us. All I am afraid of is that in the fort we might be . . . killed through a window at night. But you can arrange that all right.

Bonney added some advice on how to catch Evans and Campbell, including places to look ("Watch Fritz's, Captain Baca's ranch and the brewery. They will either go to Seven Rivers or to the Jicarilla mountains."), how to look ("give a spy a pair of glasses and let him get on the mountain back of Fritz's"), and what to look for ("if they are [there,] there will be provision carried to them").

Bonney's closing was reminiscent of prior letters from Dudley and Chapman, with the difference that Bonney had a sense of humor: "It is not my place to advise you, but I am anxious to have them caught, and perhaps know how men hide from soldiers better than you. Please excuse my having so much to say." He was anxious to have Evans and Campbell caught, of course, to prevent their enforcing the terms of the treaty: death to snitches.

Sheriff George Kimball, who had defeated the despised Peppin in November's election, made the mock arrest as planned on March 23. As sheriff, Kimball was competent and even-handed, the ideal dull-gray lawman. He locked up the Kid and O'Folliard in the abandoned store attached to Juan Patrón's house.

In his regular report to Secretary Schurz, Wallace commented on "a precious specimen nicknamed 'The Kid.'" The governor wrote, "I heard singing and music the other night, [and] going to the door, I found the minstrels of the village actually serenading the fellow in his prison."[1]

In his initial letter to the governor the Kid had written, "As to my character I refer to any of the citizens, for the majority of them are my friends." Wallace may have assumed this was an outlaw's empty boast. It wasn't. That singing is the best explanation of Bonney's return to Lincoln from Texas, and why he was willing to risk his life to give the testimony that would earn him the right to remain in Lincoln a free man.

Bonney kept his side of the bargain, testifying before the grand jury. Campbell, Evans, and Dolan were all indicted for their part in Chapman's murder.[2] Wallace, however, returned to Santa Fe without granting the promised pardon. District Attorney Rynerson felt no obligation to keep the governor's word: he pressed the prosecution of his star witness, obtaining a change of venue in both *U.S. v. Bonney* (for Roberts) and *Territory v. Bonney* (for Brady) so that the cases would not be heard in Lincoln County, where the locals serenaded the prisoner, but in neighboring Doña Ana County, where "the Kid" was just a sinister presence in the newspapers. Nevertheless, Bonney was not jailed.[3]

A week after the grand jury adjourned, Lieutenant Colonel Dudley's court of inquiry began. The court of inquiry, convened to investigate Dudley's actions as commanding officer of Fort Stanton, was not a trial court but something akin to a grand jury, in which three judges (fellow officers) decided whether there was any evidence of wrongdoing.

Reading the transcript of the court of inquiry today is grimly amusing. Every few pages, court is cleared while the judges hash out some intricate evidentiary issue, and then court is reconvened and the judges rule in favor of Lieutenant Colonel Dudley. The prosecution was not allowed to ask the most basic factual questions while Dudley's counsel (the territory's attorney general) contemptuously led the judges by the nose. Governor Wallace, whose request for Dudley's removal prompted the investigation, was not allowed to explain his reasons for seeking his removal, while Captain Purington was permitted to give hearsay evidence that Wallace approved of Dudley's actions.[4]

Even before the inevitable decision was announced, the civilian prosecutor complained to a newspaper reporter that military courts of inquiry

are an expensive and stupendous farce, and are conducted on mutual admiration principles, and if there is the least possible excuse for applying the white-wash to a military man, it will be done, without regard to the beauty and symmetry of the job, and this is especially so when the complaint comes from a civilian.[5]

The net result was a record that was tilted as far as possible in favor of

Lieutenant Colonel Dudley. Still, it provides crushing evidence of Dudley's unique combination of pompous self-regard and craven dishonesty. Dudley's own testimony characteristically consists entirely of nasty invective. He called each of the following witnesses liars: Justice Wilson, Isaac Ellis, Sue McSween, Sebrian Bates, two of his own soldiers, and Juan Patrón. Most of the rest of his time on the stand was spent denying a number of propositions put to him by his counsel. Each of the propositions was firmly supported by evidence from prosecution witnesses.

> *Question:* State whether or not in going to Lincoln at the time referred to you went with any purpose or intent to aid or assist Sheriff Peppin or his posse in any manner or with any idea of expectation that your presence would contribute to the success of the undertaking upon which he was engaged on the 19th of July last?
> *Answer:* I did not most positively.[6]

And so on. These flat denials were a way of calling a further dozen or so witnesses liars. It's possible, of course, that the twenty-one prosecution witnesses were all lying. But it's at least twenty-one times more likely that only one person was lying.

In the end, the judges had to decide which was more probably true: the evidence established by the detailed testimony of all those prosecution witnesses or the lieutenant colonel's flat denials. The result was never in doubt. The favorable verdict did not allow Dudley to regain command of Fort Stanton, but it eased his eventual retirement. He made general on the pension list.

Bonney was living at Fort Sumner, where the exhausted prairie fades into desert. In one of his last letters to Wallace, he would write that he and Bowdre had a ranch near Portales. In this context, however, "ranch" may have been an euphemism. Bonney was launched upon the freebooting career of a high plains small rancher, and he may have combined entrepreneurship and thievery in the manner of some of the Seven Rivers men, doing to the northern portion of Chisum's vast herds what they did to the southern.

There is no record of Bonney and Chisum ever meeting. Chisum was rich, the Kid was a punk; they had nothing in common but allegiance to a lost cause, derived from vastly different sources. But at the end of it all, Chisum was richer than ever and Bonney had nothing. Bonney wrote the governor: "J. S. Chisum is the man who got me in trouble and was benefitted thousands by it and is now doing all he can against me."[7]

Bonney wasn't exaggerating. The fall of the House and the Regulators' harassment of the Seven Rivers men were C-notes from heaven for Chisum. Bonney devoted half a year to the cause and never received so much as a cowboy's ordinary wages. He may have been promised payment by Chisum or (more likely) by McSween invoking Chisum's name, or maybe he just assumed payment would eventually be forthcoming. At any rate, he expected a little something for his time.

He never got a nickel out of Chisum. It is tempting to speculate that the Kid's grudge against Chisum led to rustling – collecting back wages on the hoof. If so, the rustling cemented the enmity. And Chisum, a rich man, knew numerous ways to swat a pesky mosquito.

The Kid's life was more than a succession of clandestine roundups and nighttime cattle drives. He enlivened dusty Fort Sumner. Contemporary sources give us the names of a half-dozen Hispanic women whose names were linked in gossip with Bonney's, and it seems safe to assume other names never made it into print.[8]

A *Las Vegas Gazette* reporter described the Kid after his capture at Stinking Springs:

> He is about five feet, eight or nine inches tall, slightly built and lithe, weighing about 140; a frank and open countenance, looking like a school boy, with the traditional silky fuzz on his upper lip, clear blue eyes, with a roguish snap about them, light hair and complexion. He is, in all, quite a handsome fellow . . . and he has agreeable and winning ways.

Pete Maxwell's niece Paulita reported that Bonney "danced remarkably well." The *Gazette* reporter added that Bonney's "only imperfection [was] two prominent front teeth, slightly protruding like squirrels' teeth." Those teeth also made an impression on Miguel Antonio Otero, who charitably avoided rodent comparisons. Otero wrote that the buck teeth gave Bonney a perpetual grin. Paulita Maxwell also described him as "always smiling."[9]

Bonney may have killed a man at Fort Sumner in January 1880. He was never prosecuted and the papers mentioned the killing in one-line police blotter reports, giving only the victim's name, which indicate by their brevity that the victim was not widely mourned. Robert Utley argues that the version presented in the ghostwritten portion of Pat Garrett's *Authentic Life of Billy the Kid* is true, despite its dime-novel neatness. It seems a drunk named Joe Grant was making himself obnoxious in a bar. The Kid admired Grant's revolver and, examining it, noticed three chambers were empty. He rotated the cylinder so an empty chamber was beneath the hammer. As he was leaving the saloon, his back turned to Grant, he heard a distinct click. He spun around before Grant could reach a loaded chamber. Always a good marksman, he shot Grant in the chin.[10]

A meddlesome Southerner with the unlikely name of Azariah Wild showed up in Lincoln County in the fall of 1880 to make life difficult for the Kid. Wild was a Treasury Department agent sent to investigate widespread counterfeiting in southern New Mexico. The untidiness of Lincoln County life incensed Wild, and he awarded himself a roving commission to clean it up.[11]

Wild scoured Lincoln County for a few honest men to support his crusade and found . . . John Hurley and Robert Olinger. Hurley, a member of William Morton's murdering sub-posse, committed perjury a remarkable number of times in his very brief testimony before Special Agent Angel.

As for Bob Olinger, he and the Kid went back a long way. According to Pat Garrett, who should know (he gave Olinger the job of guarding the Kid in jail), "There existed a reciprocal hatred between these two, and neither attempted to disguise or conceal his antipathy for the other." Each blamed the other for deaths that had occurred during the fighting. Bonney had an additional grudge: in the late summer of 1879, Olinger killed John Jones, with whose family Bonney supposedly had stayed when he first arrived in Lincoln County.[12]

That Wild chose these men as his untouchables shows how out of touch he was. He was one of those bustling reformers, contemptuous of the objects of their solicitude, whose arrogance makes them easy prey for manipulation by the locals they intend to set straight. Hurley and Olinger, seizing an opportunity to settle old scores, convinced the gullible Wild that Billy the Kid was the crime boss of southern New Mexico.

Wild began spreading genuine U.S. Treasury notes around Lincoln

County, being especially generous to those who brought him information concerning the Kid. Before long, most of the unsolved crimes in Lincoln County had been pinned on Bonney.

Leaving aside Wild's purchased information, the evidence of the Kid's criminal career following McSween's death and the rout of the Regulators is spotty at best. He may have killed Grant, but if so, he acted in self-defense. He gambled, but that was less a crime than a profession. It is commonly supposed that he rustled from Chisum's herds, but a sheriff's raid on Bonney's and Bowdre's Portales ranch found no stolen cattle.

Pat Garrett's biographer Leon Metz writes that "the highways of Lincoln County were unsafe for travel because the Kid or his comrades were moving across the hills, pillaging and spoiling."[13] Metz intends to correct romantic Robin Hood portrayals of the Kid, but his corrective, unsupported by any evidence, is just a photo negative.

The best evidence of the Kid's banditry is John Chisum's hostility. Chisum believed the Kid was up to no good, and he was in a position to know.

Sheriff Kimball never pursued Bonney, which prompted Chisum to sponsor his own candidate for sheriff in the 1880 election – Pat Garrett. Garrett was born into a prosperous slave-owning family in eastern Alabama in 1850. But just two years later, Pat's grandfather, the family patriarch, died and the family began a rapid decline. First it moved from Alabama to northern Louisiana. Then came the Civil War and its hardships. In 1868 Pat's father died, and the family was turned off the farm, penniless.[14]

Young Pat was extraordinarily tall for his day. He stood 6' 5", and his gangly build and long neck made him seem still taller. He had dark hair and prominent cheekbones; he wore a handlebar mustache and was, in his raw-boned way, quite handsome. Still a teenager, he drifted westward, trying his hand as a farmer in Dallas County, Texas, before finding success as a buffalo hunter. He was among the last to make his living killing buffalo, sometimes slaughtering as many as two hundred a day.

Such bloodthirsty efficiency soon put him and the other buffalo hunters out of work. Garrett compounded his problems in 1876 by killing one of his partners (he claimed that the partner, a much smaller man, started the fight). He continued drifting westward, all the way to Fort Sumner, New Mexico.

The Kid spent time in Fort Sumner during the late 1870s, too, and that less-than-amazing coincidence has given rise to a persistent legend (full of fraudulent irony) that he and Garrett were comrades who had a falling out. They weren't.

John Chisum recommended Garrett to Lew Wallace as "a very suitable man" to clean up Lincoln County. Garrett was supported in the 1880 election by another prominent citizen – Jimmy Dolan. The old alliances had entirely dissolved. The new alliances were established on more customary grounds: Garrett was supported by Anglos, Kimball by Hispanics.

Bonney, according to a well-known anecdote, campaigned for Kimball in his race against Garrett. George Curry, later an employee of Jimmy Dolan, later still appointed governor by Theodore Roosevelt, was a young man in Lincoln County in 1880. In his autobiography, written decades after the fact, he told the story of the evening before the election, when the Block Ranch bunkhouse was visited by a young Anglo man who spoke fluent Spanish with the cowboys. As the stranger prepared to leave for a preelection dance being held nearby, he asked Curry which candidate he thought would carry the precinct.

> I told him our votes would be for Pat Garrett. He asked, bluntly, why I thought Garrett would win, and I replied just as bluntly that Garrett was a brave man who would arrest Billy the Kid or any other outlaw for whom a warrant was outstanding. Mounting a sturdy cow pony, and waving a cheerful "adios," the stranger rode away. It was then that Felipe Miranda, our sheep boss, told me I had been talking with Billy the Kid.[15]

In a version of the story told by William Keleher, who interviewed Curry, the Kid told the future governor, "You are a good cook and a good fellow, but if you think Pat Garrett is going to carry this precinct for sheriff, you are a damn poor politician."[16] Curry politicked energetically for Garrett, passing out tobacco, whiskey, and premarked ballots on voting day, but when the precinct's votes were counted Garrett got exactly one vote. But because the Anglos were a numerical majority in the county as a whole, Garrett won the day.

Garrett's victory was great news for Azariah Wild. Garrett was enthusiastic about Wild's schemes. But like Hurley and Olinger before him, Garrett was pursuing his own agenda, a point Wild failed to grasp. Garrett was more than happy to use the United States Treasury Department to pay back his campaign supporters. His chief supporter, John Chisum, wished to rid himself of a pesky mosquito.

Garrett didn't take office until January 1. In a gracious gesture, Kimball named him deputy sheriff immediately following the November election, and Wild procured for him a commission as deputy U.S. marshal. Deputy Garrett and Special Agent Wild launched a multipronged attack on the Kid and his comrades in late November. Raids were launched on Fort Sumner, on a ranch near Bosque Grande, and on Bowdre's and Bonney's ranch in Portales.

They failed to find the Kid or anybody else. In fact, they failed to locate so much as a single stolen cow. Wild's grand scheme was an absolute fiasco, and its failure was a bitter blow. Henceforth he devoted his energy to writing vituperative reports condemning federal officials in New Mexico, especially Marshal Sherman. This was typical of Wild's obtuseness. He never understood that Sherman was marshal *because* he was so manifestly unfit for the job.

George Curry's campaign anecdote illustrates the Kid's dilemma. He was a hero to the Hispanic cowboys, but Curry, the Anglo newcomer, counted him a dangerous outlaw. The Kid's reputation in both communities was exaggerated. Still just twenty-one years old, he was already a legend. Men who had never set eyes on him thought they knew all about him.

In late November, while Wild's grand plan was misfiring, a group of newcomers to Lincoln County tracked down the Kid. The newcomers were miners from White Oaks, a brand-new boomtown established in northwest Lincoln County following a modest gold strike. White Oaks didn't exist during the Lincoln County War; it was founded in 1879.

A deputy sheriff from White Oaks named Bill Hudgens (whom Bonney had suggested should make the fake arrest) heard that a suspected murderer named Dave Rudabaugh, who had recently escaped from the Las Vegas jail, was camped with the Kid near White Oaks. Hudgens formed a small posse to investigate and found his men. The posse managed to kill Bonney's horse, but Bonney, Rudabaugh, and their comrades slipped away. Hudgens was persistent, however: he returned to White Oaks to obtain reinforcements, then tracked the outlaws all the way to an isolated ranch house and stagecoach stop on the plains many miles northeast of White Oaks. On November 27 Hudgens and his thirteen men surrounded the ranch house and demanded the surrender of all those inside.[17]

Bonney described the incident in a letter to Governor Wallace:

My business at the White Oaks the time I was waylaid and my

horse killed was to see Judge Leonard [his attorney] who has my case in hand. He had written to me to come up that he thought he could get everything straightened up. I did not find him at the Oaks & should have gone to Lincoln if I had met with no accident. After mine and Billie Wilson's horses were killed we both made our way to a station, forty miles from the Oaks, kept by Mr. Greathouse. When I got up next morning the house was surrounded by an outfit led by one Carlyle, who came into the house and demanded a surrender. I asked for their papers and they had none. So I concluded it amounted to nothing more than a mob and told Carlyle that he would have to stay in the house and lead the way out that night. Soon after a note was brought in stating that if Carlyle did not come out inside of five minutes they would kill the station keeper (Greathouse) who had left the house and was with them. In a short time a shot was fired on the outside and Carlyle, thinking Greathouse was killed, jumped through the window breaking the sash as he went and was killed by his own party. They [thought] it was me trying to make my escape. The party then withdrew.[18]

Other accounts agree in general outline with the Kid's. James Carlyle was a blacksmith, a well-respected man in White Oaks, and he courageously entered the house without arms to negotiate a surrender. Jim Greathouse went outside at the same time as a hostage. One of the posse men did fire a shot (probably by accident), and Carlyle did leap through the window. Disagreement exists only with regard to the crucial point: the direction of the deadly shots.

The Kid may or may not have been responsible, but in a roundabout way the blacksmith's death made his name. Galvanized by the incident, in early December *The Las Vegas Gazette* launched a campaign against the outlaws of the high plains, telling its readers that eastern New Mexico was in the grip of a gang numbering "from forty to fifty men, all hard characters, the off-scouring of society, fugitives from justice, and desperadoes by profession." And who was the leader of this formidable gang?

The gang is under the leadership of "Billy the Kid," a desperate cuss, who is eligible for the post of captain of any crowd, no matter how mean and lawless. . . .
They run stock from the Panhandle county into the White Oaks and from the Pecos country into the Panhandle, equalizing the

herds, but in true middlemen style always make heavily by the transaction. . . .

Are the people of San Miguel county to stand this any longer? Shall we suffer this horde of outcasts and the scum of society, who are outlawed by a multitude of crimes, to continue their way on the very border of our county?[19]

This was the first appearance in print of the name "Billy the Kid."

It had a magical ring: within weeks it was picked up by newspapers all over the territory, and then across the country. "Kid" was originally no more than a description, like Lefty or Curly or Shorty. But the use of "the" before such a common word made the description ironic: a killer called Kid with a child's diminutive name.

The article created a sensation. Just three weeks later *The Daily New Mexican* wrote of "Billy, 'The Kid,' . . . whom it is unnecessary to introduce to the readers of the *New Mexican*. Everybody in the Territory has probably heard of the famous outlaw." On one of the last days of the year, *The Las Vegas Gazette* pronounced its creation "the best known man in New Mexico."[20] The Kid was a star.

"Billy the Kid"

28

On December 13, 1880, Governor Wallace announced a reward of $500 to the person who delivered Billy the Kid to the Lincoln County sheriff.[1] The promise of money was reason enough for Garrett to redouble his efforts. No longer relying on the defeated and embittered Azariah Wild, he could indulge his own methods of law enforcement.

Garrett had two warrants for Bonney's arrest, both charging him with murder, both issued by Judge Bristol. Bristol issued one warrant (for Sheriff Brady) as a territorial judge, the other warrant (for Andrew Roberts) as a federal judge.

As luck would have it, several of the biggest landowners in the Texas Panhandle picked this time to send a punitive force into New Mexico. Rustling was getting out of hand. The landowners called together their cowboys and asked for volunteers. According to one of those who went, a cowboy named Cal Polk, "The boys would quit their jobs in the dead of winter before they would go out. Out of 300 men there were only 13 that would go."[2]

The reason for the reluctance is apparent in Polk's description of the plucky thirteen: "We all had 2 belts full of cartridges apiece around us and were armed to the teeth with six shooters, Bowie knives and Winchesters on our saddles."[3] The Panhandle men intended to strike with maximum violence and then scurry back across the border ahead of the law.

Garrett adopted them as his posse, exactly as Peppin had once adopted John Kinney's butcher boys. For the Texans, it was a stroke of unbelievable good fortune to be sworn in as a deputy sheriff/deputy marshal's posse. Now they could put their bosses' plan into operation without fear of hanging for it.

A few days before Christmas, Garrett and his posse rode to Fort Sumner and wasted a couple of days scouting around for Bonney. Growing impatient, Garrett picked up two local fellows whom he knew were friendly with the Kid and persuaded each to do him a favor. Juan Valdez was persuaded to write a note stating that Garrett had left town and the coast was clear. Juan Gallegos was persuaded to deliver the note to the Kid.[4]

Garrett's methods as a lawman were direct and to the point. It isn't difficult to imagine the form his persuasion took.

It helped Garrett's plan that a howling snowstorm settled over the plains that night. The Kid and his comrades had no desire to camp outside in the blizzard. The fake note gave them all the excuse they needed to seek shelter. Well after dark they rode into town, heading for Charles Bowdre's house. O'Folliard and Tom Pickett, a former Texas Ranger, were in the lead, followed by Bonney, Rudabaugh, Bowdre, and Billy Wilson.

As these six approached Bowdre's porch in the swirling snow, Garrett and his men suddenly materialized out of the darkness and opened fire.

The deputy and his posse afterward maintained that they gave the outlaws fair warning, calling for them to halt, when O'Folliard went for his gun. It's certainly possible that it happened that way, but it's at least equally possible that the Texas cowboys were in no mood to take chances.

O'Folliard and Pickett wheeled their horses around and took off at a dead run. The other four scattered. O'Folliard's horse slowed to a trot, then a walk, then gradually circled back to the house. According to Garrett, O'Folliard clung helplessly to the saddle. "Don't shoot, Garrett," he said. "I am killed." He had been hit in the left side of his chest.

Garrett and his men carried O'Folliard inside and laid him before the fire. Garrett's book recounts a hearthside conversation in which O'Folliard begged to be put out of his misery, an invitation Garrett loftily declined.

One of the Texas cowboys remembered it differently. In this version O'Folliard called Garrett a "long-legged son-of-a-bitch" and added, "God damn you, Garrett. I hope to meet you in hell." He died soon afterward.[5]

The next day the posse tracked their quarry to a sheepherder's stone hut near a sulphur seep called, predictably, Stinking Springs. There are two versions of how they followed the trail. Cal Polk's version goes like this: in the gunfight, Dave Rudabaugh's horse was slightly injured. The drops of bright blood on the fresh snow left a clear trail for the posse.[6]

Pat Garrett gave himself less credit as a tracker. According to Garrett, he just got lucky. Tom Wilcox and Manuel Brazil owned a ranch ten miles outside of town. Bonney and the rest had arrived at the ranch after the gunfight. In the morning Brazil rode into town and told Garrett everything. That night after midnight, the posse moved out, hoping to surprise their quarry asleep at the ranch. It was December 23 and bitterly cold. The moon was nearly full and reflected in the snow.

The posse reached the ranch house only to find the place deserted. But they were lucky: the full moon gave them intermittent glimpses of the tracks the horses had left in the snow. Garrett was familiar with the territory around Fort Sumner from his wandering days and knew about the sheepherder's hut.

Garrett and his men surrounded it. The outlaws' horses were tethered outside. Garrett wanted to enter the house while Bonney, Rudabaugh, Pickett, and Wilson were asleep, but his men demurred, considering it more prudent to wait outside.

In unself-conscious revelation of his straightforward approach to law enforcement, Garrett wrote: "I had a perfect description of the Kid's dress, especially his hat. I had told all the posse that if the Kid made his appearance it was my intention to kill him, for then the rest would probably surrender." He justified his shoot-on-sight order with a single sentence of explanation: "The Kid had sworn that he would never give himself up a prisoner, and would die fighting even though there was a revolver at each ear, and I knew he would keep his word."

The posse spent the rest of that wretchedly cold December night hiding in the snow, trying not to make any noise. Before sunup, a man stepped out of the hut to feed the horses. As Garrett put it: "His size and dress, especially the hat, corresponded exactly with the description I had been given of the Kid. So I gave a signal by bringing my gun to my shoulder; my men did likewise and seven bullets sped on their errand of death."

But it wasn't the Kid. Garrett reported that Charles Bowdre staggered towards him, saying in a voice choked by blood, "I wish – I wish – I wish. . . . "

The circumstances of Bowdre's death tend to confirm the suspicion that O'Folliard, too, was shot from ambush without warning. That was Garrett's way. He shot men the way he once shot buffalo, except he hunted buffalo by daylight.

Some time later, Garrett noticed one of the tethered horses moving.

Somehow, the men inside the hut had reached the reins and were slowly pulling the horse inside. They had concocted a farfetched plan to bring the horses inside so they could then burst through the doorway on horseback and race past the startled posse.

Garrett cleverly waited until the horse was halfway through the doorway before shooting. "If it hadn't been for the dead horse in the doorway I wouldn't be here," Bonney later told a *Las Vegas Gazette* reporter.

I would have ridden out on my bay mare and taken my chances of escaping. But I couldn't ride out over that, for she would have jumped back, and I would have got it in the head. We could have stayed in the house but there wouldn't have been anything gained by that for they would have starved us out. I thought it was better to come out and get a good square meal – don't you?[7]

So much for dying fighting with a revolver at each ear.

The prisoners were transported to Las Vegas, where they lodged overnight at the jail. In the morning the *Gazette* reporter visited the jail. The capture of the Kid and Rudabaugh was big news: "a large crowd strained their necks to get a glimpse of the prisoners."

Bonney . . . was light and chipper, and was very communicative, laughing, joking and chatting with the bystanders.

"You appear to take it easy," the reporter said.

"Yes! What's the use of looking on the gloomy side of everything. The laugh's on me this time," he said. Then looking about the placita, he asked: "Is the jail at Santa Fe any better than this?"

This seemed to trouble him considerably, for as he explained, "This is a terrible place to put a fellow in." He put the same question to every one who came near him and when he learned that there was nothing better in store for him, he shrugged his shoulders and said something about putting up with what he had to.

He was the attraction of the show, . . . lightly kicking the toes of his boots on the stone pavement to keep his feet warm. . . .

"There was a big crowd gazing at me, wasn't there?" he exclaimed, and then smiling continued: "Well, perhaps some of them will think me half a man now; everyone seems to think I was some kind of an animal."

The reporter added: "A cloud came over his face when he made some allusion to his being made the hero of fabulous yarns."

The Santa Fe jail was, in fact, far worse. *The Daily New Mexican* reported, "He is shut up in a stone cell to which even the light of day is denied admittance." The reporter added, "He is nevertheless cheerful," a circumstance ascribed to the hope of escape, "for it cannot fairly be presumed that he hopes to be acquitted of all his crimes."[8]

On New Year's Day, 1881, Bonney wrote a short note to Governor Wallace from the Santa Fe jail: "I would like to see you for a few moments if you can spare the time." Wallace was out of town for the holidays. When he returned, he ignored the note; he had already obtained everything he wanted from the Kid.

So Bonney wrote a second note on March 2:

Dear Sir:

I wish you would come down to the jail to see me. It will be to your interest to come and see me. I have some letters which date back two years and there are parties who are very anxious to get them but I shall not dispose of them until I see you. That is if you will come immediately.

Yours Respect –
Wm H Bonney[9]

The attempted blackmail no doubt irritated Wallace, but Bonney can hardly be blamed for trying to interest the governor in his case. Bonney sought to use his sudden notoriety to his advantage by turning himself into a political liability for the governor. It was a good try, but not good enough.

Two days later, on March 4, he wrote a third note, this time spelling out what he had intended to tell Wallace in person:

Dear Sir:

I wrote you a little note the day before yesterday but have received no answer. I expect you have forgotten what you promised me this month two years ago, but I have not, and I think you had ought to have come and seen me as I have requested you to. I have done everything that I promised you I would, and you have done nothing that you promised me. I think when you think the matter over you will come down and see me, and I can then explain everything to you.

Unfortunately for the Kid, it would have cost Wallace his career to honor his promise. Billy the Kid was celebrated in newspapers across the territory and, increasingly, from coast to coast as the outlaw chief of the frontier. Bonney seemed to understand the political problem his notoriety posed for Wallace. That's why he tried blackmail before cajolery, trying to turn Wallace's problem to his advantage.

His newfound fame was a burden in other ways as well. His March 4 letter contained this complaint about the U.S. marshal:

I am not treated right by Sherman. He lets every stranger that comes to see me through curiosity in to see me, but will not let a single one of my friends in, not even an attorney. I guess they mean to send me up without giving me any show but they will have a nice time doing it. I am not entirely without friends.

Finally, on March 27, 1881, Bonney wrote to Wallace: "For the last time I ask. Will you keep your promise. I start before tomorrow." But there is more honor among outlaws than politicians. Bonney never heard from Wallace again.

The Kid kept his sense of humor even as he was transported to Mesilla for trial, accompanied by his lawyer, Ira Leonard. *The Las Vegas Gazette* reported: "At Las Cruces an inquisitive mob gathered around the coach and someone asked which is 'Billy the Kid.' The Kid himself answered by placing his hand on Judge Leonard's shoulder, and saying 'this is the man.'"[10]

Bonney was tried twice in Judge Bristol's Mesilla courtroom. Since federal cases took precedence over territorial matters, Bristol first heard the federal case charging Bonney with the murder of Andrew Roberts. The only basis for federal jurisdiction was the contention that the crime was committed on federal land. Attorney Leonard pointed out that Blazer's Mill was an island of private land inside the Mescalero Reservation, and Bristol was obliged to dismiss the case for lack of jurisdiction.

Bonney was subsequently charged for the same crime in territorial court.

On April 8, the prosecution for the murder of Sheriff Brady began. For some reason, Leonard did not represent Bonney in this matter. Perhaps Bonney thought he didn't need a lawyer, since he had been promised a pardon. Bristol appointed a public defender, Colonel A. J. Fountain, who had quit his post as editor of *The Mesilla Valley Independent* in a quarrel with his partners.

The prosecution's chief witness was Billy Mathews, who was able to testify that Brady was shot from ambush (showing premeditation) and that Bonney ran out from behind the adobe wall (showing Bonney was part of the conspiracy, even if he didn't necessarily pull the trigger). That was enough evidence to convict.

On April 13, Judge Bristol sentenced Bonney to death.

Three days later he was transported to Lincoln to be hanged. He was guarded by seven lawmen. One of the deputies had already compiled an impressive list of accomplishments as a peace officer: John Kinney, who had found that serving as deputy sheriff gave him the opportunity to exercise his peculiar talents without the troublesome risk of criminal prosecution.

Sharing duties with Kinney were Deputies J. B. Mathews, the former House man, and Bob Olinger. All three were long-time enemies of Bonney. Nonetheless, a newspaper account of the caravan emphasized Bonney's cheerfulness.[11]

Pat Garrett had campaigned as the law-and-order candidate for sheriff, sponsored by that long-suffering victim of crime, John Chisum. At first blush it seems strange that the law-and-order sheriff deputized a notorious criminal such as Kinney and a known killer such as Olinger. But Garrett served the interests of Chisum. For Chisum, "law and order" meant the protection of his financial interests. In this he was no different from Tom Catron, who wrote to Governor Axtell that "there seems to be an utter disregard of the law in the county, as well as of life and private rights," then procured Kinney's help for *his* sheriff, George Peppin.

Bonney was incarcerated on the second floor of the House, which had been converted into the Lincoln County courthouse and doubled as the jail. Garrett maintained a guard of two deputies at all times and shackled the Kid hand and foot. On April 28, Garrett was out of town and the jail was left under guard of two deputies: Jim Bell, who appears to have been a conscientious sort, and Bob Olinger.[12]

Olinger led the other prisoners across the street to the Wortley Hotel for dinner. Bonney, under special guard, had to stay behind. He asked to go to the outhouse behind the building and Bell dutifully led him out. Shortly afterward, they returned inside.

Godfrey Gauss, Tunstall's old cook, was living in a small house behind the courthouse. He happened to be standing in his yard a few minutes later and was startled to see Deputy Bell running through the courthouse's back door. Gauss later told a reporter, "He ran right into my arms, expired the same moment, and I laid him down dead."

Gauss rushed into the street looking for help just as Olinger emerged from the hotel with a full belly. Gauss yelled for Olinger to come quickly. Olinger hurried toward the courthouse. He heard someone call his name from an upstairs window. When he looked up the Kid pulled both triggers of Olinger's own double-barreled shotgun.

No one knows quite how he managed it. Garrett speculated that the Kid moved ahead of Bell while walking back from the outhouse and bounded up the stairs (despite leg shackles that slowed his walk to a shuffle), broke open the door to the armory, seized a weapon and shot Bell while he was still laboring up the stairs.

But there wasn't time for that.

Robert Utley concludes that the Kid slugged Bell with the handcuffs, then wrestled with him for his gun. This is consistent with an anonymous correspondent who sent a description of the escape to the Las Cruces newspaper *Newman's Semi-Weekly*. According to the writer, Bonney said shortly after the killings that "he did not want to kill Bell but, as he ran, he had to. He said he grabbed Bell's revolver and told him to hold up his hands and surrender; that Bell decided to run and he had to kill him."[13]

A third version says that Sam Corbet, Tunstall's old clerk, hid a revolver in the outhouse.

Garrett's version gives the only explanation for how the Kid managed to free his hands from his manacles: he "slipped the handcuffs over his hands." But why would Garrett and his men put oversized cuffs on their most heavily guarded prisoner? They could not have failed to notice that the cuffs were loose. Perhaps the instrument Sam Corbet left in the outhouse was a key or pick rather than a gun.

In the end we have to be satisfied with the implications of Bonney's letter to Lew Wallace: "I am not entirely without friends."

Bonney had no choice but to remain in Lincoln for about an hour after the killings: the shackles prevented him from going anywhere. He stood on the balcony of the courthouse armed with every gun from the armory. It was a highly public escape. Lincoln's citizens gathered in the street to watch. According to *The Las Vegas Daily Optic,* two citizens went for their guns but were restrained by others who wished to aid the escape.[14]

Bonney called to Gauss (whom he knew he could trust) to bring a miner's pick upstairs. Sitting on the balcony, where he could keep an eye on things, Bonney worked at his manacles. As soon as he freed one leg, he looped the chain to his belt and was ready to go.

He ordered that a certain horse, belonging to the deputy clerk of the probate court, be saddled up for his use. He ventured downstairs into the yard but the chain spooked the horse, who fled. Bonney had to call for someone to bring the horse back to him. On the second try he mounted the horse and was able to ride out of town.

According to Godfrey Gauss, the horse was returned the following day.

Newspapers across the country went wild. The impossible had happened: Billy the Kid, the outlaw king of the frontier, had lived up to his reputation.

It was even better than that: he outdid himself. Editors indulged in blood-soaked descriptions of his (mostly imaginary) outrages in the guise of deploring his excesses. But even in the first reports a new note was sounded. Frank admiration can already be discerned in *The Daily New Mexican*'s description of his "coolness and steadiness of nerve." The paper commented:

> The above is a record of as bold a deed as those versed in the annals of crime can recall. It surpasses anything of which the Kid has been guilty so far that his past offenses lose much of heinousness in comparison with it, and it effectually settles the question whether the Kid is a cowardly cut-throat or a thoroughly reckless and fearless man.[15]

While one newspaper deplored "the glamour of romance thrown around his dare-devil life by sensation writers," another wrote that his supposed adventures "are thrilling enough for a dime novel." A living person was metamorphosing into a work of fiction. After describing the Kid's "pleasant expression of countenance," *The Santa Fe Weekly Democrat* reported:

> He came from Texas to Lincoln about a year ago, across the Pan Handle with a gang of notorious outlaws, one of whom was supposed to have been Jesse James. Fired by the romantic details of the deeds of desperadoes in the far West, as pictured in dime novels, he determined to emulate their example and become a desperado himself.

The Daily New Mexican also assured its readers that the Kid

> was first led to adopt the life of an outlaw by reading dime novels. He is only twenty-two years old now, and when he first "turned out" was a mere boy thirsting for notoriety as a desperado. He has been very successful in achieving this, and stands at the top of the ladder of fame, a fit subject for a novel himself.

Completing the metamorphosis into fiction were the fiction writers themselves, who descended on Bonney like impatient buzzards. "The sensational happenings in New Mexico of late have attracted considerable attention abroad," reported one paper, "and we understand Col. E.Z.C. Judson, 'Ned Buntline,' is now on his way to New Mexico to interview various men to secure material for blood and thunder literature."[16]

Mathews experienced the peculiar pleasure of reading his own admiring obituaries when the papers reported that the Kid had gunned him down on the outskirts of Lincoln.[17] Despite the publicity, the Kid remained in eastern New Mexico. Eugenio Salazar later said he counseled the Kid to flee into Mexico; doubtless others gave much the same advice. Yet Bonney remained on the high plains around Fort Sumner.

Presumably he didn't intend that people – in particular Pat Garrett – should know that he remained behind. According to a report published after his death, Bonney "allowed his beard to grow and stained his skin to look like a Mexican."[18]

Garrett was unable to pick up his trail despite repeated visits to Fort Sumner, in San Miguel County. No one provided any information. In mid-June *The Daily New Mexican* reported: "A man who came to Santa Fe yesterday from Lincoln County says that Billy, the Kid has got more friends in that county than anybody."[19]

Garrett wasn't sheriff of San Miguel County. His determined pursuit of Bonney wasn't a matter of duty; it was something he did while neglecting his duty. He was a bounty hunter, intent on collecting a second $500 reward.

On July 13, Garrett and his deputies, John Poe (another employee of the Panhandle ranchers) and Tip McKinney, were wrapping up a fruitless search of the Fort Sumner area when they decided to pay a visit to Pete Maxwell, although it was long after dark.[20]

A group of men were conversing quietly in Spanish among the trees of an orchard near the Maxwell house. Garrett, Poe, and McKinney made a wide detour around the orchard, keeping out of sight.

Maxwell was already in bed. In traditional hacienda style, each room, including Maxwell's bedroom, opened onto a veranda. Poe and McKinney took up positions on the veranda as Garrett went in to question Maxwell.

At this point, one of the men who had been quietly conversing in Spanish in the orchard approached the house barefoot, without a hat, a butcher knife in hand. Maxwell had hung a newly butchered calf from the veranda rafters to season and the man intended to cut a steak. The man was startled to see two heavily armed cowboys lounging in the darkness outside Maxwell's bedroom door. There was mutual lack of recognition. The man stepped through Maxwell's open bedroom door and urgently whispered, "¿Quién es?" "Who is it?"

Garrett shot without warning and then flung himself to the floor. Maxwell dived over the side of the bed, dragging the bedclothes with him. Both men held their breath, trying not to reveal their locations, afraid the Kid was crouching in the darkness with his pistol at the ready. But the Kid was dead.

Epilogue

Garrett immediately traveled to Santa Fe, once again seeking to claim the $500 reward. This time he cleaned up: not only did he get the reward, but John Chisum added $1,000 to the pot and Las Vegas citizens chipped in another $500.[1] A famous man, Garrett subsequently served in various capacities as local public official in southern New Mexico and El Paso. He drank far too much, and the drink made him violent and quarrelsome. At age fifty-seven, he was shot through the head while urinating on a public road. His killer was never caught.

Tom Catron obsessively pursued his political comeback. He lost a race for territorial legislature in 1882, but he won two years later. In 1894 he was elected congressional delegate, subsequently losing his bid for reelection. In 1906 he became mayor of Santa Fe, and in 1912, the year of statehood, the legislature sent him to Washington as United States senator. He was seventy-two years old and viewed the Senate as a particularly pleasant retirement village. He served just one term. He died in 1921 and was remembered when the legislature created Catron County in vacant west central New Mexico.

Like Catron, Jimmy Dolan was intelligent and resourceful enough to land on his feet. He married Charles Fritz's daughter Caroline and made money grubstaking White Oaks prospectors. He even dabbled in local politics, getting himself elected to the territorial legislature in the late 1880s. But his horrific death at age forty-nine sounds like the fulfillment of a curse: according to *The White Oaks Eagle* he died of a "hemorrhage of the bowels."[2]

Jesse Evans left New Mexico for Texas in 1879, but the following year he killed a Texas Ranger and was sentenced to ten years in the penitentiary. After eighteen months he escaped and covered his tracks with his customary skill; to this day no one knows what happened to him.

John Kinney reached the pinnacle of his success in the years immediately following the Lincoln County War, when his rustling and meat-packing operation extended its influence from Colorado to Mexico. But his success made him conspicuous and he was put on trial for rustling in 1883. He was convicted even though former district attorney William Rynerson testified on his behalf as an alibi witness. Kinney spent about three years in the pen and the experience encouraged him to go straight. When he died in 1919 at a ripe old age, he was remembered fondly in his adopted hometown of Prescott, Arizona, as a frontier lawman, Texas Ranger, and gregarious courthouse lounger.

Samuel Axtell never ceased campaigning for another patronage job. He pleaded with his mentor Collis Huntington to bring all of his Washington influence to bear. In 1882, his perseverance (or Huntington's investment) paid off. President Chester A. Arthur's private secretary wrote Huntington to inform him of Axtell's appointment as New Mexico's chief justice. The president, the letter added, "desires me to say that it has been extremely gratifying to him to have been able to oblige you in this matter."[3]

The novel Lew Wallace finished while serving as governor of New Mexico, *Ben-Hur,* sold more copies than any previous American novel. After leaving Santa Fe, Wallace served as American ambassador to Turkey. He died in 1905 at the age of seventy-seven, one of America's most admired men.

Sue McSween remarried in June 1880, not quite two years after her first husband's death. Her new husband, George Barber, had been a member of the coroner's jury that identified the six killers of John Tunstall. He later completed the appraisal of McSween's and Tunstall's property for Sheriff Copeland. After eleven years of marriage, Sue divorced Barber and lived out the rest of her long life in White Oaks. She died on January 3, 1931.

Notes

ABBREVIATIONS

The abbreviation NMRCA refers to the New Mexico State Records Center and Archives.

Historical Records refers to the "Historical Records" section of National Archives record group 60, General Records of the Department of Justice, File No.44-4-8-3.

Dudley Court of Inquiry refers to "Proceedings of a Court of Inquiry in the Case of Lt. Col. N.A.M. Dudley," National Archives record group 153, Records of the War Department, Records of the Judge Advocate General, file QQ 1284.

AGO microfilm refers to National Archives microcopy 666, Letters Received by the Office of the Adjutant General (Main Series) 1871–80, roll 397 (1878).

Frank Warner Angel filed at least four reports examining matters in New Mexico. The following shorthand references are used in the notes:

Angel Report – "Report on the Origin of the Troubles in Lincoln County," National Archives record group 60, Department of Justice General Records, File No.44-4-8-3.

Angel Report on Axtell – "In the Matter of the Investigation of the Charges against S. B. Axtell, Governor of New Mexico," National Archives record group 48, Interior Department Appointment Papers: Territory of New Mexico, 1850–1907.

Angel Report on Godfroy – "The Examination of Charges against L. F. Godfroy, Indian Agent, Mescalero, N.M.," National Archives record group 75, Bureau of Indian Affairs, New Mexico, Letters Received, 1878.

Angel Report on the Cause and Circumstances – "In the Matter of the Cause and Circumstances of the Death of John H. Tunstall, a British Subject: Report of Frank Warner Angel, Special Agent," National Archives record group 60, Department of Justice General Records, File No.44-4-8-3.

1. This figure is given in *The Mesilla News,* June 29, 1878.

2. The 1860 census found 273 people at "Rio Bonito," then part of Socorro County.

3. Darlis A. Miller, *The California Column in New Mexico* (Albuquerque: University of New Mexico Press, 1982); Arrell Morgan Gibson, "James H. Carleton," in *Soldiers West: Biographies from the Military Frontier,* ed. Paul Andrew Hutton (Lincoln: University of Nebraska Press, 1987), pp.59–77.

4. 17 Stat. 139 (1872). When originally organized in 1869, Lincoln County did not extend as far south as the Texas border. In February 1878, the county was expanded to the proportions described in the text (New Mexico Laws 1868–69, chap.8; New Mexico Laws 1878, chap.34). For maps of the changing county lines, see Warren A. Beck and Ynez Haase, *Historical Atlas of New Mexico* (Norman: University of Oklahoma Press, 1969).

5. Examples of McSween's stationery can be found in the correspondence file for the District Court Clerk, Third Judicial District, Lincoln County District Court, 1875, NMRCA.

6. *The Atcheson Champion,* Aug. 24, 1873, quoted in William A. Keleher, *Violence in Lincoln County 1869–1881* (Albuquerque: University of New Mexico Press, 1957), p.54.

7. Lily Klasner, *My Girlhood among Outlaws* (Tucson: University of Arizona Press, 1972), p.94. The basic facts of Murphy's life are told in his obituaries: *The Mesilla Valley Independent,* Nov. 2, 1878; *The Mesilla News,* Nov. 2, 1878; *The Weekly New Mexican,* Oct. 26, 1878.

8. *The New York Times,* Sept. 18–20, 1873; Willford I. King, *The Causes of Economic Fluctuations: Possibilities of Anticipation and Control* (New York: The Ronald Press Co., 1938), pp.60–63; Charles P. Kindleberger, "The Panic of 1873," in *Crashes and Panics: The Lessons from History,* ed. Eugene N. White (Homewood, Ill.: Dow Jones-Irwin, 1990), pp.69–84; Robert Sobel, *Panic on Wall Street* (1968; New York: Truman Talley Books/E. P. Dutton, 1988), pp.154–96.

9. Marion Turner letter to editor, *The Las Vegas Gazette,* May 4, 1878; Angel Report on Godfroy, James H. Farmer testimony, p.7. The House generally did not contract with the government; rather, it served as an agent or subcontractor for businessmen with the wherewithal (and political connections) to bid (Angel Report on Godfroy, Dolan testimony, p.40). The House also made off-contract sales to the fort and reservation (John P. Wilson, *Merchants, Guns and Money: The Story of Lincoln County and Its Wars* [Santa Fe: Museum of New Mexico Press, 1987], pp.41, 56–60).

10. An inventory of the mercantile stock of Murphy & Co.'s competitor, J. H. Tunstall & Co., is contained in the court file for *Fritz and Scholand v. McSween,* Lincoln County civil case no.141 (1878), NMRCA.

11. Angel Report, Patrón testimony, pp.273, 276.

12. Ibid., Van Sickle testimony, p.320.

13. Ibid., Gauss testimony, pp.303–4. Gauss's English was apparently idiosyncratic enough to confuse the stenographer; most of the punctuation given here is not found in the original.

14. Ibid., McSween testimony, p.6.

CHAPTER 2

1. Angel Report, McSween testimony, exhibit 3, p.85. The court files of numerous collection suits filed by McSween on behalf of the House are stored in NMRCA. See, for example, Lincoln County civil suits nos. 65, 66, 67, 68, 70, 72 (1875).

2. Utah Territory enacted legislation decreeing that its probate courts were courts of general jurisdiction, competent to hear any case whatsoever, cutting federal courts out of the loop altogether. The feds fought back. Eventually the Supreme Court held that probate judges in the territories could hear only probate matters and that all other disputes (except small claims) had to go before the federal judges (*Ferris v. Higley*, 87 U.S. [20 Wal.] 375, 384 [1874]).

3. These powers were conferred by the Kearny Code, as augmented by the Act of July 12, 1851, passed at the inaugural session of the legislative assembly. See General Laws of New Mexico (1882), chap.21, §§ 3, 7–10, 18. The County Commission Act of 1876 transferred many of the probate judge's powers to newly formed county commissions (N.M. Laws of 1875–76, chp.1). Prior to 1869, the county treasurer served at the pleasure of the probate judge (Comp. Laws of N.M. [1865], chap.21, § 5).

4. Justices of the peace (or *alcaldes*) had jurisdiction over contract matters involving $90.00 or less, and probate judges heard appeals from J.P. courts in matters involving $50.00 or less (Kearny Code, Courts and Judicial Powers, §§ 24 and 43). The probate courts' appellate jurisdiction was abolished in 1876 when J.P. courts were overhauled (N.M. Laws 1875–76, chap.27).

5. Fritz died in June 1874. McSween testified that probate was opened the following April (Angel Report, McSween testimony, p.14). Other accounts give April 1876 as the correct date (Donald R. Lavash, *Sheriff William Brady: Tragic Hero of the Lincoln County War* [Santa Fe: Sunstone Press, 1986], p.57; William A. Keleher, *Violence in Lincoln County 1869–1881* [Albuquerque: University of New Mexico Press, 1957], p.33). The Lincoln County probate records for the period seem to be lost. Keleher quotes from them, but without revealing his source.

6. Angel Report, McSween testimony, pp.15, 19. Murphy disputed these figures.

7. Ibid., Patrón testimony, pp.274–75.

8. *The Daily New Mexican*, May 8, 1875.

9. Angel Report, Patrón testimony, p.274.

10. Two dollars per day was the wage commanded by ranch foremen, as shown by William Morton's letter, quoted in chapter 15. Most cowboys got less. *The Albuquerque Weekly Journal* of May 5, 1881, published stock prices for New Mexico. For a mixed herd, the average price per head was ten to twelve dollars.

11. July 19, 1877, letter from Donnell, Lawson & Co. to McSween, Angel Report, McSween testimony, exhibit 7.

12. McSween letter of Dec. 14, 1876, to Charles Fritz, reproduced in Keleher, *Violence in Lincoln County 1869–1881*, p.35.

13. Angel Report, McSween testimony, p.17.

CHAPTER 3

1. Most accounts of the Kid's childhood rely on Pat Garrett's *The Authentic Life of Billy the Kid, The Noted Desperado of the Southwest* (Santa Fe: New Mexican Printing and Publishing Co., 1882). The portions of Garrett's book recounting his firsthand experiences were apparently written by Garrett himself and are candid to the point of self-exposure. However, major portions of the book, including the depiction of the Kid's childhood, were added by a ghostwriter, Ash Upson, to pad Garrett's memoirs to book length. Upson, in turn, relied on contemporary newspaper accounts of the Kid's early life, including *Newman's Thirty-Four*, Jan. 26, 1881; *Newman's Semi-Weekly*, Apr. 2, 1881; *The Daily New Mexican*, May 3, 1881; *The Las Vegas Daily Optic*, May 4, 1881; *The New Southwest and Grant County Herald*, July 23, 1881. Where the journalists obtained their biographical data is anybody's guess. My guess is that when they weren't cribbing from one another, they just made it up. A pulp novel based on the Kid's life was rushed into print just weeks after his death. It combined reportage with fiction, in uncertain proportions, and contributed mightily to the legend. Don Jenardo, *The True Life of Billy the Kid*, The Five Cent Wide Awake Library, no. 451 (New York: Frank Tousey, publisher, Aug. 29, 1881). It was reprinted in 1945 in a limited edition of 1,000 copies, with a preface by J. C. Dykes, as Happy Hours Brotherhood Reprint No.5 (n.p.).

Scholarly analyses of Garrett's book can be found in Dykes's introduction to the University of Oklahoma Press edition of *The Authentic Life;* Robert S. Utley, *Billy the Kid: A Short and Violent Life* (Lincoln: University of Nebraska Press, 1989), p.199; Ramon F. Adams, *A Fitting Death for Billy the Kid* (Norman: University of Oklahoma Press, 1960), p.20; and Jon Tuska, *Billy the Kid: A Handbook* (Lincoln: University of Nebraska Press, 1983), pp.114–20.

The account of the Kid's pre-Lincoln County life in this chapter and in chapter 6 is taken largely from Utley's biography and Robert N. Mullins's monograph, *The Boyhood of Billy the Kid*, Southwestern Studies Monograph 17 (El Paso: Texas Western Press, 1967).

2. Some of these stories are collected in *They "Knew" Billy the Kid: Interviews with Old-Time New Mexicans,* ed. Robert F. Kadlec (Santa Fe: Ancient City Press, 1987), pp.1–11.

3. *The Grant County Herald,* Sept. 26, 1875. The Sept. 4, 1875, edition contains another news story involving two men later to figure in the Lincoln County War: John Riley shot Juan Patrón in the back, later claiming self-defense. The *Herald* pointed out the logical inconsistency between the plea and the nature of Patrón's wound.

4. *The Grant County Herald,* Sept. 1, 1877; *The Mesilla Valley Independent,* Sept. 1, 1877. Both papers reprinted a story originally carried in the Tucson, Arizona *Citizen.*

5. Utley accepts the story (*Billy the Kid,* pp.21–22); so do a host of lesser writers. The legend was first told in the chapters of Garrett's *The Authentic Life of Billy the Kid* ghostwritten by Upson – in itself a powerful argument against authenticity.

6. Lily Klasner, *My Girlhood among Outlaws* (Tucson: University of Arizona Press, 1972), p.174.

7. Dudley court of inquiry transcript, Sue McSween testimony, p.221.

CHAPTER 4

1. General biographical information is drawn from Frederick W. Nolan, *The Life and Death of John Henry Tunstall* (Albuquerque: University of New Mexico Press, 1965).

2. For example, during the very months Tunstall was establishing himself in New Mexico, the future tycoons Henry Villard and James Hill, who had entered the industry as representatives of German and Dutch investors, bought their first railroads with capital raised in Frankfurt and London (Dietrich G. Buss, *Henry Villard: A Study of Transatlantic Investments and Interests* [New York: Arno Press, 1978], pp.30–111; Albro Martin, *James J. Hill and the Opening of the Northwest* [1976; St. Paul: Minnesota Historical Society Press, 1991], pp.121–54).

3. Nolan, *The Life and Death of John Henry Tunstall,* pp.89–148.

4. Tunstall letter home of Oct. 15, 1875, reproduced in ibid., p.88. Tunstall made this remark with reference to his plan, seriously entertained but soon abandoned, to make his fortune on one of the Aleutian Islands.

5. This description and the following account are taken from Tunstall's letter home of Nov. 16, 1876, reproduced in ibid., pp.190–93.

6. Tunstall letter home of Mar. 27, 1877, reproduced in ibid., pp.205–6.

7. Ibid.

8. Ibid., p.207.

9. Tunstall letter home of Apr. 27–28, 1877, reproduced in ibid., p.213.

10. McSween letter to John Crouch (district court clerk), Dec. 16, 1875, in the

correspondence file for the District Court Clerk, Third Judicial District, Lincoln County District Court, 1875, NMRCA. Wilson's execution was described in a more straightforward fashion by *The Daily New Mexican* of Dec. 21, 1875. Casey's daughter, Lily Klasner, believed that the execution was deliberately bungled, and that Wilson was supposed to make his escape after being let down from the gallows (Klasner, *My Girlhood among Outlaws* [Tucson: University of Arizona Press, 1972], pp.124–36).

11. The Desert Lands Act, 19 Stat. 377 (1877), required an initial filing fee of twenty-five cents per acre, or $160.00 per section, payment of which authorized a person to settle on government land. After the land was irrigated, title could be obtained for an additional fee of one dollar per acre. Richard Burton paid $175.00 for his mail coach ticket in 1860 (Burton, *The Look of the West, 1860: Across the Plains to California,* [Lincoln: University of Nebraska Press, 1963], p.10, an abridged version of Burton's 1862 travel account, *The City of the Saints and Across the Rocky Mountains to California*).

12. William A. Keleher, *Violence in Lincoln County 1869–1881* (Albuquerque: University of New Mexico Press, 1957), p.17; Robert S. Utley, *High Noon in Lincoln: Violence on the Western Frontier* (Albuquerque: University of New Mexico Press, 1987) p.27 and n.9; Maurice Garland Fulton, *History of the Lincoln County War,* ed. Robert N. Mullin (Tucson: University of Arizona Press, 1968), p.83; Nolan, *The Life and Death of John Henry Tunstall,* p.216 and n.24. Tunstall referred to his purchase ("it is too long to go into now") in his letter of May 7, 1877, reproduced in Nolan, *The Life and Death of John Henry Tunstall,* p.217.

13. Tunstall letter home of Jan. 30, 1878, reproduced in Nolan, *The Life and Death of John Henry Tunstall,* p.264.

CHAPTER 5

1. Quoted in William A. Keleher, *Violence in Lincoln County 1869–1881* (Albuquerque: University of New Mexico Press, 1957), pp.52–53.

2. The legal documents are reproduced in ibid., pp.35–38.

3. Angel Report, McSween testimony, p.19 and exhibit 7.

4. Robert Utley concludes that "no less than Jimmy Dolan, Alex McSween teetered on the edge of bankruptcy" (Utley, *High Noon in Lincoln: Violence on the Western Frontier* [Albuquerque: University of New Mexico Press, 1987], p.36 and n.35). Utley draws this conclusion from the declining balance of McSween's account with Thomas Benton Catron's Santa Fe bank, which may prove only that McSween shifted his money to a bank that didn't finance the House. Besides, cash on hand is only one item on the asset side of a balance sheet. Still, given the number of business projects McSween was planning or involved in, he undoubtedly could have used the money.

5. Probate judges were required to convene court on the first Monday of ev-

ery other month, starting with January (Kearny Code, Courts and Judicial Powers, § 3, N.M. Comp. Laws chap.21, § 2 [1865]).

6. Mary Whatley Clarke, *John Simpson Chisum: Jinglebob King of the Pecos* (Austin, Tex.: Eakin Press, 1984), pp.7–25; John Sinclair Drago, *The Great Range Wars: Violence on the Grassland* (Lincoln: University of Nebraska Press, 1985), pp.44–45; Lily Klasner, *My Girlhood among Outlaws* (Tucson: University of Arizona Press, 1972), pp.231–330; Maurice Garland Fulton, *History of the Lincoln County War,* ed. Robert N. Mullin (Tucson: University of Arizona Press, 1968), p.33; Harwood P. Hinton, Jr., "John Simpson Chisum, 1877–84," *New Mexico Historical Review* 32 (1956): 184–90.

7. Quoted in Fulton, *History of the Lincoln County War,* p.33.

8. *The Daily New Mexican* of Nov. 18, 1875, reprinted a dispatch from the *Marion (Indiana) Chronicle* describing the

famous Chisum cattle ranche, containing about sixteen hundred sections of land, on which Mr. Chisum has at this time eighty thousand head of cattle. He claims that he can fill an order for forty thousand beeves, sent him by telegraph from New York, on ten days' notice. Be that as it may, he is the "Cow King" of [New] Mexico, to use a provincial phrase.

9. Hinton, "John Simpson Chisum," p.188; Clarke, *John Simpson Chisum,* pp.1–4.

10. Fulton, *History of the Lincoln County War,* pp.36–43; Hinton, "John Simpson Chisum," pp.199–201; letter of Andy Boyle, *The Mesilla Valley Independent,* June 23, 1877. Fulton does not reveal the source for the story of the buried ears, but to this day criminal suspects in southern New Mexico are accused of cutting off livestock ears to obliterate earmarks. See *State v. Havens,* New Mexico Court of Appeals Cause No.13,385 (1993).

11. Angel Report, McSween testimony, p.13; John P. Wilson, *Merchants, Guns and Money: The Story of Lincoln County and Its Wars* (Santa Fe: Museum of New Mexico Press, 1987), pp.56–59, 74. Wilson analyzes the House's financial condition, but his figures apparently do not include the value of non-cash transactions.

CHAPTER 6

1. Tunstall letter home of Nov. 29, 1877, reproduced in Frederick W. Nolan, *The Life and Death of John Henry Tunstall* (Albuquerque: University of New Mexico Press, 1965), p.212. Smallpox was epidemic in New Mexico in 1877. See Lily Klasner, *My Girlhood among Outlaws* (Tucson: University of Arizona Press, 1972), p.162; *The Daily New Mexican,* July 20, 30, and 31, 1877; *The Mesilla News,* Sept. 8, 1877; *The Grant County Herald,* Jan. 27, 1877; *The Albuquerque Review,* Oct. 1, 13, 20, and Nov. 24, 1877.

2. *The Mesilla Valley Independent,* Sept. 29, 1877. The theft had been reported in the previous week's issue of the *Independent.* The prior story erro-

neously reported, "Two of the stolen animals belonged to Mr. Brewer, and two were the property of Mr. Widenman." The thieves were identified as "Jesse Evans and a companion in crime whose name we did not learn" (*The Mesilla Valley Independent*, Sept. 22, 1877).

McSween probably exaggerated the value of the stolen animals. According to the long-time territorial secretary, "The price of horses, broke to saddle or harness, varies from $35 for the ordinary stock pony to $75 for a good carriage horse" (William G. Ritch, *Aztlan: The History, Resources and Attractions of New Mexico,* 6th ed. [Boston: D. Lothrop & Co., 1885], p.61).

3. Ed Bartholomew, *Jesse Evans: A Texas Hide-burner* (Houston: Frontier Press of Texas, 1955), p.6; Grady E. McCright and James H. Powell, *Jessie Evans: Lincoln County Badman* (College Station, Tex.: Creative Publishing Co., 1983), p.201. As the titles of these two books reveal, there is disagreement about the spelling of Evans's first name. A signature spelling the name "Jessie," which looks like it was scrawled by a child, is reproduced in McCright and Powell, p.203. Because we cannot be certain the signature is authentic, or that Evans was literate enough to choose between alternative spellings, I have used the traditional form.

4. Philip J. Rasch, "The Story of Jessie J. Evans," *Panhandle Plains Historical Review* 33 (1960): 108–11; McCright and Powell, *Jessie Evans,* pp.20–56. McCright and Powell reproduce a number of *Mesilla Valley Independent* articles and editorials thundering against "the banditti."

5. Robert N. Mullin, "Here Lies John Kinney," *Journal of Arizona History* 14, no. 3 (1973): 223. *The Mesilla Valley Independent* of Nov. 3, 1877, reported that "Kenny" shot an unarmed man in the face. The next week's issue carried a well-written letter from Kinney claiming that the shooting was done in self-defense. After that, *The Independent* spelled his name correctly.

6. Rynerson letter of Sept. 24, 1877, to acting governor Ritch, Papers of Governor Axtell, letters received, NMRCA.

7. Quoted in Tunstall's Nov. 28, 1877 letter home, reproduced in Nolan, *The Life and Death of John Henry Tunstall,* p.246.

8. Brewer had settled on the ranch abandoned by the Horrell clan, whose bloody story is told in P. J. Rasch, "The Horrell War," *New Mexico Historical Review* 31 (1956): 223–31. Brewer eventually obtained title from the government (Angel Report, Widenmann testimony, p.190).

9. Angel Report, Widenmann testimony, pp.189–90.

10. Bowdre and Scurlock were rough characters in their own right (*The Mesilla Valley Independent,* Aug. 25 and Sept. 8, 1877).

11. Tunstall letter home of Nov. 29, 1877, reproduced in Nolan, *The Life and Death of John Henry Tunstall,* pp.243–44. Robert Widenmann, who claimed to have the story directly from Brewer, testified that Brewer went alone to Mesilla to obtain warrants and enlist the sheriff's aid while Bowdre and Scurlock

continued on the outlaws' trail and eventually confronted them (Angel Report, Widenmann testimony, pp.190–91). His testimony virtually paraphrases a report published in *The Mesilla Valley Independent* on Sept. 22, 1878. The similarity between the newspaper report and Widenmann's testimony can be explained in two ways: either they corroborate each other, in which case this version must be considered the more reliable, or else Widenmann parroted what he had read in the paper. I am inclined to the latter view, since the newspaper report garbles key details – for example, it states the horses belonged to Brewer and Widenmann rather than Tunstall and McSween. In addition, it is difficult to see why Tunstall would fabricate the details he repeated to his parents, since the story is satisfactorily dramatic either way.

12. The following account is taken from Tunstall's letter home of Nov. 29, 1877, reproduced in Nolan, *The Life and Death of John Henry Tunstall*, pp.244–47. For a discussion of Brewer's legal authority as deputy constable, see my article, "An Excess of Law in Lincoln County: Thomas B. Catron, Samuel B. Axtell and the Lincoln County War," *New Mexico Historical Review* 68 (1993): 133–51.

13. This quote and the following account are taken from Tunstall's epic-length letter home of Nov. 29, 1877, reproduced in Nolan, *The Life and Death of John Henry Tunstall*, pp.243–49.

14. They missed a golden opportunity even if the account given in *The Independent* is accepted. *The Independent* reported that the horses were stolen "in Mr. Brewer's presence" (*The Mesilla Valley Independent*, Sept. 22, 1878).

15. "Rat" was western slang for an undersized horse or mule (Richard Burton, *The Look of the West 1860: Across the Plains to California* [Lincoln: University of Nebraska Press, 1963], p.17).

CHAPTER 7

1. This quote and the following account are taken from Tunstall's letter home of Nov. 29, 1877, reproduced in Frederick W. Nolan, *The Life and Death of John Henry Tunstall* (Albuquerque: University of New Mexico Press, 1965), pp.244, 251–52.

2. Donald R. Lavash, *Sheriff William Brady: Tragic Hero of the Lincoln County War* (Santa Fe: Sunstone Press, 1986), pp.15–32. Lavash counts nine Brady children, but Colonel Dudley's weekly report of July 13, 1878, described Mrs. Brady as the mother of eight (AGO microfilm, frame 442).

3. Angel Report, McSween testimony, pp.11–12.

4. Ibid.

5. Tunstall letter home of Nov. 29, 1877, reprinted in Nolan, *The Life and Death of John Henry Tunstall*, p.253.

6. Some historians credit the accusation that Tunstall helped engineer the escape. See Robert S. Utley, *High Noon in Lincoln: Violence on the Western Fron-*

tier (Albuquerque: University of New Mexico Press, 1987), p.35; Lavash, *Sheriff William Brady*, p.70. Nolan is equivocal in *The Life and Death of John Henry Tunstall*, pp.255–56.

7. Tunstall letter home of Nov. 29, 1877, reproduced in Nolan, *The Life and Death of John Henry Tunstall*, p.250.

8. Angel Report, Patrón testimony, p.277.

9. This quote and the following account are taken from Tunstall's Nov. 29, 1877, letter home, reproduced in Nolan, *The Life and Death of John Henry Tunstall*, pp.253–55.

CHAPTER 8

1. The petition is reproduced in William A. Keleher, *Violence in Lincoln County 1869–1881* (Albuquerque: University of New Mexico Press, 1957), pp.40–41.

2. Catron was a political power in New Mexico for more than a half-century, ending his career as one of New Mexico's first U.S. senators. He is remembered for his acquisition of title to numerous Spanish and Mexican land grants. In northern New Mexico today, his reputation might be compared to Cromwell's in Connaught. See John R. Van Ness, "Hispanic Land Grants: Ecology and Subsistence in the Uplands of Northern New Mexico and Southern Colorado," in *Land, Water and Culture: New Perspectives on Hispanic Land Grants,* ed. Charles L. Briggs and John R. Van Ness (Albuquerque: University of New Mexico Pres, 1987), pp.197–98; Malcolm Ebright, *The Tierra Amarilla Grant: A History of Chicanery* (Santa Fe: The Center for Land Grant Studies, 1980), pp.25–27; Anselmo F. Arellano, *La Tierra Amarilla: The People of the Chama Valley* (Tierra Amarilla, N.M.: Chama Valley Schools, 1978), pp.35–36. Catron's biographer, Victor Westphall, attempted to correct the record, but overcompensated. His *Thomas Benton Catron and His Era* (Tucson: University of Arizona Press, 1973) is highly defensive, but contains much valuable biographical data. Disbarment proceedings were brought against Catron late in his career, but the New Mexico Supreme Court decided, by a divided vote, to allow him to keep his license. Justice Laughlin's dissent gives a fascinating look at Catron's style of legal hardball: *In re Catron*, 8 N.M. 253, 273, 43 P. 724, 731 (1895) (Laughlin, J., dissenting).

3. Tunstall letter home of Apr. 28, 1877, reproduced in Frederick W. Nolan, *The Life and Death of John Henry Tunstall* (Albuquerque: University of New Mexico Press, 1965), p.212.

4. *The Albuquerque Review,* Jan. 26, 1878.

5. Westphall, *Thomas Benton Catron and His Era,* pp.131–32; Simeon H. Newman, III, "The Santa Fe Ring: A Letter to the *New York Sun,*" *Arizona and the West* 12 (1970): pp.269–88 (quoting S. H. Newman's July 31, 1875, letter to the editors of *The New York Sun*). For concrete example of Catron's use of

threatened prosecution as a technique of persuasion, see ibid. at 274 and Angel Report, McSween testimony, pp.46–47.

6. Newman, "The Santa Fe Ring," p.274. The incident for which Newman was prosecuted occurred in March 1872, the month in which Catron switched jobs from territorial attorney general to U.S. attorney.

7. Oscar Doane Lambert, *Stephen Benton Elkins* (Pittsburgh: University of Pittsburgh Press, 1955); Otis K. Rice, *West Virginia: A History* (Lexington: University Press of Kentucky, 1985), pp.207–8; Keleher, *The Maxwell Land Grant: A New Mexico Item* (1964; Albuquerque: University of New Mexico Press, 1984), pp.147–50; E. Lawrence Marquess, "The West Virginia Venture: Empire Out of Wilderness," *West Virginia History* 14 (1952): 5. Elkins's son was the Republican Davis Elkins, who was appointed to the Senate in 1911 to complete his father's term, and then in 1918, following ratification of the 17th Amendment, was elected in his own right.

8. Edgar A. Walz to Catron, June 8, 1897, reproduced in Westphall, *Thomas Benton Catron and His Era,* p.25.

9. Catron, Elkins, and José Leandro Perea were the three principal owners (ibid., p.67).

10. McSween Jan. 10, 1878, letter to the *Eco del Rio Grande,* reproduced in Maurice Garland Fulton, *History of the Lincoln County War,* ed. Robert N. Mullin (Tucson: University of Arizona Press, 1968), p.99.

11. Angel Report, McSween testimony, p.23. The Chisum narrative described in the following note confirms that Catron was the "certain party." The newspaper editor may have edited out Catron's name for fear of reprisal.

12. Quoted in Lily Klasner, *My Girlhood among Outlaws* (Tucson: University of Arizona Press, 1972), p.274. Chisum was subsequently indicted for resisting arrest, pleading not guilty at the March 1878 term of court. A year later, the state dropped charges (San Miguel County criminal case #912 [1877], NMRCA).

CHAPTER 9

1. Although it was originally filed in the criminal case, the affidavit can now be found in the file of the civil case *Fritz and Scholand v. McSween,* Lincoln County civil case #141 (1878), NMRCA.

2. In the nineteenth century, and indeed until 1961, it was settled doctrine that the Fourth Amendment "restrains the issue of warrants only under the laws of the United States, and has no application to state processes" (*Smith v. Maryland,* 59 U.S. [18 How.] 71, 76 [1855]). However, a different rule applied to territories. In 1881, when Judge Bristol was still a member, the New Mexico Supreme Court held: "In a territory the constitution and laws of the United States . . . stand exactly in the relation a state constitution occupies in a state" (*In the Matter of the Attorney General,* 2 N.M. 49, 58 [1881]; *Accord Territory v. Cu-*

tinola, 4 N.M. [Gild.] 305, 316, 14 P. 809, 813 [1887]; *Murphy v. Ramsey,* 114 U.S. 15, 44 [1885]; *National Bank v. County of Yankton,* 101 U.S. [11 Otto] 129, 133 [1879] *American Ins. Co. v. 356 Bales of Cotton,* 26 U.S. [1 Pet.] 511, 543 [1828]).

3. In a 1877 case, Justice Joseph P. Bradley of the United States Supreme Court, sitting as circuit justice, determined that arrest warrants based on affidavits made on "information and belief" violated the Fourth Amendment (*In re Rule of Court,* 20 Fed. Cas. 1336, 1337 [C.C.N.D. Ga. 1877] [No.12, 126]). Justice Bradley's opinion contains a lucid discussion of the rationale for this constitutional requirement. The same result was reached in *Comfort v. Fulton,* 39 Barb. 56, 57–58 (N.Y. App. Div. 1861). The full Supreme Court didn't get around to deciding the issue until 1901, when it agreed with Justice Bradley: "A citizen ought not to be deprived of his personal liberty upon an allegation which, upon being sifted, may amount to nothing more than a suspicion" (*Rice v. Ames,* 180 U.S. 371, 374 [1901]).

4. This and the following quotation are from Angel Report, Dolan testimony, pp.244–47.

5. McSween Jan. 10, 1878, letter to the *Eco del Rio Grande,* reproduced in Maurice Garland Fulton, *History of the Lincoln County War,* ed. Robert N. Mullin (Tucson: University of Arizona Press, 1968), p.99. This letter was apparently written from jail.

6. Angel Report, Dolan testimony, p.242 (the second of two pages numbered 242).

7. McSween Jan. 10, 1878, letter to the *Eco del Rio Grande,* reproduced in Fulton, *History of the Lincoln County War,* p.99.

8. July 19, 1877, letter from Donnell, Lawson & Co., Bankers, to McSween; Angel Report, McSween testimony, exhibit 7; ibid., exhibits 2 and 3.

9. Bristol's grand jury charge was printed in *The Las Vegas Gazette* on May 4, 1878. This issue of *The Gazette* is an exhibit to Angel's Report. On November 12, 1881, Fritz and Scholand won a judgment in the amount of $3,300.00, an amount that presumably included interest and costs (*Fritz and Scholand v. McSween,* Lincoln County civil case #141 [1878], NMRCA).

10. The appraisal can be found in the case file for *Fritz and Scholand v. McSween.*

11. Angel Report, McSween testimony, p.25.

12. "Pintor Ornamental," actually. The advertisement ran in the Jan. 12, 1878, edition of the Las Vegas *Anunciador de Nuevo Méjico.* On March 16, 1877, Barrier was indicted on two counts of larceny involving forty pounds of paint and 1,200 pounds of white lead (*Territory v. Barrier,* San Miguel County criminal cases #863, 864 [1877]). The quantities involved suggest the matter was a business dispute.

13. Governor Axtell's annual message was printed in *The Mesilla Valley Independent,* Jan. 5, 1878.

14. *The Mesilla Valley Independent,* Jan. 26, 1878; the letter is reproduced in Angel Report, McSween testimony, exhibit 9.

15. A copy of the returned check is exhibit 1 to McSween's Angel Report testimony.

16. Angel Report, Dolan testimony, pp.235–36.

17. Ibid., pp.243, 237.

18. Ibid., pp.236–37. The $26,000 figure is reached by adding together the minimum value of the mortgage and the value of the notes endorsed by the bank.

19. *The Mesilla Valley Independent,* Feb. 2, 1878. A clipping of Dolan's reply can be found in Angel Report, McSween testimony, exhibit 9.

20. Details of this journey are taken from Angel Report, McSween testimony, pp.25–26, and Barrier testimony, p.290.

21. District Attorney Rynerson had sponsored Shield for admission to the Third Judicial District bar just four months previously (Records of Lincoln County district court for Oct. 3, 1877, NMRCA).

22. For instance, the Jan. 12, 1878 issue of the *Anunciador de Nuevo Méjico,* under the punning headline "Ruidoso Negocio" [Ruidoso Business, or literally Noisy Business] ran a short dispatch that began, "Last week, the arrest of Messrs. John S. Chisum and N. A. *[sic]* McSween from Lincoln County caused a great excitement in the courthouse of the justice of the peace." (Many thanks to Patricia Gandert for the translation.)

23. Angel Report, Barrier testimony, pp.290–91.

24. Quoted from the caption beneath Bristol's photograph in Robert S. Utley, *High Noon in Lincoln: Violence on the Western Frontier* (Albuquerque: University of New Mexico Press, 1987), following p.50.

25. Despite his thirteen years of service, Bristol rated just two passing references in Arie W. Poldervaart's history of the New Mexico Supreme Court, *Black-Robed Justice* (Santa Fe: Historical Society of New Mexico, 1948), pp.83, 105.

26. Bristol's statement was prompted by Widenmann's testimony, under oath, that no such partnership existed (*The Mesilla News,* July 6, 1878).

27. Angel Report, Barrier and Shield joint affidavit, p.185.

28. Ibid., McSween testimony, p.33. There is no evidence that McSween and Tunstall were partners other than the bare assertions of Judge Bristol and Jimmy Dolan's employee, James Longwell (ibid., Longwell testimony, p.254).

CHAPTER 10
1. Grady E. McCright and James H. Powell, *Jessie Evans: Lincoln County Badman* (College Station, Tex.: Creative Publishing Co., 1983), p.72; *The Mesilla Valley Independent,* Jan. 26, 1878.

2. Details of the return journey are taken from Angel Report, McSween testimony, pp.26–30; Barrier testimony, pp.291–92.

3. Ibid., Dolan testimony, pp.240–41.

4. Ibid., McSween testimony, p.28. In McSween's telling, the incident bears a striking resemblance to the 1873 incident when Dolan threatened to shoot a Fort Stanton officer. On that occasion, too, Dolan took the precaution of leveling his gun on his adversary before challenging him to a fight (Frederick W. Nolan, *The Life and Death of John Henry Tunstall* [Albuquerque: University of New Mexico Press, 1965], p.186).

5. Angel Report, McSween testimony, p.29. Barrier largely corroborated McSween's testimony, but he did not mention *The Independent* (ibid., Barrier testimony, p.292).

6. Ibid., Dolan testimony, pp.240–42.

7. Ibid.

8. Ibid., p.242 (the first of the two pages with that number). The meeting is described in Barrier's testimony, p.292, and McSween's testimony, p.30.

9. Ibid., McSween testimony, pp.30–31.

10. McSween letter to Secretary Schurz, Feb. 11, 1878, National Archives record group 75, Office of Indian Affairs, letters received, microcopy 234, roll 576.

11. 7 Cong. Rec. 3620 (May 21, 1878).

12. 7 Cong. Rec. 3840 (May 27, 1878) (remarks of Rep. Thomas Patterson [D. Colo.]); p.4235 (June 7, 1878) (remarks of Sen. Allen Thurman [D. Ohio]); p.3839 (May 27, 1878) (remarks of Rep. Henry Blackstone Banning [D. Ohio]).

13. Angel Report on Godfroy. Angel, who seems to have liked Godfroy ("an educated and cultured gentleman surrounded by a loving and refined family"), acknowledged that the count was made "under unfortunate circumstances." He amplifies the point at p.95 (Angel letter to Watkins, July 2, 1878). Godfroy complained to his superiors that, as a result of Angel's insistence that the Apaches come to him to be counted, his census entirely missed a band of two hundred camped a short distance from the agency (*Annual Report of the Commissioner of Indian Affairs to the Secretary of the Interior* [Washington, D.C.: U.S. Government Printing Office, 1878], p.107). But that still meant Godfroy drew rations for 328 more people than he could account for.

14. Angel Report on Godfroy, Gallegos testimony, p.34; Dolan testimony, pp.42–43, 45.

15. The attachment action is *Fritz and Scholand v. McSween*, Lincoln County civil case #141 (1878), NMRCA. The petition and writ are both dated February 7, 1878.

16. The bond is included in the case file. It was notarized by A. J. Fountain, the deputy clerk of court who was also editor of *The Mesilla Valley Independent*. After Rynerson left his position as district attorney, he represented Fritz and Scholand in the lawsuit.

17. A detailed discussion of the New Mexico attachment statute and an analysis of the legality of actions taken by Judge Bristol and Sheriff Brady can be found in my article, "An Excess of Law in Lincoln County: Thomas B. Catron,

Samuel Axtell and the Lincoln County War," *New Mexico Historical Review* 68 (1993): 133–52.

18. Angel Report, McSween testimony, p.33. It appears that the writ was actually served on February 9 (ibid., Mathews testimony, p.210; Widenmann testimony, p.193; affidavit of F. G. Christie, dated Apr. 15, 1878, filed in Lincoln County civil case #141 [1878], NMRCA). Whether the correct date is February 8 or 9th makes little difference, since the trip from Mesilla to Lincoln normally took four days (*The Mesilla News,* June 29, 1878).

19. Angel Report, Dolan testimony, p.240. The date is indirectly corroborated by McSween and Barrier, who testified they also left Mesilla on February 5.

20. Affidavit of George Peppin, dated Apr. 15, 1878, in Lincoln County civil case #141 (1878), NMRCA. The common law of partnerships is discussed in my article, "An Excess of Law in New Mexico."

21. "Lincoln County Postscript: Notes on Robert A. Widenmann by His Daughter, Elsie Widenman," ed. Bruce T. Ellis, *New Mexico Historical Review* 50 (July 1975): 215. Widenmann's daughter changed the spelling of the family name during World War I to make it less conspicuously German.

22. Ibid., p.275.

23. Schurz was just twenty when he emerged as a leader of the 1848 revolution. Recent accounts of his spectacular career include *Carl Schurz: Revolutionär und Staatsmann/Revolutionary and Statesman,* ed. Ruediger Wersich (Munich: Heinz Moos Verlag, 1979); Hans L. Trefousse, *Carl Schurz: A Biography* (Knoxville: University of Tennessee Press, 1982).

24. Angel Report, Widenmann testimony, pp.193–94.

25. The inventory, written by Deputy F. G. Christie, is filed in Lincoln County civil case #141 (1878), NMRCA. No valuation is placed on any of the listed property.

26. Angel Report, Widenmann testimony, pp.193–94.

27. Ibid., "In the Matter of the Lincoln County Troubles," p.2. This evaluation overestimated Peppin's leadership abilities.

28. Quoted in *Missionaries, Outlaws and Indians: Taylor F. Ealy at Lincoln and Zuni, 1878–1881,* ed. Norman J. Bender (Albuquerque: University of New Mexico Press, 1984), p.26.

29. Angel Report, Longwell testimony, p.248. Longwell's name is frequently spelled Longwill – including in the first line of his own affidavit – but his signature spells the name with an "e."

30. Ibid., Widenmann testimony, p.194.

CHAPTER 11

1. Slough's triumph as military commander is detailed in Ray C. Colton, *The Civil War in the Western Territories* (Norman: University of Oklahoma Press,

1959), pp. 58–72. For the jaundiced view of a soldier who served under him, see Ovando J. Hollister, *Colorado Volunteers in New Mexico, 1862,* ed. Richard Harwell (Chicago: The Lakeside Press, 1962), pp. 75–76, 132–33. Slough's death was reported in *The New Mexican* on Dec. 17, 1867, although the newspaper's front-page "Official Directory" continued to list him as territorial chief justice for weeks to come. The following account of his murder is derived from Gary L. Roberts, *Death Comes for the Chief Justice: The Slough-Rynerson Quarrel and Political Violence in New Mexico* (Niwot: University Press of Colorado, 1990).

2. Angel Report, McSween testimony, pp. 46–47. A copy of the bond submitted to Rynerson is exhibit 15 to McSween's testimony.

3. Ibid., pp. 32–33.

4. Ibid., pp. 50–52; Barrier testimony, pp. 293–94.

5. *Territory v. Barrier,* Lincoln County criminal case #260 (1878), NMRCA. There is no record that this prosecution progressed beyond the filing of the information. William A. Keleher reprints a newspaper article erroneously stating that Barrier was charged with contempt of court (*Violence in Lincoln County 1869–1881* [Albuquerque: University of New Mexico Press, 1957], p. 63).

6. Angel Report, Bonney testimony, p. 314. Benito Cruz, the murder victim mentioned in Bonney's testimony, was killed by the Boys in the course of a robbery. Cruz's eighty-year-old father-in-law was also shot, lingering for several months before dying. The killer was recognized: "He is a man named Ponciano and is said to have been connected with the bandits not long since" (*The Mesilla Valley Independent,* Sept. 15, 1877; Dec. 1, 1877). At the request of District Attorney Rynerson, Acting Governor W. G. Ritch (the territorial secretary) offered a $500 reward for the arrest and conviction of Cruz's murderers (*The Mesilla Valley Independent,* Oct. 6, 1877).

Robert S. Utley suggests that Bonney's testimony was actually written by Rob Widenmann (*High Noon in Lincoln: Violence on the Western Frontier* [Albuquerque: University of New Mexico Press, 1987], p. 81; *Billy the Kid: A Short and Violent Life* [Lincoln: University of Nebraska Press, 1989], p. 83). Utley bases his suspicion on the resemblance between the handwriting of the two statements. While Utley's thesis cannot be disproved, it is shaky. First, Widenmann gave two statements, written in different hands, demonstrating the fallibility of handwriting as a guide to authorship. Second, all of the testimony in Angel's report – from thirty-nine different witnesses – is in very few hands. If graphological similarity proves forgery, then most of the testimony must be discounted, not just Bonney's. Third, the witness statements are, by and large, neither depositions nor affidavits in the modern sense. With a few exceptions, most of the statements appear to be paraphrases of testimony, perhaps worked up from shorthand notes. Nevertheless, Bonney's and Widenmann's statements are sufficiently similar in content that we can't rule out the possibility that Widenmann drafted both. However, it seems at least as likely that the two witnesses merely coordinated their stories. Enough of Bonney's correspondence has survived to prove he was literate and articulate, with no need to rely on a ghostwriter.

7. Biographical information is taken from Mathews' front-page obituary in *The Roswell Register,* June 10, 1904.

8. Angel Report, Mathews testimony, pp.210–11.

9. *The Mesilla News,* July 6, 1878.

10. Angel Report, Mathews testimony, pp.213 ½–14.

11. Ibid., Bonney testimony, p.315.

12. Ibid., Gauss testimony, pp.297–98.

13. Angel's concise comments on various New Mexicans, written for the benefit of incoming Governor Lew Wallace, are reprinted in "Frank Warner Angel's Notes on New Mexico Territory, 1878," ed. Lee Scott Theisen, *Arizona and the West* 18 (Winter 1976): 333–70. The comment about Widenmann can be found on p.368. Angel also described Widenmann as "well connected in the east & well educated" (ibid.).

14. Angel Report, Widenmann testimony, p.195.

15. Ibid., Bonney testimony, p.315.

16. Ibid., Mathews testimony, p.211.

17. Ibid., Gauss testimony, p.298; Middleton testimony, p.308.

18. Angel Report, on the Cause and Circumstances, p.2.

19. Angel Report, Hurley testimony, pp.261–62.

20. Ibid., Widenmann testimony, p.198.

CHAPTER 12

1. Larry D. Ball, *The United States Marshals of New Mexico and Arizona Territories, 1846–1912* (Albuquerque: University of New Mexico Press, 1978), p.79. Sherman was not treated with great respect in the territorial press. In a scathing editorial, *The Grant County Herald* wrote, "He is highly connected, and credited with power to command unlimited influence; but it strikes us that the people of New Mexico have endured him quite long enough." *The Herald* accused Sherman of drawing pay for phantom and no-show employees, forging signatures on paychecks, and being "stupidly drunk in open court." The paper dared Sherman to sue (he didn't), and concluded: "Insignificant as we are upon this frontier, we will try to make it apparent to John Sherman, Sr. that he cannot afford to carry so utterly worthless a subject of nepotism – even in New Mexico" (*The Grant County Herald,* June 21, 1879). In its December 1, 1877, issue, *The Mesilla Valley Independent* reported accusations that Sherman paid federal grand jurors in vouchers that could be redeemed only at certain stores and only at a steep discount. Sherman then allowed the shopkeepers to cash in the vouchers at their face value, splitting the illicit profit (the scheme is detailed in *The*

Herald's editorial). Sherman denied the charges, but he was strongly condemned in the report of the grand jurors, who felt swindled (*The Mesilla Valley Independent*, Dec. 22, 1877). A year and a half later, a different federal grand jury issued a report blasting him for neglect of duties (*The Mesilla Valley Independent*, June 28, 1879; *The Grant County Herald*, July 4, 1879). *The Mesilla Valley Independent* reported in its June 21, 1879, issue that Sherman had somehow forgotten to transport prisoners to court for trial. And so on.

2. Axtell to Collis P. Huntington, Sept. 19, 1878, Axtell papers, letters sent 1875–84, NMRCA.

3. Organic Act Establishing the Territory of New Mexico, 9 Stat. 446 (Sept. 9, 1850), § 12. One of the charges leveled against Sherman was that he delegated the duties of marshal to part-time duties (*The Grant County Herald*, June 21, 1879). For a discussion of the unlikelihood that Schurz concerned himself with Widenmann's appointment as deputy, see "Lincoln County Postscript: Notes on Robert A. Widenmann by His Daughter, Elsie Widenman," ed. Bruce T. Ellis, *New Mexico Historical Review* 50 (July 1975): 219.

4. Angel Report, Widenmann testimony, p.192.

5. Ibid., p.193.

6. Ibid., Bonney testimony, p.315; Widenmann testimony, p.196.

7. Ibid., Bonney testimony, pp.315–16.

8. Ibid.

9. Ibid., Widenmann testimony, p.197.

10. Ibid., McSween testimony, p.36.

11. Ibid., Widenmann testimony, p.199.

12. Ibid., McSween testimony, pp.36–37.

13. Ibid., p.37.

14. Ibid., Widenmann testimony, pp.199–200.

15. Ibid., Gauss testimony, p.299.

16. Widenmann testified that "Sheriff Brady's bondsmen . . . were known to be insolvent" (ibid., Widenmann testimony, p.198).

17. Ibid., pp.200–201.

18. Ibid., Mathews testimony, p.213.

19. Ibid., Dolan testimony, p.258.

20. Ibid., Gauss testimony, pp.300–302.

21. Ibid., p.302.

22. Ibid., Gallegos testimony, pp.219–20.

23. Ibid., Kruling testimony, p.266.

24. Ibid., Gauss testimony, p.301.

25. Ibid., p.300.

26. An inventory of the cattle is contained in the court file for Lincoln County civil case #141 (1878), NMRCA.

27. McSween said the property attached was "worth over $40,000," which I

suspect is an exaggeration in the opposite direction (Angel Report, McSween testimony, p.33).

28. Ibid., Widenmann testimony, p.201.

29. Ibid., Bonney testimony, p.318.

30. Ibid., Middleton testimony, p.309.

31. Ibid., Widenmann testimony, p.202; Bonney testimony, p.318.

32. Four posse members told Special Agent Angel that Evans, Morton, and Hill were in the lead (ibid., Perry testimony, p.226; W. Olinger testimony, p.229; R. Beckwith testimony, p.231; Cochraine testimony, p.232). Two other posse members identified Morton as the leader without mentioning the two Boys (ibid., Gallegos testimony, p.218–19; Kruling testimony, p.267). Albert Howe, who was not present but heard the story from a posse member named George Kitt, testified that Kitt said Hill and Morton were in the lead (ibid., Howe testimony, p.286).

33. Ibid., Bonney testimony, pp.318–19.

CHAPTER 13

1. Angel Report, Gallegos testimony, pp.217–18.

2. Ibid., Widenmann testimony, p.203.

3. Ibid., Gallegos testimony, pp.218–19.

4. Angel Report, on the Cause and Circumstances, p.4. *The Mesilla Valley Independent* of May 11, 1878, editorialized: "We could not see, nor can we yet see any occasion for the killing of Tunstall. The party had captured all the stock they wished to attach without opposition."

5. Angel Report, Hurley testimony, pp.263–64. Gallegos later retracted his story (ibid., Gallegos testimony, p.221).

6. Ibid., Olinger testimony, pp.229–30.

7. Ibid., Perry testimony, pp.228–29. Perry added: "After our return to the Felix I heard either Baker, Evans, or Hill say the death of Tunstall was a small loss, that he ought to have been killed – or something to that effect. I cannot say which one said this of the three. One of these three said that Tunstall had tried to have them killed while they were in jail at Lincoln" (ibid., pp.227–28). This testimony further refutes Brady's accusation that Tunstall helped the Boys escape.

8. Ibid., Howe testimony, pp.286–87. A similar story was told to Florencio Gonzáles by another posse member, the ex-sheriff Alexander Hamilton ("Ham") Mills (ibid., Gonzáles testimony, p.330).

9. Ibid., Olinger testimony, p.229.

10. Ibid., McSween testimony, p.40; Perry testimony, p.227; Olinger testimony, pp.230–31. Prominent Cimarron attorney Frank Springer related the story of the hat with greater clarity than is found in the testimony in an April 9, 1878, letter to Congressman Rush Clarke of Pennsylvania, which Clarke passed on to Secretary of War George W. McCrary (AGO microfilm, frame 302).

McSween added that Tunstall's skull had been "broken in pieces by a blow from some instrument" (Angel Report, McSween testimony, p.41). Perry and Olinger denied this story, and the post surgeon, Dr. Appel, who performed the autopsy, testified that in his opinion the damage to Tunstall's skull was caused solely by the bullet wound and fall (ibid., Appel testimony, p.2).

11. Ibid., Appel testimony, p.3. Dr. Appel described the passage of both bullets and concluded: "It is my opinion that both of the wounds could be made at one and the same time – and if made at the same time were made by different persons from different directions and were both most likely made while Tunstall was on horseback inasmuch as the direction of the wounds were slightly upwards."

12. Ibid., Gonzáles testimony, p.327.

13. Ibid., Bonney testimony, p.319.

14. Dolan's employee James Longwell testified that McSween's house began filling up with armed and dangerous men even before news of Tunstall's death reached town (ibid., Longwell testimony, p.250). The suggestion was that an all-out attack was planned. If so, news of Tunstall's death would have been a spark touched to powder, but there was no explosion. It seems far more likely that the citizens gathered upon hearing word of the murder.

15. Ibid., McSween testimony, p.42.

16. The letter is exhibit 19 to ibid., pp.173–75.

17. Governor Axtell's assertion that Rynerson could stand on the letter was quoted by David Shield, who was not an unbiased source, although I am not aware of any instance where it can be shown he lied. Shield's affidavit is contained in Angel's Report on Axtell, p.111. The accusation that Widenmann stole the letter was originally made by Riley himself, according to Fort Stanton's Lieutenant Millard Filmore Goodwin (Angel Report, Goodwin testimony, p.372 [exhibit E to Purington's official report]). Captain Purington repeated the charge in his official report (ibid., p.344). The charge was given wide circulation in the April 6, 1878, edition of *The Weekly New Mexican*. Widenmann denied the charge after reading Purington's official report (Angel Report, Widenmann testimony p.335). After providing his lengthy testimony, McSween swore out the separate affidavit quoted in the text, stating that the letters left by Riley "were the ones with which Widenmann is charged with having taken from the house of J. J. Dolan & Co. two days after Riley left them at my house" (ibid., McSween testimony, p.342). By alleging that Widenmann stole the letter, of course, Riley acknowledged its authenticity.

The memorandum book, which detailed the House's beef purchases, may have been the evidence on which the Lincoln County grand jury indicted Riley for receiving stolen property (Lincoln County criminal case #262 [1878]).

Historian John P. Wilson argues unconvincingly that the letter is a forgery. He states that "the original letter is probably in McSween's own handwriting," but he appears to be referring to the copy attached as exhibit 19 to McSween's testimony, which McSween specifically testified was not the original (Wilson, *Merchants, Guns and Money: The Story of Lincoln County and Its Wars* [Santa Fe: Museum of New Mexico Press, 1987], p.84). Historian John P. Wilson also asserts that Justice of the Peace John B. (or Green) Wilson did not become *alcalde* or justice of the peace until the very date of the letter, February 14, 1878; thus Rynerson could not have known he was alcalde when he wrote the letter (ibid). In fact, Wilson was appointed exactly one year previously, on February 14, 1877 (Records of the Lincoln County Commission, NMRCA). A copy of Wilson's commission is included in Angel Report on Axtell, p.70; another copy is attached to Ambassador Edward Thornton's letter to Secretary of State William Evarts, Mar. 27, 1878, Historical Records.

CHAPTER 14

1. Angel Report, McSween testimony, p.40.

2. Ibid., Gonzáles testimony, p.326.

3. Wilson's given name, presumably a family name, was Green. John B. or Juan Bautista was his baptismal name, bestowed in 1859 but not used by Wilson in business matters until after 1875 (Dudley Court of Inquiry, Wilson testimony, p.209). See, for example, his signature as "Green Wilson" on a settlement agreement contained in the court file for *Murphy v. Miranda*, Lincoln County civil case #65 (1875), NMRCA. Three years later, he signed his name "John B. Wilson" (see, for example, his affidavit, contained in Angel Report, McSween testimony, exhibit 13, pp.143–45). The Dec. 31, 1875, issue of *The Daily New Mexican* included this somewhat cryptic item, reproduced in its entirety: "Green Wilson of Lincoln county, wants his name changed by act of the Legislative Assembly to 'Juan Bautista.' A bill was introduced to that effect and somebody cruelly moved to lay it in the table and it was laid." In the 1870s, names were legally changed by special legislation rather than by judicial decree, but I have found no legislation pertaining to Wilson. However, when the House, represented by W. L. Rynerson, sued him for a $200 debt, the suit was styled *L. G. Murphy & Co. v. Green Wilson (now known as John B. Wilson)*, Lincoln County civil case #133 (1878). Adding to the confusion about his name is the tendency of some contemporaries to refer to him as Squire Wilson, in reference to his office.

4. N.M. Laws of 1875–76, chap.1, § 40.

5. N.M. Laws of 1866–67, chap.42.

6. Angel Report, McSween testimony, exhibits 9a and 11; Widenmann testimony, p.205.

7. Ibid., McSween testimony, exhibit 12.

8. The verdict form was included as an appendix to the Act of January 30, 1867 (N.M. Laws 1866–67, chap.42, § 3). References to the coroner were anach-

ronistic. The statute giving corners the duty to investigate violent deaths had been repealed in 1864. Since that time the job had been left to justices of the peace, but the old terminology had carried over.

9. The statute authorized Justice Wilson to conduct an inquest only after receiving requests in writing from two citizens. This was the purpose of the affidavits. The jury verdict states that witnesses testified, which presumably refers to live testimony. However, we have no record of the testimony. Middleton's affidavit identified only one killer, "George Henderson" [George Hindemann] (Angel Report, McSween testimony, exhibit 9a, p.131). Brewer and Bonney's joint affidavit named Dolan, Baker, Evans, Davis, Ham Mills, Morton, Thomas Moore, Hindemann, Rivers, and Gallegos (ibid., exhibit 11, p.147). Mathews later told Special Agent Angel that neither Mills, Moore, nor Dolan were part of the sub-posse that pursued the horses (ibid., Mathews testimony, p.215).

10. Widenmann later claimed to have seen Dolan at the murder site (ibid., Widenmann testimony, p.203). He repeated this assertion at Jesse Evans's habeas corpus hearing, where Judge Bristol made it plain he did not believe Widenmann could have identified anyone under the circumstances he described (bullets flying, horses at dead run, distance of two hundred yards, etc.) (*The Mesilla News,* July 6, 1878). When it published the inquest jury's verdict, *The Mesilla Valley Independent* of March 9, 1878, added this postscript: "It is due to Mr. J. J. Dolan to state that he denies being present when Mr. Tunstall was killed."

11. Wilson affidavit of Aug. 31, 1878; Angel Report, McSween testimony, exhibit 13.

12. Angel Report, McSween testimony, p.45. A copy of the warrant is reproduced ibid., exhibit 14.

13. A copy of Widenmann's letter, dated Feb. 20, 1878, is exhibit D to Captain Purington's June 25, 1878, letter to Angel (Angel Report, p.348). Purington and Widenmann engaged in an acrimonious exchange, through Angel, concerning this incident.

14. Angel Report, Martínez testimony, p.340.

15. Riley complained to Lieutenant Goodwin (ibid., Goodwin testimony, p.372). Goodwin passed the complaint on to Captain Purington, who included it in his official report (Angel Report, p.344).

16. Angel Report, Widenmann testimony, p.335.

17. Angel Report, Ibid., pp.335–36; Martínez testimony, p.340.

18. Ibid., Martínez testimony, p.340.

19. Ibid., pp.340–41.

20. Ibid., Goodwin testimony, pp.370–71. Goodwin used the phrase "civil" to distinguish civilian from military authority. The "writs" were actually arrest warrants.

21. Ibid., Martínez testimony, p.311.

22. Ibid., Goodwin testimony, p.371.

23. Ibid., Martínez testimony, p.311.

24. Ibid., Goodwin testimony, p.371.

25. Ibid., Martínez testimony, pp.311–11 (two pages are numbered 311). Some historians assume Martínez paid two different visits on the House on February 21, 1878. *See* Robert S. Utley, *High Noon in Lincoln: Violence on the Western Frontier* (Albuquerque: University of New Mexico Press, 1987), pp.54–55; Maurice Garland Fulton, *History of the Lincoln County War* ed. Robert N. Mullin (Tucson: University of Arizona Press, 1968), pp.126, 130–31; Jon Tuska, *Billy the Kid: A Handbook* (Lincoln: University of Nebraska Press, 1983), pp.26–27. This seems inherently unlikely to me. Why would Martínez pass up the opportunity to make the arrests under the troopers' protection only to make a quixotic attempt while badly outnumbered later the same day? The fact that Widenmann was accompanied by "two citizens" while Martínez was accompanied by Widenmann's two companions, Bonney and Waite, reinforces my conviction that only one visit was involved. Nevertheless, my interpretation is inconsistent with Constable Martínez's testimony that he arrested John Riley on his first visit (Angel Report, Martínez testimony, p.340). But, as far as we know, Martínez had no warrant for Riley's arrest, and it is unclear what he would have arrested him for. Riley was not charged with any crime relating to Tunstall at the next term of district court (although he was indicted for receiving stolen cattle).

26. Angel Report, Martínez testimony, p.311.

27. *Missionaries, Outlaws and Indians: Taylor F. Ealy at Lincoln and Zuni, 1878–1881*, ed. Norman J. Bender (Albuquerque: University of New Mexico Press, 1984), pp.1–11.

28. Untitled manuscript by Taylor F. Ealy, quoted in ibid., p.6.

29. The following account of the Ealy's arrival in Lincoln is drawn from Mary Ealy's dispatch of March 16, 1878, to *The Rocky Mountain Presbyterian*, reproduced in ibid., pp.12–14.

30. Untitled manuscript by Taylor F. Ealy, quoted in ibid., p.18. The double belts of cartridges are a somewhat suspect touch, since one of the selling points of Colt's Frontier Six-Shooter was that it used the same ammunition as Winchester's Central Fire Carbine. See the advertisement in *The Weekly New Mexican,* June 15, 1878.

31. Untitled manuscript by Taylor F. Ealy, quoted in *Missionaries, Outlaws and Indians,* p.19.

32. Mary Ealy in *The Rocky Mountain Presbyterian*, quoted in ibid., p.14.

CHAPTER 15

1. Taylor F. Ealy, unpublished manuscript, reproduced in *Missionaries, Outlaws and Indians: Taylor F. Ealy at Lincoln and Zuni, 1878–1881*, ed. Norman J. Bender (Albuquerque: University of New Mexico Press, 1984), p.19.

2. Purington's official report begins on p.344 of the Angel Report.

3. Order #18, exhibit F to Purington's official report, Angel Report, p.374. On February 21, 1878, Purington reported that he had ordered troops into town and the previous night they had been fired on by "the mob" (AGO microfilm, frame 98).

4. Angel Report, p.352.

5. Purington letter to Angel, June 25, 1878, Angel Report, p.348. See also ibid., Longwell testimony, p.250.

6. Ibid., Gonzáles testimony, p.328. Brady defeated Gonzáles in the 1871 race for the territorial house of representatives, so there may have been bad blood between the two (Donald R. Lavash, *Sheriff William Brady: Tragic Hero of the Lincoln County War* [Santa Fe: Sunstone Press, 1986], p.35).

7. Angel Report, Gonzáles testimony, p.328.

8. AGO microfilm, frames 54–57.

9. Ibid., frames 63–66, 111.

10. Angel Report, Barrier testimony, pp.293–94.

11. Ibid., pp.294–95. District Attorney Rynerson filed a criminal information charging Barrier with refusing to serve process, a statutory offense (Lincoln County criminal case #260 [1878]). The available records indicate that the prosecution never went past the filing of charges. William A. Keleher quotes a *Las Vegas Gazette* article that erroneously reported Barrier was charged with contempt of court (Keleher, *Violence in Lincoln County 1869–1881* [Albuquerque: University of New Mexico Press, 1957], p.63).

12. Angel Report, McSween testimony, p.52.

13. Lincoln County criminal cases #253 (riot) and 254 (resisting sheriff), NMRCA. For some reason, Frank MacNab was charged separately with riot in case #264. In addition, Widenmann was indicted for resisting the sheriff in cases #251 and 252.

14. Brady letter to Rynerson, dated Mar. 5, 1878, printed in *The Mesilla Valley Independent*, Mar. 30, 1878.

15. Angel Report, Mathews testimony, p.211; Gauss testimony, p.297. Mathews's list included someone named "McCormick."

16. Ibid., Mathews testimony, p.210. Mathews emphasized that the Boys "were not part of the posse" but merely riding with it.

17. Ibid., p.213.

18. *The Mesilla Valley Independent*, Mar. 30, 1878.

19. This incident is examined in detail in Robert S. Utley, *High Noon in Lincoln: Violence on the Western Frontier* (Albuquerque: University of New Mexico Press, 1987), pp.130–31 and 225n.

20. The use of the name "Regulator" originated with the South Carolinians (Richard Maxwell Brown, *The South Carolina Regulators* [Cambridge, Mass.: Harvard University Press, 1963], pp.39 and 187n).

21. Brown, *Strain of Violence: Historical Studies of American Violence and Vigilantism* (New York: Oxford University Press, 1975), pp.96–97.

22. For the powers of a special constable in New Mexico in 1878, see Acts of July 14, 1851, and Jan. 13, 1876, N.M. Comp. Laws (1884), §§ 2612, 2333. It was a criminal offense to refuse to serve a warrant issued by a justice of the peace (Act of Feb. 15, 1854, N.M. Comp. Laws [1884], § 808).

23. Angel Report, Kruling testimony, p.269; Widenmann testimony, p.204.

24. Letter dated Mar. 10, 1878, from "* * *" to editor, printed in *The Mesilla Valley Independent,* Mar. 16, 1878.

25. Letter dated Mar. 9, 1878, from "Pecos" to editor, printed in *The Las Vegas Gazette,* Mar. 16, 1878, quoted in Keleher, *Violence in Lincoln County 1869–1881,* pp.97–98.

26. W. S. Morton letter to H. H. Marshall, dated Mar. 8, 1878, printed in the Apr. 13, 1878, issue of *The Mesilla Valley Independent.* We learn from *The Independent*'s Mar. 16, 1878, dispatch that, while in Roswell, Morton "expressed fears that he would be lynched."

27. Angel Report, Middleton testimony, pp.309–10.

28. Ibid., p.310. Frank MacNab was quoted to the same effect in *The Mesilla Valley Independent,* Mar. 16, 1878.

29. Letter dated Mar. 14, 1878, from "X.Y.Z." to editor, printed in *The Albuquerque Review,* Mar. 30, 1878. The letter did not say how many times McCloskey was shot.

30. *The Weekly New Mexican* of May 4, 1878 inflated the total number of bullet wounds to eleven in each body – one for each Regulator, including (improbably) McCloskey. Utley accepts this bullet count in *High Noon in Lincoln,* p.58.

31. Act of February 16, 1854, N.M. Comp. Laws (1884), § 688. "In our criminal law as in most others, the punishment for some offenses is fixed absolutely by the statute, being an undeviating penalty. Such, for example, is the punishment of death for murder in the first degree" (*Territory v. Romine,* 2 N.M. [Gild.] 114, 127 [1881]).

32. *The Albuquerque Review,* Mar. 30, 1878. "X.Y.Z." did not identify the source of this information. The editor noted, "The above letter is from a respectable citizen of Lincoln, and we publish it just as written."

CHAPTER 16

1. To be fair, Axtell was governor at the time of John Lee's prosecution for the Mountain Meadows Massacre, to this day a controversial matter. The Gentile press accused him of excessive sympathy for the Latter Day Saints. See Hubert Howe Bancroft, *History of Utah* (San Francisco: The History Co., 1889), p.667, and Orson F. Whitney, *History of Utah 1832–1888,* 4 vols. (Salt Lake City:

George Q. Cannon & Sons Co., 1892–1904), 2:732. Typical of the censure is the *Salt Lake Daily Tribune* article abusing "Bishop Axtell," reprinted in *The (Albuquerque) Republican Review,* July 10, 1875. Axtell himself wrote that the Gentile press "pretended to consider my appointment to this territory [i.e., New Mexico] as a punishment" (Axtell letter to editor, *Daily New Mexican,* Nov. 29, 1875). For more general biographical information, see *The Weekly New Mexican,* Nov. 23, 1878, and Calvin Horn, *New Mexico's Troubled Years: The Story of the Early Territorial Governors* (Albuquerque: Horn & Wallace, 1963), p.174.

2. Angel Report on Axtell. Angel "cleared" Axtell of the "charge" that he was Mormon.

3. Ibid.

4. 17 Stat. 416 (1873).

5. Angel Report on Axtell, attachments, p.5.

6. Ibid., Shield affidavit, p.110.

7. Ibid.

8. Angel Report on Axtell, attachments, p.8; Angel Report, McSween testimony, exhibit 16.

9. N.M. Laws 1875–76, chap.1, § 40.

10. Angel Report on Axtell, attachments, p.4.

11. The legal issues raised in this chapter are examined in detail in my article "An Excess of Law in Lincoln County: Thomas B. Catron, Samuel B. Axtell and the Lincoln County War," *New Mexico Historical Review* 68 (1993): 133–51.

12. *Cimarron News and Press,* Apr. 11, 1878. An original of this edition is included as an exhibit to the Dudley Court of Inquiry transcript. The proceeding referred to by McSween was a quo warranto action.

13. *The Weekly New Mexican,* Mar. 23, 1878. A Spanish translation of the letter appeared in the Mar. 30, 1878, issue.

14. *The Weekly New Mexican,* Apr. 6, 1878.

15. *The Weekly New Mexican,* Mar. 30, 1878.

16. *Cimarron News and Press,* Apr. 11, 1878.

17. The campaign for justice (or at least compensation) waged by Tunstall's family is detailed in Frederick W. Nolan, "A Sidelight on the Tunstall Murder," *New Mexico Historical Review* 31 (1956): 206–22.

18. *The Weekly New Mexican,* Mar. 30, 1878; *The Mesilla Valley Independent,* Mar. 30, 1878.

19. Thornton to Secretary of State Evarts, Mar. 9, 1878, included with the Angel Report in Historical Records. Thornton was technically a minister, not ambassador.

20. Ibid.

21. Evarts to Attorney General Devens, Mar. 13, 1878, Historical Records.

22. Phillips (acting Attorney General) to Catron, Mar. 18, 1878, Historical Records.

23. Thornton to Evarts, Mar. 27, 1878, Historical Records.

24. Ibid.

25. Evarts to Devens, Apr. 3, 1878, Historical Records.

26. Phillips to Evarts, April 9, 1878, Historical Records.

27. The circumstances of Angel's appointment are described in Devens to Evarts, Jan. 10, 1879, Historical Records.

CHAPTER 17

1. Angel Report, McSween testimony, pp.52–54.

2. Ibid., p.55.

3. Wagner letter dated Mar. 14, 1878, printed in the Mar. 16, 1878, issue of *The Mesilla Valley Independent.*

4. Ibid. See also *The Cimarron News and Press,* Mar. 28, 1878 (a copy can be found in AGO microfilm, frame 302).

5. *The Mesilla Valley Independent,* Mar. 23, 1878.

6. Grady E. McCright and James H. Powell, *Jessie Evans: Lincoln County Badman* (College Station, Tex.: Creative Publishing Co., 1983), p.111.

7. Ibid., p.112; *The Mesilla Valley Independent,* Mar. 30 and Apr. 6, 1878; Captain Purington to AAAG, Mar. 29, 1878, AGO microfilm, frame 114. Further news of Evans's incarceration at Fort Stanton can be found in *The Mesilla News* of June 22, 1878, and July 6, 1878.

8. *The Mesilla Valley Independent,* Mar. 23, 1878.

9. Taylor F. Ealy to Albert Ealy, Mar. 13, 1878, reproduced in *Missionaries, Outlaws and Indians: Taylor F. Ealy at Lincoln and Zuni, 1878–1881,* ed. Norman J. Bender (Albuquerque: University of New Mexico Press, 1984), p.25.

10. "Frank Warner Angel's Notes on New Mexico Territory, 1878," ed. Lee Scott Theisen, *Arizona and the West* 12 (Winter 1976): 351.

11. Newspapers reported that Dolan's leg was broken when he was thrown from a horse (*The Mesilla Valley Independent,* Mar. 23, 1878; *The Weekly New Mexican,* Mar. 16, 1878).

12. *The Mesilla Valley Independent,* Mar. 23, 1878. The following year, Dolan testified that in mid-July, four months after the accident, he still "could not walk, having a broken leg. I was a cripple at the time, recovering" (Dudley Court of Inquiry, Dolan testimony, p.436).

13. Angel Report, Widenmann testimony, p.205.

14. National Archives record group 153, Records of the Adjutant General, QQ 448, Order No.14, dated Mar. 8, 1878.

15. The story of the Ninth Cavalry's New Mexico service is told in William H. Leckie, *The Buffalo Soldiers: A Narrative of the Negro Cavalry in the West* (Norman: University of Oklahoma Press, 1967), pp.172–222.

16. National Archives record group 153, Records of the Adjutant General, QQ 448, General Court Martial Orders, No.1, Fort Leavenworth, Kansas, Jan. 17, 1878. See Leckie, *The Buffalo Soldiers,* pp.181–83.

17. National Archives record group 153, Records of the Adjutant General,

QQ 448, L. H. Woodard of San Antonio, Texas, to W. McKee Dunn, Bureau of Military Justice, Washington, Jan. 9, 1878.

18. National Archives record group 153, Records of the Adjutant General, QQ 448, Order of Jan. 17, 1878; Leckie, *The Buffalo Soldiers,* p.181n.; Huston Chapman to Governor Lew Wallace, Nov. 25, 1878, Dudley Court of Inquiry, exhibit 24; "Frank Warner Angel's Notes on New Mexico Territory, 1878," p.349.

19. National Archives record group 153, Records of the Judge Advocate General, court-martial case files, II 499.

20. Leverson to President Hayes, Apr. 2, 1878. Leverson's voluminous letters are found in Historical Records.

21. Leverson to President Hayes, Apr. 1, 1878, Historical Records. The first page of this letter is written on Juan Patrón's stationery while the third page is on stationery bearing the letterhead: "Legislative Chamber/23d Session/Santa Fe, N.M. —— 1878." Leverson wrote other letters on Tunstall's stationery.

22. Leverson to President Hayes, Apr. 2, 1878, Historical Records; hereafter Leverson April 2 letter.

23. Leverson to Senator Anthony, Mar. 20, 1878, Historical Records.

24. Leverson to President Hayes, Apr. 1, 1878, Historical Records.

25. Hon. Rush Clarke to Secretary of War, May 28, 1878, enclosing Apr. 5, 1878, letter from Taylor Ealy and Apr. 9, 1878, letter from Frank Springer (AGO microfilm, frame 298).

26. Angel Report, McSween testimony, pp.55–56.

27. Leverson April 2 letter.

28. Report No.2 of the Lincoln County grand jury, printed in *The Mesilla Valley Independent,* May 4, 1878.

29. AAAG to Commanding Officer, Fort Stanton, by order of the district commander, Mar. 24, 1878 (AGO microfilm, frame 111).

30. Leverson April 2 letter.

31. Angel Report, McSween testimony, p.55.

32. Leverson April 2 letter.

CHAPTER 18

1. Angel Report, Barrier testimony, p.294.

2. Leverson to President Hayes, Apr. 2, 1878, Historical Records; hereafter Leverson April 2 letter.

3. A good description of the work of cattle detectives can be found in Andy Russell and Ted Grant, *Men of the Saddle: Working Cowboys of Canada* (Toronto: Van Nostrand Reinhold, 1978), pp.45–47.

4. Bill O'Neal, *Henry Brown: The Outlaw-Marshal* (College Station, Tex.: Creative Publishing Co., 1980). The story of Marshal Brown's final job can be found on pp.125–41; his letter to his wife is reproduced on pp.137–38. O'Neal

and some other historians accept that Marshal Brown and Lincoln County's Brown were one and the same (William A. Keleher, *Violence in Lincoln County 1869–1881* [Albuquerque: University of New Mexico Press, 1957], pp.324–25; Robert S. Utley, *High Noon in Lincoln: Violence on the Western Frontier* [Albuquerque: University of New Mexico Press, 1987], p.166). Lincoln County's Henry Brown signed his affidavit with "his X mark" (Angel Report, Brown testimony, p.306).

5. *Newman's (Las Cruces) Thirty-Four,* Mar. 30, 1881. This particular Henry Brown was reported to be the son of "ex-Governor Browne" of Tennessee. Tennessee had no fewer than three governors named Brown (but none named Browne) between 1845–79, but only one, Neill Smith Brown, had a son named Henry, who was probably too old to be the Kid's companion. See Robert Sobel and John Raimo, *Biographical Directory of the Governors of the United States, 1789–1978* (Westport, Conn.: Meckler Books, 1978).

6. Dudley court of inquiry, Susan McSween testimony, p.221; Dudley testimony, p.923; Lincoln County criminal case #274 (1879).

7. Angel Report, McSween testimony, pp.55–56; *The Mesilla Valley Independent,* Apr. 27, 1878; John Riley letter to editor, *The Weekly New Mexican,* Apr. 20, 1878.

8. The following account is pieced together from several sources. *The Mesilla Valley Independent* of Apr. 27, 1878, contains a lengthy narrative by its editor, A. J. Fountain, who visited Lincoln soon after the events described. Fountain interviewed witnesses and participants, but for obvious reasons did not always identify his sources. Rev. Ealy's recollections can be found in *Missionaires, Outlaws and Indians: Taylor F. Ealy at Lincoln and Zuni, 1878–1881,* ed. Norman J. Bender (Albuquerque: University of New Mexico Press, 1984), pp.30–31. Justice Wilson's son, Gregorio, was interviewed twice about the day's events a half-century after they occurred (Maurice Garland Fulton, *History of the Lincoln County War,* ed. Robert N. Mullin [Tucson: University of Arizona Press, 1968], p.159; *They "Knew" Billy the Kid: Interviews with Old-Time New Mexicans,* ed. Robert F. Kadlec [Santa Fe: Ancient City Press, 1987], p.20). Sheriff Brady's son was also interviewed in 1938 (*They "Knew" Billy the Kid*), p.16.

9. *The Mesilla Valley Independent* of Apr. 13, 1878, stated that Wilson was "slightly wounded in the rear of his person."

10. The cup of water was Stockton's sole contribution to the Lincoln County War. His turbulent career after he left Lincoln is described in F. Stanley, *The Private War of Ike Stockton* (Denver: World Press, 1959).

11. Utley, *High Noon in Lincoln,* pp.61, 204n; *The Mesilla Valley Independent,* Apr. 27, 1878.

12. *The Weekly New Mexican,* Apr. 13, 1878.

13. Fulton, *History of the Lincoln County War,* p.159; *They "Knew" Billy the Kid,* p.21; Angel Report, Martínez testimony, p.311.

14. *The Mesilla Valley Independent,* Apr. 27, 1878.

15. Quoted in *Missionaries, Outlaws and Indians,* p.31. For cavalry technique, see Utley, *Frontier Regulars: The United States Army and the Indian, 1866–1891* (1973; Bloomington: Indiana University Press, 1977), p.49; Anonymous, "Red Indian Warfare," *Journal of the Royal United Service of India* 35 (Feb. 1891): 198. Middleton's use of approved technique should be contrasted with the disputed contention that the Regulators shot from horseback while pursuing Morton and Baker.

16. Quoted in *Missionaries, Outlaws and Indians,* p.30.

17. Ibid.; Fulton, *History of the Lincoln County War,* p.161.

18. Purington to AAAG, Mar. 29, 1878 (AGO microfilm, frame 114).

19. AAAG to Commanding Officer, Fort Stanton, by order of the district commander, Mar. 24, 1878 (Ibid., frame 111). A copy is exhibit G of Purington's official report (Angel Report, p.376).

20. Angel Report, Widenmann testimony, pp.332–33.

21. Ibid., McSween testimony, p.56.

22. Leverson April 2 letter.

23. Angel Report, McSween testimony, pp.57–58.

24. Purington letter to Angel, June 25, 1878, Angel Report, p.349.

25. Leverson April 2 letter.

26. Angel Report, Widenmann testimony, p.33. McSween testified he heard the remark, and Rev. Ealy passed it on to his uncle the congressman, who told the secretary of war (Ibid., McSween testimony, p.59; AGO microfilm, frame 296). Purington denied that he had made the remark (Purington letter to Angel, June 25, 1878, Angel Report, p.349). See also Angel Report, Sampson testimony, p.387; Galvin testimony, p.385; Robinson testimony, pp.389 and 391; Lusk testimony, p.357.

27. Angel Report, McSween testimony, p.59; Widenmann testimony, p.333.

28. Ibid., McSween testimony, p.57. McSween's account was corroborated by Sergeant Houston Lusk (Ibid., Lusk testimony, p.358).

29. Ibid., McSween testimony, pp.59–60.

30. Ibid., Purington letter, p.350; ibid., Lusk testimony, p.358.

31. Ibid., McSween testimony, p.60.

CHAPTER 19

1. Blazer, along with Florencio Gonzáles and Paul Dowlin, was appointed to the comission by the legislature pending elections (Act of January 13, 1876, N.M. Laws of 1875–76, chap.1).

2. *The Mesilla Valley Independent,* Apr. 27, 1878.

3. William A. Keleher and Colin Rickards state that the county offered a reward of $200 for the arrest of Brady's killers (Keleher, *Violence in Lincoln County 1869–1881* [Albuquerque: University of New Mexico Press, 1957], p.113; Rickards, *The Gunfight at Blazer's Mill,* Southwestern Studies Mono-

graph no. 40 [El Paso: Texas Western Press, 1974], p.24). The minutes of the Lincoln County Commission in the NMRCA do not bear out this assertion. If a reward was offered, it was apparently offered by the House rather than the county.

4. Angel Report, Mathews testimony, p.213.

5. Ibid., Middleton testimony, p.307; Brown testimony, p.306.

6. This description and the following account are based on *The Weekly New Mexican*, Apr. 13, 1878; Rickards, *The Gunfight at Blazer's Mill*; Paul A. Blazer, "The Fight at Blazer's Mill: A Chapter in the Lincoln County War," *Arizona and the West 6* (Autumn 1964): 203–10; George Coe and Nan Hillary Harrison, *Frontier Fighter: The Autobiography of George W. Coe, Who Fought and Rode with Billy the Kid* (Boston: Houghton Mifflin, 1934), pp.64–71. The most detailed firsthand account is the extended interview with Frank Coe contained in Walter Noble Burns's half-novel, half-history, *The Saga of Billy the Kid* (Garden City, N.J.: Garden City Publishing Co., 1926), pp.92–100. Unfortunately, we cannot know for certain to which half the interview belongs. Also interesting is the Federal Writers' Project interview with A. N. Blazer and Lucius Dills in *They "Knew" Billy the Kid: Interviews with Old-Time New Mexicans*, ed. Robert F. Kadlec (Santa Fe: Ancient City Press, 1987), p.24. The bare facts are set out in the May 12, 1879, federal indictment in the case of *United States v. Bowdre, et al.*, contained in Historical Records. The Apr. 23, 1878, territorial indictment in the case of *Territory v. Bowdre*, Lincoln County criminal case #256 (1878) apparently has not survived.

7. Burns, *The Saga of Billy the Kid*, p.95. *The Weekly New Mexican* of Apr. 13, 1878, reported that Frank Coe engaged Roberts in conversation, but only as a trick to get Roberts to drop his guard.

8. Burns, *The Saga of Billy the Kid*, p.96.

9. Ibid., p.97.

10. Burns's chapter on the Blazer's Mill fight is entitled "Thirteen to One"; Robert S. Utley, *High Noon in Lincoln: Violence on the Western Frontier* [Albuquerque: University of New Mexico Press, 1987], p.63.

CHAPTER 20

1. McSween letter to the editor, *The Cimarron News and Press*, Apr. 18, 1878, quoted in Maurice Garland Fulton, *History of the Lincoln County War*, ed. Robert N. Mullin (Tucson: University of Arizona Press), pp.176–77.

2. Dolan letter to the editor, *The Weekly New Mexican*, May 25, 1878.

3. Ibid.; Dolan letter to the editor, *The Weekly New Mexican*, June 1, 1878; Dolan letter to the editor, *The Mesilla News*, June 15, 1878; Marion Turner letter to the editor, *The Las Vegas Gazette*, May 4, 1878; Riley letter to the editor, *The Weekly New Mexican*, Apr. 20, 1878, referring to *The Trinidad Enterprise and Chronicle*.

4. AGO microfilm, frames 68–76.

5. Sherman to Sheridan, Apr. 12, 1878 (ibid., frame 68).

6. Sheridan to Adjutant General Platt, May 2, 1878 (ibid., frame 79).

7. Ibid., frame 80.

8. N.M. Laws of 1867, chap.32, § 2. Although the 1884 official statutory compilation placed this statute under the heading of "civil procedure," it applied equally to criminal matters (N.M. Comp. Laws [1884], § 1906).

9. Riley and Copeland ranched cooperatively in the mid-1870s. *The Grant County Herald* of Sept. 4, 1875, describes their joint involvement in a violent incident that seriously injured Juan Patrón. The incident is related in greater detail, but without citation of sources, in Fulton, *History of the Lincoln County War*, pp.29–31.

10. Lincoln County Commission records, Apr. 10, 1878, NMRCA.

11. Dudley to AAAG, May 4, 1878, AGO microfilm, frame 125.

12. Lincoln County district court minute book for 1878, NMRCA; Organic Act, § 10.

13. The charge was printed in *The Las Vegas Gazette*, May 4, 1878, a copy of which was submitted with Special Agent Angel's report.

14. Angel Report, Barrier and Shield joint affidavit, p.185.

15. William A. Keleher, *Violence in Lincoln County 1869–1881* (Albuquerque: University of New Mexico Press, 1957), p.119.

16. The two grand jury reports are printed in *The Las Vegas Gazette* and *The Mesilla Valley Independent* issues for May 4, 1878.

17. Judicial records relating to these and the following indictments are housed in the NMRCA.

18. *The Las Vegas Gazette*, May 4, 1878.

19. *The Mesilla News*, July 27, 1878; Victor Westphall, *Thomas Benton Catron and His Era* (Tucson: University of Arizona Press, 1973), p.82.

20. The description of the meeting and the text of the proclamation are taken from *The Mesilla Valley Independent*, May 4, 1878.

21. Some weeks later a Dolan partisan wrote, "It appears that Gen. Dudley is a good deal sharper than McSween & Co. give him credit for, and all their flattery and fulsome praise did not budge the General a peg" (letter from "Van" to the editor, *The Weekly New Mexican*, May 18, 1878).

22. *The Cimarron News and Press*, May 2, 1878, quoted in Keleher, *Violence in Lincoln County 1869–1881*, p.116.

CHAPTER 21

1. Seventeen Seven Rivers men signed a petition attached to Dudley's May 4, 1878, report to the AAAG (hereafter Dudley May 4 report), AGO microfilm, frame 125. Others may well have been present.

2. The following account is taken from *The Weekly New Mexican*, May 11 and 18, 1878; *The Mesilla Valley Independent*, May 11, 1878; *The Albuquerque*

Review, May 11, 1878; Wilbur Coe, *Ranch on the Ruidoso: The Story of a Pioneer Family in New Mexico, 1871–1968* (New York: Alfred A. Knopf, 1968), pp.38–42; George Coe and Nan Hillary Harrison, *Frontier Fighter: The Autobiography of George W. Coe, Who Fought and Rode with Billy the Kid* (Boston: Houghton Mifflin, 1934), pp.82–88; and the Donicino Molina interview in *They "Knew" Billy the Kid: Interviews with Old-Time New Mexicans,* ed. Robert F. Kadlec (Santa Fe: Ancient City Press, 1987), p.28.

3. Dudley to AAAG, May 18, 1878 (AGO microfilm, frame 235). Saunders survived, only to die a few years later during an operation to repair damage caused by the gunshot.

4. The following description is based on the sources cited in note 2 above and also on letters from "Van" and "El Gato" in *The Weekly New Mexican,* May 18 and June 1, 1878, and on Lieutenant Smith's May 1, 1878, report, which is attachment J to Dudley's May 4 report.

5. An entertaining account of Frank Coe's escape, which also purports to explain how Jimmy Dolan broke his leg (but which unfortunately is contradicted by the historical record), is found in Coe, *Ranch on the Ruidoso,* pp.43–44.

6. Act of July 14, 1851, N.M. Comp. Laws (1865), chap.89, § 2.

7. Dudley court of inquiry, Easton testimony, pp.188–90; Dudley to AAAG, May 4, 1878, AGO microfilm, frame 132.

8. Kearny Code, Practice at Law in Criminal Cases, § 1, codified as N.M. Comp. Laws (1865), chap.57, § 1; N.M. Laws of 1875–76, chap.27, § 80 *et seq.*

9. Easton to Dudley, May 1, 1878, attachment O to Dudley's May 4 report; "El Gato" letter to the editor, *The Weekly New Mexican,* June 1, 1878.

10. McCrary to Dunn, June 3, 1878 (AGO microfilm, frame 123).

11. Dunn to McCrary, June 8, 1878 (ibid., frame 200). The order was actually dated June 7, which (if it wasn't a simple mistake) means that the judge advocate general gave his legal opinion informally the day before presenting it in writing.

12. Dudley May 4 report; "Soapweed" letter to *The Cimarron News and Press,* dated May 4, 1878, quoted in Maurice Garland Fulton, *History of the Lincoln County War,* ed. Robert N. Mullin (Tucson: University of Arizona Press, 1968), pp.218–19.

13. Dudley May 4 report.

14. Riley to Dudley, May 14 and 17, attachments to Dudley to AAAG, May 25, 1878, AGO microfilm, frame 285; *The Weekly New Mexican,* June 1 and 8, 1878; *The Cimarron News and Press,* June 6, 1878, quoted in Fulton, *History of the Lincoln County War,* pp.225–26; Victor Westphall, *Thomas Benton Catron and His Era* (Tucson: University of Arizona Press, 1973), pp.87–88.

15. The horses were later returned on the condition that Walz not allow them to be used in the fighting ("Regulator" to Walz, July 13, 1878, AGO microfilm, frame 522). Copeland's disclaimer is exhibit E to Dudley's May 25 report (ibid., frame 285).

16. Catron to Axtell, May 28, 1877 (ibid., frame 250).

17. Ibid., frame 257; *The Weekly New Mexican,* June 1, 1878.

18. N.M. Laws of 1875–76, chap.16, § 2. Angel's report on Axtell incorrectly stated that the county commissioners failed to establish the amount of the bond; the failure was Bristol's alone. It was arguably the perogative of the commission rather than the governor to name a replacement sheriff, just as the commission had named Copeland in the first place; the statutes were ambiguous on this point.

19. N.M. Laws of 1875–76, chap.16, § 1.

20. Order of June 1, 1878 (AGO microfilm, frame 265). Victor Westphall argues that Catron wrote his letter after Axtell's proclamation was issued, and after Axtell requested Colonel Hatch to send the troops to Roswell (*Thomas Benton Catron and His Era,* p.89). It would have been a waste of time for Catron to have done so, since by that time he had received everything he asked for.

21. Angel Report on Axtell, p.5.

22. Dudley to AAAG, July 13 and Aug. 27, 1878 (AGO microfilm, frames 444, 689).

CHAPTER 22

1. Angel Report on Axtell; Jim Berry Pearson, *The Maxwell Land Grant* (Norman: University of Oklahoma Press, 1961); Norman Cleaveland, *Colfax County's Chronic Murder Mystery* (Santa Fe: Rydal Press, 1977); Morris F. Taylor, *O. P. McMains and the Maxwell Land Grant Conflict* (Tucson: University of Arizona Press, 1979). A highly colored account of the Colfax County troubles can be found in M. E. McPherson's pamphlet, "In the Matter of the Charges vs. Gov. S. B. Axtell and Other New Mexican Officials" (August 1877), a copy of which is in the Museum of New Mexico archives.

2. Axtell described Catron as "a good friend of mine and a very worthy man" (Axtell Aug. 18, 1878, letter to Huntington, Governor Axtell papers, letters sent, 1875–84, NMRCA).

3. Angel Report on Axtell, under heading "Charge Eleventh." Axtell admitted writing the letter but claimed these lines were interpolated. See also Norman Cleaveland with George Fitzpatrick, *The Morleys: Young Upstarts on the Southwest Frontier* (Albuquerque: Calvin Horn Publisher, 1971), pp.149–58.

4. *The Mesilla Valley Independent,* Aug. 3, 1878.

5. *The Weekly New Mexican,* Aug. 7, 1878. *The Weekly New Mexican* was called "the Santa Fe Ring Organ" by its rival, *The Santa Fe Democrat,* Oct. 14, 1880. *The Albuquerque Review* of Aug. 25, 1877, reported that "*The New Mexican* . . . appears to be the official champion of these Santa Fe gentlemen."

6. Quoted in Robert N. Mullin, "Here Lies John Kinney," *Journal of Arizona History* 14 (Autumn 1973): 223. In a letter to Acting Governor Ritch requesting the offer of a reward for Benito Cruz's killers, District Attorney Rynerson wrote

that the killers, Kinney and his men, "passed through Mesilla about 10 o'clock [on September 22, 1877]. Sheriff had warrant for them in his pocket at the time. No effort is made to arrest them" (Rynerson to Ritch, Sept. 24, 1877, Papers of Governor Axtell, letters received, NMRCA). Kinney's career was well documented in contemporary newspaper reports, including: *The Albuquerque Review,* Oct. 27 and Nov. 10, 1877; *The Mesilla Valley Independent,* Oct. 27 and Nov. 3, 1877, May 18, 1878; *The Mesilla News,* May 18, 1878.

7. The El Paso (or San Elizario) Salt War has never received the attention it deserves. The basic facts can be found in C. L. Sonnichsen, *The El Paso Salt War* (El Paso: Carl Hertzog and the Texas Western Press, 1961), a reprint of the chapter from *Ten Texas Feuds* (Albuquerque: University of New Mexico Press, 1957); W. W. Mills, *Forty Years at El Paso, 1858–1898* (El Paso: Carl Hertzog, 1962); C. L. Douglas, *Famous Texas Feuds* (Dallas: The Turner Co., 1936); Walter Prescott Webb, *The Texas Rangers: A Century of Frontier Defense* (Austin: University of Texas Press, 1965). The Salt War received widespread attention in New Mexico newspapers, including *The Albuquerque Review,* Oct. 20, 1877, Jan. 5 and 19, 1878; *The Mesilla Valley Independent,* Oct. 6 and Dec. 15, 1877. A dispatch from *The Independent* was read on the floor of the House by El Paso's Congressman: 7 Cong. Rec. 3670–71 (Remarks of Rep. Gustave Schleicher [D. Tex.], May 22, 1878).

8. In 1877, the chief town on the American side of the Mexican-Texas border was called Franklin. Even then, however, people referred to the region's settlements collectively as El Paso (or Paseo), the name used here to avoid confusion.

9. N.M. Laws of 1853–54, chap.7. The preamble to the statute states that it was passed in response to an attempt by a Texan to claim title to salt beds in southern New Mexico. Article 13 of the Texas Constitution of 1876 was found unconstitutional in *Texas Mexico Railway Co. v. Locke,* 12 S.W. 80, 88 (Tex. 1889); *Lerma v. Stevenson,* 40 F. 356, 359 (C.C.W.D. Texas 1889). See also *Gonzales v. Ross,* 120 U.S. 605, 626–30 (1887), which states, "If [the 1876 state constitution's] effect is to make titles void which were before good, a grave constitutional question may arise, with regard to its validity."

10. *The Mesilla Valley Independent,* Oct. 6, 1877.

11. *The Weekly New Mexican* editorialized, in connection with Lincoln County's troubles: "In the late El Paso and San Elizario troubles, quite a number of the outlaw class rode down to the scene of the disturbance, for where the carcasses are, there jayhawkers gather. There they were Texas Rangers and fought for God and liberty" (*The Weekly New Mexican,* Mar. 23, 1878).

12. The Jan. 19, 1878, issue of *The Albuquerque Review* reported that a shortage of grain was expected "for the reason that not less than nine-tenths of the farmers of [the El Paso region] have abandoned their ranches and crossed to the Mexican side of the river."

13. *The Mesilla Valley Independent,* May 4, 1878.

14. *The Mesilla Valley Independent,* Aug. 24, 1878, and Sept. 7, 1878; letter from "Scrope" (possibly Jimmy Dolan in a good mood) to the editor, *The Mesilla News,* June 29, 1878. "Scrope" continued: "Few persons of any means or prominence are to be met with here, most of them I learn being abroad on the green hills taking a little recreation after their arduous duties in this neighborhood. Should they not return before next term of court it will be a matter of impossibility to find 15 good men in this country to make up a grand jury." Judge Bristol subsequently decided not to hold the October term of court in Lincoln County for the very reason "Scrope" suggested. (*The Mesilla Valley Independent,* Sept. 28, 1878).

15. 7 Cong. Rec. 3677 (remarks of Rep. Milton Southard [D. Ohio], May 22, 1878); p.4245 (remarks of Sen. Augustus Summerfield Merriman [D. N.C.], June 7, 1878); p.3717 (remarks of Rep. Carter Henry Harrison [D. Ill.], May 23, 1878). For background, see Robert V. Bruce, *1877: Year of Violence* (Indianapolis: Bobbs-Merrill Co., 1959). The use of the military as posse comitatus was sanctioned by an 1854 opinion of the attorney general authorizing use of soldiers to capture fugitive slaves (6 Op. Att'y Gen. 466 [1854]). The legal basis for the opinion was a simple syllogism: all citizens have a duty to serve in posses; soldiers are citizens; therefore soldiers have a duty to serve in posses. The constitutionality of that view was persuasively challenged in a congressional floor speech of rare scholarship. See 7 Cong. Rec. 3581 et. seq. (remarks of Rep. William Kimmel [D. Md.], May 20, 1878).

16. 20 Stat. 152 (1878).

17. AGO microfilm, frames 29, 247, 269, 349.

18. *The Mesilla Valley Independent,* Aug. 24, 1878.

19. Dudley to AAAG, June 29, 1878 (AGO microfilm, frame 408).

20. Dudley reported that he received the order on June 28, 1878 (ibid).

21. Letter from "Julius" to the editor, *The Mesilla News,* July 6, 1878; dispatch in *The Weekly New Mexican,* July 27, 1878, reprinted from *The Las Vegas Gazette.*

22. Letter from "Lincoln" (almost certainly McSween) to the editor, *The Cimarron News and Press,* July 25, 1878, quoted in Maurice Garland Fulton, *History of the Lincoln County War,* ed. Robert N. Mullin (Tucson: University of Arizona Press, 1968), p.244.

23. Quoted in Fulton, *History of the Lincoln County War,* p.246. Captain Blair got into unusual legal trouble in early 1879, pleading guilty to bigamy (*Newman's [Las Cruces] Thirty-Four,* Feb. 26, 1879; *The Mesilla Valley Independent,* Mar. 1, 1879).

24. On July 4, the women of San Patricio submitted a petition, in Spanish, to Colonel Dudley, imploring him "in the name of God and the Constitution" to protect them (Dudley court of inquiry, exhibit 51).

CHAPTER 23

1. Dudley court of inquiry, Ellis testimony, p.166; Washington testimony, pp.266–67; Philipowski testimony, p.303; Montaño testimony, pp.350–51; Martin Chávez testimony, pp.357–58; Corbet testimony, pp.365–66; Bush testimony, pp.377–78; Baca testimony, p.439; Peppin testimony, p.536; *The Mesilla News,* July 27, 1878. There may also have been some men in Patrón's house, next door to Montaño's house.

2. Dudley court of inquiry, Long testimony, p.589.

3. Ibid., Baca testimony, pp.440–47, 461–62, 464.

4. Ibid. and exhibit 47.

5. Ibid., Appel testimony, pp.843–45 and exhibit 58; Dudley to AAAG, midnight, July 20, 1878 (hereafter Dudley July 20 report), AGO microfilm, frame 459.

6. Dudley court of inquiry, Peppin testimony, pp.533–34; Easton testimony, p.192; Dudley July 20 report, AGO microfilm, frame 459.

7. Dudley court of inquiry, Easton testimony, p.174; Peppin testimony, p.535.

8. Ex-Justice Easton said Peppin's force consisted of men "I never knew to do much of anything and others who I had never seen previous to the fight" (Dudley court of inquiry, Easton testimony, p.186). He added that he wasn't referring to the Seven Rivers men, who were "hard working and industrious men" (ibid., p.193).

9. Dudley court of inquiry, Peppin testimony, p.581 and exhibit 48; Dudley July 20 report, AGO microfilm, frame 469.

10. Dudley July 20 report, AGO microfilm, frames 449, 484.

11. Dudley to Peppin, July 16, 1878, Dudley court of inquiry, exhibit 49; Dudley July 20 report, AGO microfilm, frame 469.

12. Peppin to Dudley, July 16, 1878, Dudley court of inquiry, exhibit 57; Dudley July 20 report, AGO microfilm, frame 473.

13. Dudley court of inquiry, exhibit 57; Dudley July 20 report, AGO microfilm, frame 475.

14. Ibid.

15. Dudley July 20 report, AGO microfilm, frame 475.

16. Dudley court of inquiry, Baca testimony, p.477–78; Appel testimony, p.834; Dudley to AAAG, July 27, 1878, AGO microfilm, frame 567.

17. Dudley court of inquiry, Ellis testimony, p.160. Details of the following incident are taken from Ruth Ealy, *Water in a Thirsty Land* (privately printed, 1955), quoted in *Missionaries, Outlaws and Indians: Taylor F. Ealy at Lincoln and Zuni, 1878–1881,* ed. Norman J. Bender (Albuquerque: University of New Mexico Press, 1984), pp.51–52.

18. Dudley July 20 report, AGO microfilm, frame 496.

19. Dudley court of inquiry, Dudley testimony, p.918.

20. Ibid., Dolan testimony, p.433. Samuel Beard, an employee of Dowlin's mill, testified earlier that he overheard such a conversation (ibid., Beard testimony, p.133).

21. Ibid., Dolan testimony, p.437. The technical basis for the objection was that the question went beyond the scope of the direct examination, since Dudley's attorney had only asked Dolan about a conversation occurring at that precise time and place in which Dudley used those precise words. It would be difficult for most lawyers to make such an objection with a straight face.

22. Ibid., Appel testimony, p.836; Montaño testimony, p.351.

23. Ibid., Ellis testimony, 163–65; Washington testimony, pp.267, 277; Philipowski testimony, pp.303–5; Romero y Valencia testimony, pp.347–48; Bates testimony, p.290; O'Brien testimony, p.318; Montaño testimony, pp.350–53; Martin Chávez testimony, pp.357–60; Corbet testimony, pp.365–67; Bush testimony, pp.377–78.

24. Ibid., Easton testimony, p.184; Sue McSween testimony, pp.218–21; Bonney testimony, p.326; Bush testimony, p.373; Peppin testimony, 538–40.

25. Ibid., Wilson testimony, pp.203–6. Dudley denied making the threat (ibid., Dudley testimony, pp.919–20). Numerous witnesses contradicted him, including two soldiers (ibid., Washington testimony, pp.262–63; Bates testimony, p.283; Dixon testimony, pp.300–301; Bush testimony, p.379; Lusk testimony, p.392). The warrant itself is exhibit 32.

26. Ibid., Nash testimony, p.674.

27. Ibid., Chávez y Chávez testimony, p.345.

28. McSween to Dudley, July 19, 1878, Dudley court of inquiry, exhibit 56; Dudley July 20 report, AGO microfilm, frame 500.

29. Dudley July 20 report, AGO microfilm, frame 500.

30. Dudley court of inquiry, Easton testimony, pp.174–75; Washington testimony, pp.267–68; Bates testimony, p.289; Bonney testimony, p.332; Chávez y Chávez testimony, p.335; Baker testimony, p.364; Bush testimony, p.377, 384; Lusk testimony, p.390; Mathews testimony, p.657–59; Nash testimony, pp.665–67.

31. The following account is taken from Sue McSween's court of inquiry testimony, beginning on p.216.

32. Bates confirmed this testimony (Dudley court of inquiry, Bates testimony, pp.283–84). A soldier, James Bush, testified that Dudley told Peppin, Hurley, and Robert Beckwith that they had a "perfect right" to make Bates and Dixon work against their will (ibid., Bush testimony, p.374).

33. Ibid., Peppin testimony, p.547.

34. Ibid., Lusk testimony, p.390.

35. Ibid., Philipowski testimony, pp.303–4; Baker testimony, pp.362–64. The teamster John O'Brien confirmed that Dudley ordered his men to shoot Sue (ibid., O'Brien testimony, p.317).

36. Dudley confirmed Sue's testimony on this point (ibid., Dudley testimony, p.923).

37. Mrs. Philipowski testified that Dudley told Sue "she should be ashamed mentioning the name of McSween" (ibid., Philipowski testimony, p.304).

38. Ibid., Long testimony, p.592. Powell denied being with Long when he set the fire, but admitted he and Long hid together, as discussed in the text below (ibid., Powell testimony, p.619). If Powell hadn't accompanied Long from the beginning, however, he wouldn't have wound up hiding with Long.

39. Ibid., Long testimony, p.594; Powell testimony, p.618. Both Long and Powell testified that the shots came from the Tunstall store, and Nash testified that some Regulators sneaked back across the river and into the store (ibid., Nash testimony, p.671). Late in life, George Coe alleged that he was one of the intrepid few to occupy the store (Coe and Nan Hillary Harrison, *Frontier Fighter: The Autobiography of George W. Coe, Who Fought and Rode with Billy the Kid* [Boston: Houghton Mifflin, 1934], p.115). Despite this corroboration, however, I'm skeptical. We know that Coe and his pals were not in the store when the showdown came a few hours later, but Coe doesn't explain how they escaped. Moreover, Bonney testified that he saw Long and another man try to set the fire (Dudley court of inquiry, Bonney testimony, p.323). It is highly unlikely that Bonney watched without defending himself. I think the shots that chased Long and Powell into the outhouse came from inside the McSween house.

40. Dudley court of inquiry, Boyle testimony, pp.627–28; Nash testimony, p.669.

41. Ibid., Peppin testimony, p.545.

42. The following account is derived from Rev. Ealy's court of inquiry testimony, beginning on p.401.

43. Dudley court of inquiry, exhibits 39 and 40.

44. Ibid., Bates testimony, pp.284–85.

45. Ibid., Bonney testimony, pp.322, 326, 327–28; Chávez y Chávez testimony, pp.335–40, 346; Boyle testimony, p.690; Nash testimony, pp.671–72.

46. Ibid., Corbet testimony, pp.368–70.

47. Ibid., Easton testimony, pp.177–78. See also Bates testimony, p.285; Corbet testimony, p.368; Peppin testimony, pp.551, 556; Appel testimony, p.868. John Kinney was indicted for stealing pants, boots, shirts, and a coat from the Tunstall store (Lincoln County criminal cases #284, 299 [1879]). For an account of the Tunstall family's ultimately futile efforts to obtain compensation for the looting, see Frederick W. Nolan, "A Sidelight on the Tunstall Murder," *New Mexico Historical Review* 31 (1956): 206–22.

48. Dudley court of inquiry, Dudley testimony, p.927.

CHAPTER 24

1. Boyle told the story in a letter to the editor, *The Grant County Herald*, Aug. 24, 1878 (reprinted from *The Mesila News*), and then again in his testimony at

the Dudley court of inquiry, pp.627–28. Between the two tellings, he was indicted for horse theft (Lincoln County criminal case #278 [1879], NMRCA). The story of the fake surrender was widely reported, as was the "fact" that ten McSween men were killed, including "Antrim (alias the Kid)" (*The Mesilla News,* July 27 and Aug. 3, 1878; *The Grant County Herald,* Aug. 10, 1878; *The Mesilla Valley Independent,* Aug. 3, 1878; *The Weekly New Mexican,* Aug. 10, 1878).

2. *The Albuquerque Review,* Aug. 3, 1878.

3. Selman's career is described in Leon Claire Metz, *John Selman: Texas Gunfighter* (New York: Hastings House, 1966).

4. Robert S. Utley, *High Noon in Lincoln: Violence on the Western Frontier* (Albuquerque: University of New Mexico Press, 1987), pp.114–15.

5. *The Mesilla Valley Independent,* Sept. 7 and 28, Oct. 12, 1878; *The Albuquerque Review,* Oct. 1, 1878 (reprinted from *The Las Vegas Gazette*); Dudley court of inquiry, Wallace testimony, pp.72–74.

6. "Rapine in New Mexico: A Desperate Gang of Renegades from Texas Committing Murders and Outrages," *The New York Times,* Oct. 13, 1878. *The Philadelphia Times* had covered the slaughter of the five-day battle. The Philadelphia paper's ludicrously garbled report (McSween and Dolan were competing sheriffs) was reprinted and ridiculed in *The Albuquerque Review* of Aug. 10, 1878. Lawrence Murphy didn't get the joke; he wrote a letter criticizing *The Review* for mixing up the facts (*The Albuquerque Review,* Aug. 24, 1878). He also sent a complaining letter to *The Weekly New Mexican,* published in the Aug. 17, 1878, issue.

7. George Coe and Nan Hillary Harrison, *Frontier Fighter: The Autobiography of George W. Coe, Who Fought and Rode with Billy the Kid* (Boston: Houghton Mifflin, 1934), p.134.

8. Dudley to AAAG, Aug. 10, 1878 (AGO microfilm, frame 603).

9. AAAG to Dudley, Aug. 15, 1878; Dudley to AAAG, Aug. 22, 1878 (AGO microfilm, frames 640, 644).

10. Angel report on Godfroy, Dolan testimony, p.44.

11. This account is taken from Captain Blair's report, an enclosure to Dudley's Aug. 10, 1878, report (AGO microfilm, frame 609).

12. *El Nuevo Méjicano,* Aug. 31, 1878 (Spanish-language reprint from *The Weekly New Mexican,* Aug. 24, 1878).

13. Dudley to AAAG, Aug. 27, 1878 (AGO microfilm, frame 677).

14. Some historians accept that the Regulators (or perhaps their ally, Constable Atanacio Martínez) killed Bernstein (Maurice Garland Fulton, *History of the Lincoln County War,* ed. Robert N. Mullin [Tucson: University of Arizona Press, 1968], pp.282–83; Robert S. Utley, *High Noon in Lincoln: Violence on the Western Frontier* [Albuquerque: University of New Mexico Press, 1987], pp.113–14). For a careful review of all the evidence, see Frederick Nolan, *The*

Lincoln County War: A Documentary History (Norman: University of Oklahoma Press, 1992), pp.339–42.

15. The negotiations are described in Catron to Devens, Aug. 17, 1878, and Elkins to Devens, Sept. 13, 1878, Historical Records.

16. Catron to Devens, Aug. 19, 1878, Historical Records.

17. Wing to Catron, Sept. 7, 1878, Historical Records. Devens waspishly observed that Catron "appears to have considered the matter of answering not of sufficient importance as to take precedence of his private matters" (Devens to Elkins, Sept. 16, 1878, Historical Records).

18. Devens to Evarts, Jan. 10, 1879, Historical Records.

19. Correspondence to author from John K. Vandereedt, Civil Reference Branch, National Archives, dated May 6, 1993. The report is reprinted without archival citation in Norman Cleaveland, *An Introduction to the Colfax County War, 1875–78* (Albuquerque: privately printed, 1975), pp.41–44.

20. Victor Westphall, *Thomas Benton Catron and His Era* (Tucson: University of Arizona Press, 1973), p.130. Westphall's conclusion that the report never existed is belied by Catron's interest in it. Catron was unlikely to be uninformed about a matter of such importance to himself.

CHAPTER 25

1. Angel Report on Axtell, pp.2 and 7.

2. Angel's thirty-one questions and Axtell's article of response are found in ibid., pp.1–11. After conceding the letter outlining the murder plot "sounds like me," Axtell charged that the incriminating lines were interpolated by forgers (ibid., p.9). But several months previously Axtell had written a letter to one of the intended victims of the plot apologizing for "any ambiguity" in his letter suggesting he meant the man harm (ibid., p.56). There would have been no ambiguity if the incriminating lines were forged.

The Axtell-Angel exchange was widely covered in the newspapers: *The Mesilla Valley Independent*, Aug. 31, 1878; *The Mesilla News*, Aug. 31, 1878; *The Weekly New Mexican*, Sept. 14 and 21, 1878; *The Grant County Herald*, Aug. 24 and 31, 1878. Axtell sent his response to *The (Santa Fe) Rocky Mountain Sentinel* because that paper publicly offered to print it (see *The Grant County Herald*, Aug. 24, 1878).

3. Axtell to Huntington, Sept. 19, 1878 (Governor Axtell's papers, letters sent, 1875–84, NMRCA).

4. Axtell to Huntington, Aug. 12, 1878 (ibid.). Axtell's letters reveal that he used his position as governor to obtain information about the railroad operations of Huntington's rivals, which he relayed in exchange for railway passes.

5. Biographical information about Wallace is derived from Lew Wallace, *Autobiography* (New York: Harper & Bros., 1906); Irving McKee, *"Ben-Hur" Wallace: The Life of General Lew Wallace* (Berkeley: University of California

Press, 1947); Robert Morsberger, *Lew Wallace: Militant Romantic* (New York: McGraw-Hill, 1980).

6. Shelby Foote, *The Civil War: A Narrative,* 3 vols. (New York: Random House, 1958), 1:209.

7. John S. C. Abbott, *The History of the Civil War in America,* 2 vols. (New York: Ledyard Bill, 1863), 1:507. This instant history was sold by subscription only. An advertisement in the back of the book listed twenty or so prominent "patrons and subscribers," among whom was Lew Wallace.

8. Quoted in McKee, *"Ben-Hur" Wallace,* p.57.

9. Ulysses S. Grant examined both sides of the issue in chapter 24 of his *Personal Memoirs.* He was critical of Wallace in the text, but somewhat more forgiving in a note he appended to the end of the chapter in 1885, just weeks before his death (Grant, *Memoirs and Selected Letters* [New York: Library of America, 1990], pp.226, 236).

10. For a muckraking account of the Wallace-McLin exchange, see A. M. Gibson, *A Political Crime: The History of the Great Fraud* (New York: William S. Gottsberger, 1885), pp.101–3, 112.

11. Wallace's letter to President Hayes is reproduced as an illustration to William A. Keleher, *Violence in Lincoln County 1869–1881* (Albuquerque: University of New Mexico Press), p.174. The term "second-class" wasn't (just) a value judgment; diplomatic postings were divided into classes according to the salary paid the ambassador.

12. *The Grant County Herald,* Sept. 28, 1878.

13. Susan E. Wallace, *The Land of the Pueblos* (New York: John B. Alden, 1888), pp.51–52, 248.

14. Quoted in Keleher, *Violence in Lincoln County 1869–1881,* p.188. The original is in the Wallace papers, Indiana Historical Society. On Aug. 9, 1878, *The New York Times* reported that the secretary of war had ordered military commanders in New Mexico to prepare for the imposition of martial law, but nothing ever came of it.

15. 20 Stat. 806 (Oct. 7, 1878). The President's proclamation was reported in *The New York Times,* Oct. 8 and 9, 1878, and printed in the Oct. 12, 1878, edition of the following newspapers: *The Mesilla Valley Independent, The Weekly New Mexican,* and *The Mesilla News.*

16. Wallace to Schurz, Nov. 13, 1878, quoted in Keleher, *Violence in Lincoln County 1869–1881,* p.193.

17. The amnesty proclamation was printed in the Nov. 23, 1878, issues of *The Mesilla News* and *The Mesilla Valley Independent.*

18. *The Mesilla Valley Independent,* Nov. 23, 1878.

19. *The Mesilla News,* Nov. 23, 1878; Wallace to Dudley, Nov. 30, 1878, Dudley court of inquiry, exhibit 26; Dudley court of inquiry, Wallace testimony, p.86.

20. *The Weekly New Mexican* of Dec. 14, 1878, published in English and Spanish. Much of the letter was reprinted, with editorial comment, in *The Mesilla Valley Independent,* Dec. 21, 1878. The letter is exhibit 2 to the Dudley court of inquiry.

21. Dudley, or one of the officers on his staff, wrote an pseudonymous letter to the editor and leaked official correspondence to *The Mesilla News* in an effort to discredit Wallace (letter from "Looker On," *The Mesilla News,* Mar. 22, 1879).

CHAPTER 26

1. "Frank Warner Angel's Notes on New Mexico Territory, 1878," ed. Lee Scott Thiesen, *Arizona and the West* 18 (1976): 360.

2. Chapman to Wallace, Oct. 24, 1878, Dudley court of inquiry, exhibit 4.

3. Dudley court of inquiry, exhibit 14 (Wallace to Hatch, Oct. 28, 1878); exhibit 13 (Dudley to Wallace, Nov. 9, 1878); exhibit 3 (Wallace to Dudley, Nov. 16, 1878); Wallace testimony, p.64.

4. Dudley court of inquiry, exhibits 8, 6C, 7, 10, and 11. Testifying through an interpreter at Dudley's court of inquiry, Baca said, "I can understand a good deal [of English] but can speak only few words" (ibid., Baca testimony, p.466).

5. Quoted in William A. Keleher, *Violence in Lincoln County 1869–1881* (Albuquerque: University of New Mexico Press, 1957), p.204, and Frederick Nolan, *The Lincoln County War: A Documentary History* (Norman: University of Oklahoma Press, 1992), p.452.

6. Chapman to Wallace, Nov. 25 and 29, 1878, Dudley court of inquiry, exhibits 24 and 25. Wallace discussed the letters in his court of inquiry testimony, pp.80–82.

7. Records of board of officers, Dudley court of inquiry, exhibit 28; *The Mesilla Valley Independent,* Jan. 11, 1879; *Newman's (Las Cruces) Thirty-Four,* Jan. 1, 1878.

8. *Newman's (Las Cruces) Thirty-Four,* Jan. 1, 1879 and Jan. 19, 1881; *The Santa Fe Democrat,* Feb. 3, 1881.

9. *Mesilla Valley Independent,* Dec. 14, 1878. The victims were identified as "Jack Irvin and Moore," formerly with the Texas Rangers in El Paso.

10. The following account is derived from the courtroom testimony reported in *The Mesilla Valley Independent,* July 5, 1879, and from the reports in *The Independent,* Mar. 1 and 22, 1879; *The Mesilla News,* Mar. 1 and Apr. 5, 1879; *Newman's (Las Cruces) Thirty-Four,* Mar. 5, 1879.

11. *The Daily New Mexican,* May 4, 1881.

12. Dolan's shifting account is told in *The Mesilla Valley Independent,* Mar. 22, 1879; Dolan letter to the editor, *The Mesilla News,* Apr. 5, 1879; report of Dolan's testimony, *The Mesilla Valley Independent,* July 5, 1879.

13. Dudley court of inquiry, Wallace testimony, pp.106–7.

14. The Bonney-Wallace correspondence is reproduced, in whole or part, in virtually every book on the Lincoln County War. See, for example, Nolan, *The Lincoln County War,* pp.382–84; Keleher, *Violence in Lincoln County 1869–1881,* pp.210–15; Robert S. Utley, *Billy the Kid: A Short and Violent Life* (Lincoln: University of Nebraska Press, 1968), pp.117–19; Maurice Garland Fulton, *History of the Lincoln County War,* ed. Robert N. Mullin (Tucson: University of Arizona Press, 1968), pp.336–39. The originals are housed with the Wallace Papers in the Indiana Historical Society in Indianapolis. See the bibliographic discussions in Utley, *Billy the Kid,* p.246n; Nolan, *The Lincoln County War,* p.570n.

15. *The Indianapolis World,* June 8, 1902, quoted in Fulton, *History of the Lincoln County War,* pp.337–38.

CHAPTER 27

1. Wallace to Schurz, Mar. 31, 1879, quoted in William A. Keleher, *Violence in Lincoln County 1869–1881* (Albuquerque: University of New Mexico Press, 1957), p.216; Robert S. Utley, *Billy the Kid: A Short and Violent Life* (Lincoln: University of Nebraska Press, 1989), p.119; Frederick Nolan, *The Lincoln County War: A Documentary History* (Norman: University of Oklahoma Press, 1992), p.384. The original is in the Wallace Papers, Indiana Historical Library, Indianapolis. See note 14 above for the Bonney-Wallace correspondence.

2. Campbell and Dolan were indicted for murder, Evans as accessory (Lincoln County criminal case #279 [1879]).

3. Lincoln County criminal case #243 (1878). The file contains this handwritten note: "Indictment in this cause in Doña Ana County for trial of 'Kid' on change of venue." *The Las Vegas Gazette* quoted Bonney as saying: "I went up to Lincoln to stand my trial on the warrant that was out for me, but the Territory took a change of venue to Doña Ana, and I knew that I had no show, and so I skinned out" (*The Las Vegas Gazette,* Dec. 28, 1880, reproduced in *New Mexico Magazine* 22 [1954]: 41, and in the unattributed collection, *Billy the Kid: Las Vegas Newspaper Accounts of His Career, 1880–1881* [Waco, Tex.: W. M. Morrison Books, 1958], p.14).

4. Dudley court of inquiry, Wallace testimony, pp.88–93; Purington testimony, pp.858–59.

5. Ira Leonard, quoted in *The (Las Vegas) New Mexico Herald,* July 30, 1879. In the same issue, Dudley characteristically attributed complaints against him to "petty malice and personal hatred."

6. Dudley court of inquiry, Dudley testimony, p.918.

7. Bonney letter to the editor, *The Las Vegas Gazette,* Dec. 22, 1880, quoted in Keleher, *Violence in Lincoln County 1869–1881,* p.289.

8. Utley, *Billy the Kid,* p.127. George Coe wrote of the Kid's "many affairs with the señoritas" (George Coe and Nan Hillary Harrison, *Frontier Fighter: The Autobiography of George W. Coe, Who Fought and Rode with Billy the*

Kid [Boston: Houghton Mifflin, 1934], p.147). George's cousin remembered the Kid as "a lady's man, the Mex girls were crazy about him" (Frank Coe to William Steele Dean, Aug. 3, 1926, quoted in *They "Knew" Billy the Kid: Interviews with Old-Time New Mexicans,* ed. Robert F. Kadlec [Santa Fe: Ancient City Press, 1987], p.66).

9. *The Las Vegas Gazette,* Dec. 28, 1880, reproduced in *New Mexico Magazine,* p.40, and in *Billy the Kid: Las Vegas Newspaper Accounts,* p.13; Paulita Maxwell Jaramillo, quoted in Walter Noble Burns, *The Saga of Billy the Kid* (Garden City, N.Y.: Garden City Publishing Co., 1926), p.185; Miguel Antonio Otero, *The Real Billy the Kid: With New Light on the Lincoln County War* (New York: Rufus Rockwell Wilson, Inc., 1936), p.176; Otero, *My Life on the Frontier 1864–1882* (New York: The Press of the Pioneers, 1935), p.211. Although Burns appears to have rendered Mrs. Jaramillo's reminiscences into what he considered an appropriately picturesque idiom, he actually interviewed her. The evidence concerning her relationship with the Kid is examined in Utley, *Billy the Kid,* pp.127 and 248–49n.

10. Pat F. Garrett, *The Authentic Life of Billy the Kid,* ed. J. C. Dykes (Norman: University of Oklahoma Press, 1954), pp.87–88; Utley, *Billy the Kid,* pp.131–32.

11. The following account of Wild's Lincoln County career is derived from Garrett, *The Authentic Life of Billy the Kid,* p.98; Leon C. Metz, *Pat Garrett: The Story of a Western Lawman* (Norman: University of Oklahoma Press, 1974), pp.58–67; Utley, *Billy the Kid,* pp.134–38.

12. Garrett, *The Authentic Life of Billy the Kid,* p.134; Eve Ball, *Ma'am Jones of the Pecos* (Tucson: University of Arizona Press, 1969), pp.117–20. Olinger's side of the quarrel is told in Lily Klasner, *My Girlhood among Outlaws* (Tucson: University of Arizona Press, 1972), p.187.

13. Metz, *Pat Garrett,* p.59.

14. Biographical information about Garrett is derived from Metz, *Pat Garrett,* and Colin Rickards, *Sheriff Pat Garrett's Last Days* (Santa Fe: Sunstone Press, 1986).

15. *George Curry 1861–1947: An Autobiography,* ed. H. B. Henning (Albuquerque: University of New Mexico Press, 1958), pp.18–19.

16. William A. Keleher, *The Fabulous Frontier* (1962; Albuquerque: University of New Mexico Press, 1982), pp.72–73.

17. The following account is derived from *The Daily New Mexican,* Dec. 7, 1880; *The Las Vegas Gazette,* Nov. 30, 1880, quoted in Keleher, *The Fabulous Frontier,* p.69; *The Lincoln County Leader,* Dec. 7, 1889, quoted in ibid., pp.70–71; Utley, *Billy the Kid,* pp.142–43.

18. Bonney to Wallace, Dec. 12, 1880, published in *The Las Vegas Gazette,* Dec. 22, 1880, reproduced in Keleher, *Violence in Lincoln County 1869–1881,* pp.288–89.

19. *The Las Vegas Gazette,* Dec. 3, 1880, reproduced in Keleher, *Violence in Lincoln County 1869–1881,* pp.286–87.

20. *The Daily New Mexican,* Dec. 29, 1880; *The Las Vegas Gazette,* Dec. 28, 1880, reproduced in *Billy the Kid: Las Vegas Newspaper Accounts,* p.12. The *New Daily Mexican* article referred collectively to the Kid, Rudabaugh, and Billy Wilson as the "famous outlaws."

CHAPTER 28

1. It is sometimes asserted the the omission of the words "dead or alive" from the reward notice was significant (William A. Keleher, *Violence in Lincoln County 1869–1881* [Albuquerque: University of New Mexico Press, 1957], p.290; Jon Tuska, *Billy the Kid: A Handbook* [Lincoln: University of Nebraska Press, 1983], p.85). In fact, New Mexico's governor was only authorized to offer rewards (in the maximum amount of $500) for the "apprehension and delivery" of fugitives; he couldn't just place a bounty on a man's head (N.M. Laws [1873–74], chap.12). The form of reward notice used by Wallace was typical. Compare, for example, the reward offered for the arrest and conviction of Benito Cruz's murderers (*The Mesilla Valley Independent,* Oct. 6, 1877). However, Governor Axtell bent the law on September 7, 1878, when he offered a reward for his old Colfax County antagonist Tom Bow, adding:

But if said Tom Bow is necessarily killed in the attempt to arrest him, or if he should be wounded and afterwards die of his wounds before he could be tried for said offense; then, in that case, upon satisfactory proof to me, that he resisted the arrest and also that he committed the crime, I will cause the reward to be paid from the Territorial Treasury the same as upon conviction in Court.

Papers of Governor Axtell, reward notices, NMRCA. In effect, this unauthorized procedure permitted the ultimate trial in absentia – first the execution, then the determination of guilt.

2. Manuscript autobiography of Cal Polk, dated Jan. 25, 1896, published in *The Capture of Billy the Kid,* ed. James H. Earle (College Station, Tex.: Creative Publishing Co., 1988), p.18.

3. Ibid., p.19.

4. Pat F. Garrett, *The Authentic Life of Billy the Kid,* ed. J. C. Dykes (Norman: University of Oklahoma Press, 1954), pp.116–20. The following account is derived from Garrett's book; Cal Polk's autobiography; James East's letter of May 1, 1920, reproduced in *The Capture of Billy the Kid,* pp.26, 82–83; *The Daily New Mexican,* Dec. 23, 1880; and Leon C. Metz, *Pat Garrett: The Story of a Western Lawman* (Norman: University of Oklahoma Press, 1974), pp.73–75.

5. Quoted in Robert S. Utley, *Billy the Kid: A Short and Violent Life* (Lincoln: University of Nebraska Press, 1968), p.156.

6. Cal Polk autobiography, pp.26–27. The following account is derived from Garrett's *Authentic Life of Billy the Kid*, pp.122–28; an article in *The Daily New Mexican*, Dec. 29, 1880, which appears to have been based on an interview with Garrett or his men; *The Las Vegas Gazette*, Dec. 27, 1880, reprinted in *Billy the Kid: Las Vegas Newspaper Accounts of His Career, 1880–1881* (Waco, Tex.: W. M. Morrison Books, 1958), p.5; *The Las Vegas Daily Optic*, Dec. 27, 1880, reprinted in *Newman's (Las Cruces) Thirty-Four*, Jan. 5, 1881, and in *Billy the Kid: Las Vegas Newspaper Accounts*, p.9.

7. *The Las Vegas Gazette*, Dec. 28, 1880, reprinted in *New Mexico Magazine* 22 (1954): 41, and in *Billy the Kid: Las Vegas Newspaper Accounts*, p.14.

8. *The Daily New Mexican*, Dec. 30, 1880.

9. Originals of all but one of the Kid's jailhouse notes are housed with the Wallace Papers in the Indiana Historical Society, Indianapolis; see the explanatory note in Utley, *Billy the Kid*, p.259n. The notes are quoted in Maurice Garland Fulton, *History of the Lincoln County War*, ed. Robert N. Mullin (Tucson: University of Arizona Press, 1968), p.386; William A. Keleher, *Violence in Lincoln County 1869–1881* (Albuquerque: University of New Mexico Press, 1957), pp.300–303; Utley, *Billy the Kid*, pp.168–70; Frederick Nolan, *The Lincoln County War: A Documentary History* (Norman: University of Oklahoma Press, 1992), pp.411–12.

10. *The Las Vegas Gazette*, Apr. 5, 1881, reprinted in *Billy the Kid: Las Vegas Newspaper Accounts*, p.17.

11. *Newman's (Las Cruces) Semi-Weekly*, Apr. 30, 1881. The posse also included deputies named Wood, Williams, Reade, and Lockhart.

12. The following account is derived from Garrett, *The Authentic Life of Billy the Kid*, pp.132–39; *The Daily New Mexican*, May 3, 1881; *The Las Vegas Daily Optic*, May 2, 3, and 4, 1881; *Newman's (Las Cruces) Semi-Weekly*, quoted in *The New Southwest and Grant County Herald*, May 14, 1881; interview with Godfrey Gauss in *The Lincoln County Leader*, Mar. 1, 1890, quoted in Keleher, *Violence in Lincoln County 1869–1881*, pp.337–39.

13. Utley, *Billy the Kid*, pp.180–81; *The New Southwest and Grant County Herald*, May 14, 1881.

14. *The Las Vegas Daily Optic*, May 3, 1881.

15. *The Daily New Mexican*, May 3, 1881.

16. *The New Southwest and Grant County Herald*, July 23, 1881; *The Daily New Mexican*, May 5, 1881; *The Santa Fe Weekly Democrat*, May 5 and Jan. 27, 1881; *The Daily New Mexican*, May 3, 1881. The Ned Buntline quote was written with reference to Garrett's capture of the Kid at Stinking Springs. Ned Buntline, the incredibly prolific author of sensational dime novels and serials, was reputed in the 1870s to be the highest paid writer in America. See Jay Monaghan, *The Great Rascal: The Life and Adventures of Ned Buntline* (Boston: Little, Brown, 1952). For a first-rate study of the early pulp westerns, and Billy

the Kid's unique role as the bad outlaw protagonist, see Daryl Jones, *The Dime Novel Western* (Bowling Green, Ohio: The Popular Press, Bowling Green State University, 1978), esp. pp.75–99.

17. *The Daily New Mexican,* May 4, 1881; *The Las Vegas Daily Optic,* May 4, 1881; *The Santa Fe Weekly Democrat,* May 5, 1881. Mathews died of pneumonia in 1904 at age fifty-seven (*The Roswell Register,* June 10, 1904).

18. *The New Southwest and Grant County Herald,* July 23, 1881.

19. *The Daily New Mexican,* June 16, 1881.

20. The following account is derived from Garrett, *The Authentic Life of Billy the Kid,* pp.142–48; John Poe, *The Death of Billy the Kid* (Boston: Houghton Mifflin, 1933); *The Las Vegas Daily Optic,* July 18, 1881; *The New Southwest and Grant County Herald,* July 23, 1881.

EPILOGUE

1. *The Las Vegas Daily Optic,* July 19, 1881.

2. *The White Oaks Eagle,* Mar. 3, 1898, quoted in William A. Keleher, *Violence in Lincoln County 1869–1881* (Albuquerque: University of New Mexico Press, 1957), p.54. *The Daily New Mexican* of Mar. 2, 1878, said only that Dolan "died very suddenly . . . of internal hemmorhage."

3. Letter of June 15, 1882, Papers of Governor Axtell, letters sent 1875–84, NMRCA.

Bibliographic Essay

The starting point for all research into the Lincoln County War is the work of Frank Warner Angel. He interviewed all of the major players and most of the minor ones, giving us multiple points of view about practically every incident of the Lincoln County War. In my opinion, Angel was a first-rate attorney, but that opinion is not universally shared. For example, Robert S. Utley writes, "Angel . . . had obvious biases, and he was not skilled in taking depositions" (Utley, *High Noon in Lincoln: Violence on the Western Frontier* [Albuquerque: University of New Mexico Press, 1987], p. 237). John P. Wilson criticizes Angel for seeming "to have accepted McSween's claims almost at face value" (Wilson, *Merchants, Guns and Money: The Story of Lincoln County and Its Wars* [Santa Fe: Museum of New Mexico Press, 1987], p. 210). But Angel was hired to investigate the conduct of various federal officials. McSween and the Regulators were not federal officials, nor were they acting at the behest of federal officials, and so Angel did not investigate them.

As to Angel's forensic skill, only Perry Mason can make a witness break down on the stand and admit that he or she is lying. Angel did a superb job of getting people to commit to highly specific, seemingly trivial details in their testimony. By comparing the statements of various witnesses, it becomes possible to judge with some confidence who is being honest and who isn't. What Utley sees as Angel's bias, and Wilson as his credulity, I see as the only reasonable reading of the evidence.

Almost as useful as Angel's Reports are the territorial newspapers. New Mexico had a wealth of newspapers in the post–Civil War era. The editors relied on letters from readers for news of outlying areas, such as Lincoln. The correspondents usually felt little obligation to give equal time to both sides of any controversy. Frequently, neither did the editors, who made little distinction between news stories and editorials. The writing was literate, colorful, sometimes ornate, and frequently humorous. The Lincoln County War was a made-to-order circulation booster: there was always some new twist to report, wax indignant about, or cheer. And there was always some journalistic lapse by one's competitors to deplore. Once allowance is made for the incendiary style of journalism, the newspapers are particularly rich sources of information, providing not just facts but a taste of what people felt about the facts. Sober modern newspapers are unreadably dull a week after the publication date, but the frontier newspapers of a century ago still entertain, amuse, and even inform.

New Mexico Newspapers: A Comprehensive Guide to Bibliographical Entries and Locations, ed. Pearce C. Grove, Becky Barnett, and Sandra J. Hansen (Albuquerque: University of New Mexico Press, 1975), is a useful finding aid. Some newspaper accounts of the Kid's later career are reprinted in the unattributed collection, *Billy the Kid: Las Vegas Newspaper Accounts of His Career, 1880–1881* (Waco, Tex.: W. M. Morrison Books, 1958).

The New Mexico Records Center and Archives in Santa Fe contains a huge amount of source material that has been ignored by most historians, including docket books and court files from the Lincoln County district court, records of the Lincoln County Commission, and the papers of Governor Axtell. Voluminous testimony regarding the military's role in the Five Days' Battle is transcribed in the Dudley court of inquiry record.

Many books have been written about the Lincoln County War, but few have been any good. In 1960, Ramon F. Adams published *A Fitting Death for Billy the Kid* (Norman: University of Oklahoma Press, 1960), which canvassed every single book and article Adams could find dealing with the Kid and the Lincoln County War, and gleefully exposed their every sin against history. More recently, Jon Tuska published *Billy the Kid: A Handbook* (Lincoln: University of Nebraska Press, 1983), which summarizes the major incidents of the Lincoln County War and includes an exhaustive annotated bibliography and filmography. Yet another bibliography is J. C. Dykes, *Billy the Kid: The Bibliography of a Legend* (Albuquerque: University of New Mexico Press, 1952). Each book provides a springboard for anybody interested in diving into the vast swampland of fictional and semifictional works on the Kid and the troubles in Lincoln.

On the strictly factual side, homage must be paid to the pioneering work of Maurice Garland Fulton and William A. Keleher. Keleher's *Violence in Lincoln County 1869–1881* (Albuquerque: University of New Mexico Press, 1957) is a storehouse of information, which is both its strength and its weakness. It reprints huge blocks of the testimony collected by Frank Warner Angel and also publishes, in full, numerous newspaper articles. It has no discernable structure: the narrative makes few allowances to chronology, relegates important material to endnotes, and wanders off on bewildering digressions. But one can only admire Keleher's assiduous collection of material, including interviews with participants and their descendants.

Fulton's *History of the Lincoln County War* (Tucson: University of Arizona Press, 1968) was edited after Fulton's death by Robert N. Mullin. Like Keleher's book, it is a compendium of raw information, including interviews and reprints of newspaper articles. Fulton's book has more narrative flow than Keleher's, but sometimes the flow resembles a tidal wave: the book treats irrelevant incidents to the same detailed analysis accorded critical turning points. Fulton also had the maddening habit of recounting stories without revealing his source.

The Keleher/Fulton school of scholarship by accretion reached its high-water mark with the recent publication of Frederick Nolan's monumental *The Lincoln County War: A Documentary History* (Norman: University of Oklahoma Press, 1992), which lives up to the promise of its subtitle and also contains a particularly impressive collection of photographs, some of them never before published. Nolan is also the editor of John Tunstall's correspondence, published with extensive annotations in *The Life and Death of John Henry Tunstall* (Albuquerque: University of New Mexico Press, 1965).

Robert S. Utley is by far the most distinguished historian to write on the Lincoln County War. His first book on the subject was *Four Fighters of Lincoln County* (Albuquerque: University of New Mexico Press, 1986), a collection of lectures later incorporated into *High Noon in Lincoln*. The latter book traces the development of the conflict to the Five Days' Battle, the "high noon" of the title. Utley's narrative is both brisk and thorough, and with his unparalleled knowledge of the frontier military he is particularly good on army operations. Utley's take on the Lincoln County War is in many respects an elaboration of views originally advanced by Philip Rasch in a series of thought-provoking articles listed in *High Noon*'s bibliography.

Utley also wrote *Billy the Kid: A Short and Violent Life* (Lincoln: University of Nebraska Press, 1989), which collects every scrap of biographical information known about the Kid. Robert Mullin's monograph, *The Boyhood of Billy the Kid*, Southwestern Studies Monograph 17 (El Paso: Texas Western Press, 1967), also does a good job of separating fact from legend.

John P. Wilson's *Merchants, Guns and Money,* a history of Lincoln County's first century, is notable for its financial analysis of the Dolan and Tunstall stores.

Numerous first-person accounts of the Lincoln County troubles are available. Walter Noble Burns's *The Saga of Billy the Kid* (Garden City, N.Y.: Garden City Publishing Co., 1926), although essentially a novel, includes interviews with Frank Coe and Sue McSween, among others, which were almost certainly polished by Burns. George Coe published his (not entirely reliable) memoirs as *Frontier Fighter: The Autobiography of George W. Coe, Who Fought and Rode with Billy the Kid* (Boston: Houghton Mifflin, 1934), cowritten and probably polished by Nan Hilary Harrison. His nephew Wilbur Coe published his own book of family history as *Ranch on the Ruidoso: The Story of a Pioneer Family in New Mexico, 1871–1968* (New York: Alfred A. Knopf, 1968). Paul Blazer, grandson of the owner of the mill, recounted his family's oral tradition of the shootout in "The Fight at Blazer's Mill," *Arizona and the West* 6 (1964): 203–10. Robert Widenmann was remembered fondly by his daughter in "Lincoln County Postscript: Notes on Robert A. Widenmann by His Daughter, Elsie Widenman," ed. Bruce T. Ellis, *New Mexico Historical Review* 50 (July 1975): 213–30. The diaries, letters, and manuscript narratives of Reverend and Mrs. Ealy and their daughter Ruth are collected and masterfully annotated by Norman J. Bender in *Missionaries, Outlaws and Indians: Taylor F. Ealy at Lincoln and Zuni, 1878–1881* (Albuquerque: University of New Mexico Press, 1984). Lee Scott Theisen usefully supplemented Angel's reports with "Frank Warner Angel's Notes on New Mexico Territory, 1878," *Arizona and the West* 18 (1976): 333–70, which reprints and annotates notes Angel prepared for Lew Wallace.

Pat Garrett wrote a taut and unintentionally self-revealing narrative of his pursuit of the Kid, which was then padded to book length with a ghostwriter's rehash of fanciful newspaper articles about the Kid's early years and published as *The Authentic Life of Billy the Kid*. Numerous editions are available. I used the University of Oklahoma Press edition of 1954, edited by J. C. Dykes. John Poe, Garrett's deputy, told his story in *The Death of Billy the Kid* (Boston: Houghton Mifflin, 1933). The fragmentary memoirs of other Garrett deputies were compiled by James H. Earle in *The Capture of Billy the Kid* (College Station, Tex.: Creative Publishing Co., 1988). Robert F. Kadlec edited *They "Knew" Billy the Kid: Interviews with Old-Time New Mexicans* (Santa Fe: Ancient City Press, 1987). The quotation marks in the title are warranted.

Lew Wallace, whose *Autobiography* was published by Harper & Bros. in 1906, is the subject of two highly readable biographies: Irving McKee, *"Ben-Hur" Wallace: The Life of General Lew Wallace* (Berkeley: University of California Press, 1947), and Robert Morsberger, *Lew Wallace: Militant Romantic* (New York: McGraw-Hill, 1980). His wife, Susan E. Wallace, published *Land of the Pueblos* (New York: John B. Alden, 1888), a lively and frequently witty memoir of their time in New Mexico, written in a fresh and distinctly modern style that contrasts with her husband's biblical cadences.

Thomas Catron has also been the subject of a biography, Victor Westphall's *Thomas Benton Catron and His Era* (Tucson: University of Arizona Press, 1973), which adopts a defensive tone but contains much useful biographical information. The fabulous career of Catron's one-time partner is detailed in Oscar Doane Lambert, *Stephen Benton Elkins* (Pittsburgh: University of Pittsburgh Press, 1955). Another fabulous career is described in Harwood P. Hinton, Jr.'s "John Simpson Chisum, 1877–84," *New Mexico Historical Review* 31 (1956): 177–205, 310–37, 32 (1957): 53–65, and Mary Whatley Clarke's *John Simpson Chisum: Jinglebob King of the Pecos* (Austin: Eakin Press, 1984).

An insightful analysis of New Mexico's political culture in the post–Civil War period can be found in Gary L. Roberts, *Death Comes for the Chief Justice: The Slough-Rynerson Quarrel and Political Violence in New Mexico* (Niwot: University Press of Colorado, 1990).

Much recent scholarship has examined frontier violence in a larger context, sometimes at the risk of overly broad generalizations. Richard Maxwell Brown's *Strain of Violence: Historical Studies of American Violence and Vigilantism* (New York: Oxford University Press, 1975), the best of the lot, has already achieved classic status. Other noteworthy studies include Roger D. McGrath, *Gunfighters, Highwaymen and Vigilantes: Violence on the Frontier* (Berkeley: University of California

Press, 1984), and Richard White, *"Your Misfortune and None of My Own": A New History of the American West* (Norman: University of Oklahoma Press, 1992).

Finally, a more detailed examination of some of the legal issues raised by the Lincoln County War can be found in my article, "An Excess of Law in Lincoln County: Thomas B. Catron, Samuel B. Axtell and the Lincoln County War," *New Mexico Historical Review* 68 (1993): 133–51.

Index

French, Jim, 131–32, 134, 141, 181, 184, 186
Fritz, Caroline, 235
Fritz, Charles, 13, 25, 44, 48, 51–52, 65, 214, 235
Fritz, Maj. Emil: and the House, 6, 11, 24; death of, 11, 56; estate of, 12–13, 44, 50, 53, 92, 151, 239 n.5. *See also* Fritz insurance policy
Fritz insurance policy, 12, 25, 44, 50–51, 53
Fritz, Emilie. *See* Scholand, Emilie Fritz

Gallegos, Juan, 225
Gallegos, Lazaro, 93
Gallegos, Pantelón, 81–82, 87–89, 93, 143
Garrett, Sheriff Pat: and *Authentic Life of Billy the Kid*, 111, 218, 240 n.1; described, 219; elected sheriff, 220; and Wild, 221; pursuit of Bonney, 224–26, 233–34; capture of Bonney, 227; and Kinney, 230; kills Bonney, 234; subsequent career of, 235; mentioned, 231
Gates, Susan, 181, 185
Gauss, Godfrey, 9, 69, 71, 73–74, 80–82, 105, 231–32
Glorieta Pass, Battle of, 4, 46, 70
Godfroy, Maj. L. Frederick (Mescalero Indian Agent), 64–65, 140, 165, 194–95, 250 n.13
Gómez, Francisco, 205
Gonzáles, Probate Judge Florencio, 11–12, 25, 51–52, 58, 90, 93, 102–3, 153, 169, 260 n.6
González, Ignacio, 105, 141, 182, 191
Goodnight, Charlie, 26
Goodnight-Loving Trail, 26
Goodwin, Lt. Millard Fillmore, 95–97, 101
grand jury, 128–29, 149–52
Granillo, León, 167
Grant, Joe, 218–19
Grant County Herald, 15, 200
Grant, Ulysses S. (U.S. President), 6, 59, 76, 199, 278 n.9
Greathouse, Jim, 222

Green, Thomas, 87, 143

Hardin, John Wesley, 192
Harrison, Benjamin (U.S. President), 46, 197
Hatch, Col. Edward, 103, 126, 129, 135, 147, 159, 163, 169, 170, 193, 194, 201, 205, 209
Hayes, Rutherford B. (U.S. President), 103, 131, 136, 166, 198, 200, 201
Hereford, Mr., 153
Herford, Rev. Brooke, 147–48, 153
Herrera, Fernando, 178
Hill, Tom: captured by Brewer, 34; escapes from jail, 71; and Mathews posse, 72–73; and Tunstall killing, 81, 84, 89–90; named in inquest verdict, 94; warrant for, 95, 107; death of, 122–23, 125; mentioned, 39, 96. *See also* the Boys
Hindemann, George: and Mathews posse, 72; named in inquest verdict, 94; warrant for, 95, 107, 125; death of, 132–34, 151; mentioned, 143
Horrell clan, 244 n.8
House, the: established, 6; business practices of, 7–10, 27, 238 n.9; acquired by Dolan and Riley, 11, 24; debts of, 28, 56; closes, 152; acquired by Catron, 153; converted to courthouse, 207, 230
Howard, Charles, 166–67
Howe, Albert H., 90
Hudgens, William, 213, 221
Humphries, Lt. Henry (Humphreys), 101
Hunter & Evans, 28
Huntington, Collis, 198–99, 236
Hurley, John, 72, 75, 78, 82, 87–89, 218, 220

Indian, the. *See* Segovia, Manuel

J.J. Dolan & Co. *See* the House
James, Jesse, 208, 233
Jenardo, Don, 240 n.1
jingle-bob earmark, 27
Jones, John (of Seven Rivers), 218
Jones, Major John (of the Texas Rangers), 167

Wilson (*continued*)
34, 41; accompanies McSween to Mesilla, 58; at Shedd's Ranch, 61, 63; and Rynerson letter, 92; conducts inquest, 93–94; issues warrants, 95; right to hold office, 97, 115–17, 122, 125, 198; wounded, 132; and Dudley, 181, 216; and Wallace-Bonney meeting, 210–11; name change, 257 n.3; mentioned, 100, 105, 143, 152, 159

Wortley Hotel, 174, 175–77, 231

Wrestlers, the, 192, 207

Zamora, Francisco, 182, 186, 191

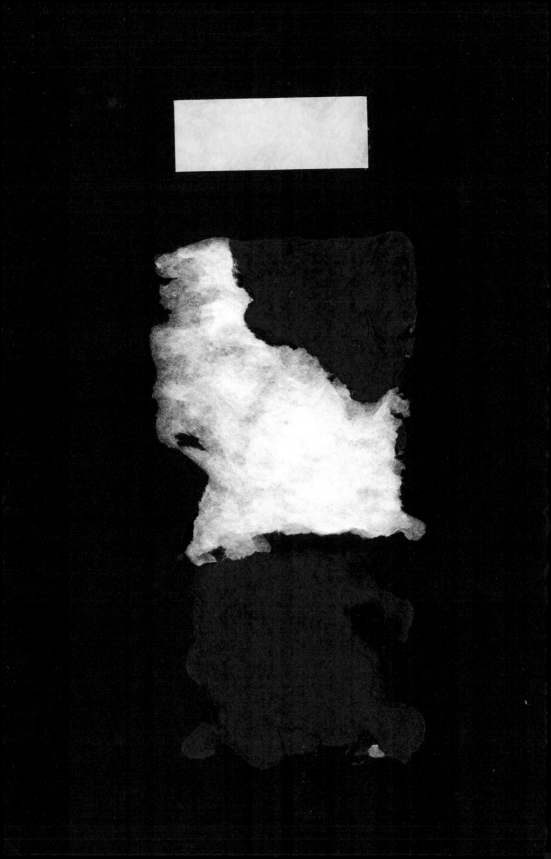